# RADICALS, BEATS AND
# BEBOPPERS

# RADICALS, BEATS AND BEBOPPERS

### JIM BURNS

PENNILESS PRESS PUBLICATIONS
www.pennilesspress.co.uk

Published by

*Penniless Press Publications 2011*

© Jim Burns

**ISBN 978-1-4476-3072-2**

*Cover: Greenwich Village New York 1995 – photo Ken Clay*

# CONTENTS

| | |
|---|---|
| ACKNOWLEDGEMENTS | 7 |
| INTRODUCTION | 9 |
| JACK CONROY: WORKER WRITER IN AMERICA | 11 |
| RADICALS AND MODERNISTS | 17 |
| WHO WAS ALBERT HALPER? | 27 |
| WILLIAM HERRICK AND THE SPANISH CIVIL WAR | 34 |
| BEN MADDOW | 43 |
| REBEL VOICES | 51 |
| JOHN HERRMANN: WRITER AND SPY | 61 |
| LEFT IN LOS ANGELES | 67 |
| WALTER LOWENFELS | 75 |
| WAS KEROUAC A COMMUNIST? | 85 |
| LAWRENCE LIPTON AND THE BEAT GENERATION | 91 |
| CARL SOLOMON | 99 |
| COOL KEROUAC | 107 |
| JACK MICHELINE: POET OF PROTEST | 112 |
| JOHN CLELLON HOLMES | 121 |
| WILLIAM BURROUGHS: HIP NOT BEAT | 130 |
| BEATITUDE | 135 |
| WHAT BECAME OF CLINT NICHOLS? | 142 |
| ANATOLE BROYARD | 148 |
| BEHIND THE SCENES | 157 |
| HOW BRAVE WE LIVE | 163 |
| THE AMERICAN CONNECTION | 166 |
| MAXWELL BODENHEIM | 173 |
| CLIFFORD ODETS: SWEET SMELL OF SUCCESS | 183 |
| ABSTRACT EXPRESSIONISM: THE BEBOP MYTH | 192 |
| ROBERT MCALMON'S POETRY | 196 |
| BIRD BREAKS DOWN | 205 |
| HARRY BISS | 212 |
| BUDDY WISE | 216 |
| BIRD LIVES! | 220 |
| INDEX | 227 |

# ACKNOWLEDGEMENTS

The essays in this book first appeared in the following publications:

Jack Conroy:Worker Writer in America, *Critical Survey* 7:2, Oxford, 1995

Radicals and Modernists, *Prop 3*, Bolton, 1997

Who was Albert Halper? *Beat Scene* 36, Coventry, 2000

William Herrick and the Spanish Civil War, *The Penniless Press* 9, Preston,1999

Ben Maddow, *The Penniless Press* 8, Preston, 1998

Rebel Voices, *The Penniless Press* 16, Preston, 2002

John Herrmann: Writer and Spy, *London Magazine* London February/March 2000

Left in Los Angeles, *The Penniless Press* 18, Preston, 2003

Walter Lowenfels, *The Penniless Press* 11, Preston, 2000

Was Kerouac a Communist? *Beat Scene* 41, Coventry, 2001

Lawrence Lipton and the Beat Generation, *Beat Scene* 39, Coventry, 2001

Carl Solomon, *Beat Scene* 46, Coventry, 2004

Cool Kerouac, *Beat Scene Press Pocket Book* 17, Coventry, 2008

Jack Micheline: Poet of Protest, *Beat Scene* 45, Coventry, 2004

John Clellon Holmes, *Beat Scene* 40, Coventry, 2002

William Burroughs: Hip not Beat, *My Kind of Angel: i.m. William Burroughs*, edited by Rupert Loydell, Stride Publications, Exeter, 1998

Beatitude, *Beat Scene* 50, Coventry, 2006

What Became of Clint Nicholls? *Beat Scene* 37, Coventry, 2000

Anatole Broyard, *The Penniless Press* 7, Preston, 1998

Behind the Scenes, *Beat Scene* 48, Coventry, 2005

How Brave We Live, *Beat Scene* 57, Coventry, 2008

The American Connection, *Beat Scene* 35, Coventry, 2000

Maxwell Bodenheim, *The Penniless Press* 10, Preston, 1999

Clifford Odets: Sweet Smell of Success, *The Penniless Press 17*, Preston, 2003

Abstract Expressionism: The Bebop Myth, *London Magazine* London December/January, 2003

Robert McAlmon's Poetry, *The Penniless Press* 14, Preston, 2001

Bird Breaks Down, *Beat Scene* 49, Coventry, 2005/2006

Harry Biss, *Jazz Journal*, Loughton, June 2007

Buddy Wise, *Jazz Journal* , Loughton, September 2000

Bird Lives!, *Ambit* 142, London, 1995

William Burroughs: Hip not Beat was first delivered as a paper at a symposium on William Burroughs at Keele University in 1994. It appears here in a slightly different form.

My thanks to all the editors concerned, especially Kevin Ring (*Beat Scene*) and Alan Dent (*The Penniless Press*). Also to Ken Clay and Joan Mottram

# INTRODUCTION

This book can be seen as a companion volume to a previous collection of essays, *Beats, Bohemians and Intellectuals*, published by Trent Books in 2000. It covers some of the same ground in that it looks primarily at American writers active from around 1930 to 1960 and a little beyond. Many of them had radical connections of one kind or another. Some people may wonder why I choose to focus mainly on less well-known writers, and the reason is simple - they are rarely written about and it seems relevant to establish a record of their existence. A couple of the essays deal with very minor figures who got into print during the heyday of the Beat movement, roughly 1957 to 1962, and while they may not appear important enough to warrant such attention they sometimes had something to say and they could be lively and entertaining.

The same can be said about two little-known jazzmen I've included. There is also a piece about Charlie Parker, but so many other critics have written articles and books about him that I've always thought it more interesting to draw attention to rank-and-file musicians who, like the writers referred to above, are often neglected. My spirits sink these days when I open a jazz magazine and see yet another article about Miles Davis or John Coltrane or someone similar to them.

I gather that the article I wrote about Anatole Broyard some years ago is quite popular, though I've been asked why it doesn't refer to his "passing for white," which I suspect intrigues certain readers. It doesn't, it's true, and the reason is that I wanted to survey his literary work. I do mention the racial element in his life in another essay, "Behind the Scenes," which discusses Chandler Brossard's *Who Walk in Darkness*, with its fictional portrait of Broyard. I also refer to the fact that a few of his fellow-writers accused him of what R.V. Cassill described as "competent malice" when he reviewed books by his more-successful contemporaries. My original essay played down that side of his work because I thought there was sufficient evidence to show that, at his best, he was a decent reviewer.

One essay, "Bird Lives!" is a personal memoir of my early and continuing love of jazz, and particularly the aspect of it known as bebop. My justification for it being here can be summed up by quoting the words of the American writer, Gilbert Sorrentino: "Bop, for me, was the entrance into the general world of culture, although at the time, I wouldn't have believed it."

9

# JACK CONROY: WORKER-WRITER IN AMERICA

Proletarian writing in the United States was always a topic likely to arouse heated debate, with few of the participants even agreeing on what the term meant. Did it indicate literature produced by genuine proletarians, or was it a description of writing which identified with them, but could be produced by middle-class authors? A definitive anthology, published in 1935 at the height of the proletarian literary movement, included writers such as John Dos Passos, Josephine Herbst, Malcolm Cowley and Albert Maltz, all of them talented and interesting, but not, by any stretch of the imagination, proletarians. The debate was never resolved, and was, perhaps, only settled when the Communist Party line moved away from insistence on the supposed virtues of proletarian values. The Popular Front ideal aimed to incorporate the work of well-known literary figures and played down the productions of genuinely proletarian writers.

One of these was Jack Conroy. Born in Missouri in 1898, he was the son of a miner and grew up in a small coal camp, which was, in Douglas Wixson's words,

> 'bound together in a community of work, shared danger, class struggle, and the special nature of mining itself. The experiences of his younger days were to have a lasting effect on Conroy, whose view of life was shaped more by a collective than an individual philosophy. He started work in a railroad workshop when he was thirteen, and soon began to move toward deeper involvement with the growing labour struggle, cooperative literary enterprises, and identification with the "people of the abyss," the disinherited'.

Conroy's father was killed in a mining accident, but he had been a union activist and a relatively well-educated man. His mother was an avid reader of fiction. Conroy himself loved the popular weekly magazines and the cheap novels which spotlighted the adventures of Diamond Dick and other heroes, though he also read Macaulay and learned long poems by heart. Wixson notes that this was a time when union journals printed poetry by workers, and had columns called 'Poems You Ought to Know', and other educational hints. And he adds: 'Conroy followed the oral culture of workers,

11

which included bawdy songs, sentimental ballads, and tales of his childhood, into railroad shop and factory. His own writing would translate those oral features of workers' lives into an authentic idiom that attracted H. L. Mencken's attention and led to publication in the *American Mercury*.' As he got older, Conroy read Kipling, Jack London, Frank Norris, Upton Sinclair, Edward Bellamy, and socialist tracts.

He was blacklisted after a major strike in 1922, and a variety of jobs followed as he wandered around the Midwest and tried to look after his family. He was, at the same time, attempting to write, and as Wixson says: 'What was a young worker to do, possessed of a lively intelligence, an interest in books, and writing ability? The natural course of an ambitious, energetic, and talented young person in America was (and is) to struggle upward, out of the working classes.' Conroy, however, had effectively renounced such a direction when he spurned attempts to make him into a white-collar employee. And a brief encounter with student life left him dissatisfied after one term. He wanted to enter into what Gorki had called 'the universities of life'.

His early published work appeared in union magazines and local papers, and by 1930 or so he was in touch with young, radical writers across the Midwest. It is at this point that Wixson's account begins to take on added interest, with a catalogue of now-forgotten writers filling the pages. Little is written these days about H. H. Lewis, Joseph Kalar, Robert Cruden, and many others like them. They did not become professional writers, nor did they necessarily have that aim in mind. Conroy may have summed up their point of view when he wrote an article, 'What if you don't want to write for money?' in 1933, the year when his first novel, *The Disinherited,* was published in New York. It was, in fact, a lightly fictionalised version of his childhood and first working experiences, and was meant to give a voice to the kind of people that Conroy knew.

*The Disinherited* brought him some fame, at least around the American Left, though sales were fairly low. And an idea of how some people viewed him can be gained from a publicity photograph which shows Conroy overalled and holding a cow by its tether, and with a hoe clutched in his other hand. This sort of representation of provincial, and particularly working-class writers was (and is) not untypical. And it raises serious questions about

12

how readers and critics rate such writers. There is, inevitably, a loss of seriousness, and a tendency to think: This is a good book because it's written by a farmer, factory-worker, or whatever, and not just because it's good'. The writers were fully aware of the irony inherent in their situation. H. H. Lewis referred to himself as 'the ploughboy poet', and penned a piece of doggerel which summed up his dilemma:

> Oh how can I struggle
> And win through strife
> Looking up a mule's prat
> All of my life.

Wixson's survey of the worker-writer movement in 1930 and 1931 is a fascinating story of neglected poets and obscure little magazines. One of the unsung heroes of those years was a printer named Ben Hagglund, described by Wixson as 'a poor man's patron of writing'. Hagglund was hampered by circumstances, and was not always the finest printer there was, but he could be 'a selfless, generous person', hiring himself out for farm work when Conroy was hard-pressed to raise money for his magazine, *Rebel Poet*, which Hagglund printed. How they managed to finance *Rebel Poet*, the later *Anvil,* and a radical anthology, *Unrest*, is described by Wixson in detail, and is illuminating in terms of explaining how worker-writers had to struggle to see their poems and stories in print.

Conroy, thanks to the publicity surrounding *The Disinherited*, and because of his energy and enthusiasm for keeping in touch with like-minded individuals, acted as something of a clearing house for radical writers and their work. He had access to the Communist Party magazine *New Masses*, to which he contributed articles and reviews, and he was in demand for introductions to small collections of verse by young left-wingers. An example of his agit-prop style when carrying out such tasks can be found in *When The Sirens Blow*, a slim book by Leonard Spier which was printed by Ben Hagglund. Conroy described Spier as 'one of the young worker-poets about whom most literary critics seldom speak unless goaded to it', and he made it clear that he considered it his role to do the goading when he added: 'The aroma of sweat and the heroism of toil are often very repugnant to the erudite gentlemen who pose as arbiters of literary worth.' These sentiments were not likely to endear Conroy to sophisticated critics of any political persuasion, and he was to pay for them in later years.

His relationship to the American Communist Party was always problematic, and Wixson has much of interest to say about it. In his words: 'While approving the Party's interventions on behalf of the unemployed and blacks, Conroy nonetheless ignored Party dictates and didactic tendencies among its orthodox ideologues.' There was some advantage in this, as there was in Conroy's location in the Midwest, because it kept him apart from the 'jealousies and backbiting among writers and critics' in New York. He was soon to encounter their influence, despite his distance from them, when his involvement with *Anvil* brought him into contact with people prepared to manipulate political ideology in order to advance their literary careers.

Wixson's detailed narrative of the rise and fall of *Anvil* is yet another intriguing look at the problems facing worker-writers. The magazine was, for a time, distributed by the Communist Party, but it also circulated thanks to the efforts of contributors and subscribers. Leonard Spier hawked it around New York bookshops, and the feminist writer Meridel Le Sueur tried selling it at factory gates. With a circulation of five thousand, and a readership higher than that, it was considered important enough for Party officials to object when Conroy printed advertisements for publications frowned on by Communists. He also dared to publish a writer accused of Trotskyism. Conroy, while never challenging the Party line in principle, didn't bother to hold to it in practice. His view was that he'd print anything he thought interestingly written and critical of the status quo, and he wasn't about to quibble over a writer's politics, provided they were generally in favour of the workers and other good causes.

Regional writers like Conroy found themselves under attack from New York literary circles, and Wixson quotes one Midwesterner as recalling that 'regional' was used almost as a dirty word. Changes in the Communist Party programme soon dictated that *Anvil* shed its regional image, and with it the policy of promoting worker-writers, in favour of printing established authors who, in the spirit of the Popular Front, were travelling with the Party, if not always joining it. The sad tale of how and why *Anvil* was incorporated into the newly established *Partisan Review*, and then disposed of altogether, is a depressing mixture of politics, personality clashes, and literary infighting, in which the less-sophisticated worker-writers, 'innocent of the city's plots and counterplots in the literary domain', came off worst.

Conroy's second, and last, novel, *A World to Win*, was neither as interesting nor as successful in critical terms as his first. It would be wrong to say that he wrote it to Party specifications, but he certainly shaped it to suit the political mood, something he had not deliberately done with *The Disinherited*. It was published in 1935, the year when he delivered a talk at the First American Writers' Congress in New York, and came across to many there as a naive and crude innocent when set among metropolitan intellectuals. That was certainly James T. Farrell's view, and he expressed it some years later in a novel, *Yet Other Waters*, in which Conroy is portrayed as a brash provincial, boosted by the Party because of his worker-status and given to wide-sweeping statements invoking the virtues of strike leaflets when compared to corrupt novels about bourgeois decadents. Farrell knew that the worker-writers were of little real interest to Communist bureaucrats and their literary allies, and that they would be dropped when it was opportune to welcome acclaimed poets and novelists to the cause. Wixson sees the ambitious left-wing writers on the New York literary scene as anxious to 'reclaim quality and value for their work according to more traditional literary standards', and further notes that 'a shift of power was taking place that sought control of the cultural discourse through systems of exclusion'.

1935 was probably the highpoint of Conroy's activities, although he continued to contribute occasional pieces to *New Masses* and the *Sunday Worker Magazine*. In 1939 he co-edited, with Nelson Algren, *New Anvil,* which was printed by the indefatigable Ben Hagglund and survived for seven issues. But he had a family to support and obtained a post on the Federal Writers' Project, a branch of Roosevelt's job-creation programme, where he spent much of his time researching folklore and transcribing traditional stories. Later, he was employed by popular encyclopedias, cooperated with the black writer Arna Bontemps on several books, and wrote articles and book reviews for various magazines and newspapers. It's significant that Wixson's large book has only sixty pages about Conroy's life between 1936 and his death in 1990.

Jack Conroy made a genuine attempt to promote authentic worker-writing, as opposed to theoretical proletarian writing, but found that it brought him into conflict with the literary establishment. His own work received some initial recognition from that establishment, but was downgraded by its spokesmen when attitudes changed. And he almost inevitably drifted into forms of employment that set him apart from the working class he had been born into and admired. His career raises numerous provocative questions about the position of the worker-writer in a society where the middle class dominates methods of literary production and determines the response to those methods.

This is an essential book for anyone interested in worker-writers, the history of the American literary Left, and questions of cultural norms. It is a little repetitious in places, but generally avoids jargon. And it is well documented, with a mass of information about writers, publishers, editors of little magazines, and printers.

*Jack Conroy and the Tradition of Midwestern Literary Radicalism, 1898-1990* by Douglas Wixon
Urbana and Chicago: University of Illinois Press, 1994) 0 252 02043 X

# RADICALS AND MODERNISTS

Cary Nelson, in his fascinating *Repression and Recovery: Modern American Poetry and the Politics of Cultural Memory 1910-1945,* pointed out that

> "the modern American poetry we have been most likely to encounter for some time - the poetry most regularly anthologised, taught, reprinted, read, and written about - is the poetry of a limited number of figures" (and that) "the process by which poets like these are elevated and others marginalised or forgotten" (can be) "regarded as immensely biased and repressive."

Nelson's book is a spirited and informative attempt to redress the balance by looking at the work of numerous neglected poets, including political radicals, surrealists, working class balladeers, and others usually left out of standard surveys of 20th Century poetry. Amongst the poets mentioned are Herman Spector, Joseph Kalar, and Sol Funaroff, all of them at one time linked to the Left and actively publishing in magazines in the 1920s and 1930s. It seems to me that their work says some interesting things about the making of poetry, and particularly about the relationship between radical politics and modernist techniques. It's too often assumed that many left-wing poets were opposed to modernist ideas on the grounds that they ignored the tastes of the masses, but this was not true of the poets concerned, nor of others like them. Spector, Kalar, and Funaroff were all well aware of what modernism meant and how they could use the techniques it pioneered in their own work.

All three, and a fourth poet, Edwin Rolfe, were featured in a small volume, *We Gather Strength*, published in New York in 1933. Mike Gold, the American Communist Party's cultural commentator, wrote the introduction for the book, and referred to them as "hungry proletarians. Their minds are filled with images of death. They alternate between deathly despair and the wild wonderful dreams of our World Revolution. Nothing is clear about them yet, except that they are actors in a great drama." It was, perhaps, a typical piece of revolutionary-hype by Gold, who would often judge a poet by the level or lack of political commitment in the work, but at one point he did also note that "the influence of modern bourgeois poetry, T.S.Eliot, Ezra Pound, William Carlos Williams," could be detected in some of the poems. Gold could be dismissive of experimental modernism - "We, are not interested in verbal acrobats - this is only another form for bourgeois idleness," he commented elsewhere - but he was prepared to extend a welcome to poets who used modernist techniques that were filtered-through a radical perspective.

*Herman Spector*

Herman Spector was born in 1905 in New York, the son of a businessman. Little is known about his early life - he dropped out of high school after three years -other than that he worked at a variety of jobs, most of them of a routine labouring or clerical kind. He began publishing poetry in the 1920s, and appeared in avant-garde magazines such as *transition* and *The Exile.* According, to Harry Roskolenko, another now-forgotten poet of that period, Spector was "the bitterest man I ever knew..... Ezra Pound, then extolling social credit economics in Mussolini's Italy, had made Spector one of his far-away proteges.." (he was) "savage, brutal and brilliant, an innovator in poetry, and Pound admired his experiments." An example of what Pound liked was Spector's *Cloaks and Suits,* a cryptic look at a businessman in the rag trades:

> The salesmen salaam and kiss his feet and vis
> iting buyers respect him because he got more
> money than what they got and Mr. Goldberger
> figures he could buy every dressmodel in the
> building - If he wanted to.....

Spector seems to have almost relished looking at life from the bottom of the social ladder, and he described himself as "the bastard in the ragged suit/ who spits, with bitterness and malice to all." Harry Roskolenko suggested that it was some sort of extension of his loathing for his upper-middle class background, and said that Spector "took shoddy jobs to aggravate the cosmic hatred in his poetry." Throughout his poems there runs a steady stream of images of "rusted iron and garbage dumps/flowers and garlic, and windows choked/with faces bereft of colour or hope," and along with them flows a strong social conscience. Pound may have been an admirer of Spector's works but the feeling wasn't necessarily mutual. In a poem published in *Partisan Review* in 1934, Spector attacked the Objectivist poets (even though some of them were fellow-communists) and alluded to Pound's influence on them:

> sadly they perish, each by each,
> whispering madness, they disappear...
> into the isolate doom, of dreams,
> into the cold gray vaults of dust,
> and who will gather the darlings up,
> arrange them in anthologies?
> what mussolini-horse will drop
> bouquets upon their mouldering graves?

The techniques that Spector used were, on the whole, derived from modernist sources, though he was not averse to using rhyme and clearly-defined stanzas to make sharp political points. But mostly, the poems broke rhythms, placed lines irregularly on the page, and aimed for a language largely taken from the streets, though there were some uneven excursions into more-literary phrases. If the technique was modernistic, though, it was rare for Spector to ever be less than clear in what he was saying. An inward-looking modernism was not for him, and his world was the one in front of his eyes as he prowled the streets:

> each morning john hawley jaunts to the job
> via streetcar in the summertime,
> absentmindedly proffers his fare
> (the motorman has a sweaty face),
> turns to the sportsection of the paper with habitual indifference.

Spector's poems appeared in many of the publications associated with the Left, but he was also a frequent contributor to *Blues*, the avant-garde magazine edited by Charles Henri Ford with assistance from Parker Tyler. There is, incidentally, a fictional portrait of Spector in *The Young and Evil*, the novel by Ford and Tyler which was published in 1933 and dealt with the Greenwich Village bohemia of the late-1920s and early-1930s. And there seems little doubt that he was something of an influence on other poets. Norman Macleod later recalled how Spector and Parker Tyler pushed him "in the direction of experiment and in trying to find my own voice and new forms - or at least to say what I was trying to say in language that was not distorted by restrictive English metrical patterns." And yet, as the 1930s left-literary scene gathered momentum, Spector seemed to slow down. By 1940 he had virtually stopped publishing or mixing with the poets and political activists he once sought out, and he had retreated to what someone described as "what was masochistically secure - Brooklyn, driving a taxi, living lower middle-class, raising his children." He did write when he could, his wife said, but didn't bother to send the results to magazines. When he died, in 1959, he was a forgotten figure. The pressures of supporting a family may have had much to do with Spector's decision to withdraw from the literary world, though there is evidence that his dark vision of society was not just a pose and that it stemmed from something inherent in his personality. Friends thought that the darkness -a form of disenchantment with both life and literature - had finally come out on top. Whatever the reasons for his withdrawal it, and the amnesia which affected much of the intellectual community in the late-1940s and the 1950s as anti-communist hysteria mixed with complacency to cause people to almost pretend that the radical 1930s hadn't existed, meant that only a few scholars and maverick figures like Kenneth Rexroth acknowledged Spector's contribution to the poetry of that era.

*Joseph Kalar*

Some of the pressures that Spector felt were also experienced by Joseph Kalar. He was born in 1906 in Minnesota, and although he trained as a teacher he worked only briefly in the profession before attempting to make a living as a journalist. Unsuccessful, he took manual jobs as a lumber worker and sawmill mechanic and began contributing to a variety of radical magazines. Kalar was very much part of a Midwestern school of writing which, for a time in the 1930s, had its own outlets in publications like *The Anvil* and *The Rebel Poet*. There was a tradition of social protest poetry in the Midwest, though much of it was based firmly on conventional forms. Kalar, however, was familiar with the kind of poetry published in expatriate magazines like *transition* and *This Quarter*, and seems to have had a fairly wide awareness of modernist experiments. Like Spector, he wanted to use the technical innovations of the modernists to express radical ideas, as in *Bank*, a poem commenting on the effect that banks had on people's lives:

> Be proud be proud whimpers
> the bank be proud with
> compound interest and
> mortgages on farms lean

and not so lean.

What is obvious is that Kalar used techniques taken from the modernists, but did so in order to accent the fragmentation of society as economic factors caused job losses, evictions, family breakdown, and other social ills. What he said was clear enough, though the way he said it may have seemed strange to those more at home with conventional metrical forms, obvious rhymes, and the general tradition of verse making.

Kalar was a member of the American Communist Party, though his sometimes idiosyncratic views brought him into conflict with the editors of *New Masses,* the magazine which published several of his poems. And, unlike Spector, he didn't have the opportunity to mix with sophisticated radicals, like those in New York. As Douglas Wixson has pointed out,

> "the ideological sources of Midwestern literary radicals like Kalar..... derived from indigenous traditions of protest, (and the) legacy was grass-roots democratic expression, a spirit of egalitarianism and individualism-neighbourliness that seemed at times at odds with the demand for revolutionary change."

From the evidence of his poems Kalar rarely, if ever, wrote lines that waved banners or made great calls for any kind of violent upheaval. His work largely focuses on the miseries of unemployment, low pay, poor conditions, and hunger. There are occasional nods in the direction of communism, but it is the immediate problem that engages Kalar's attention most of the time:

> Hunger is with us.
> Factory smoke is sour
> with the memory of work
> to be done
> and a wild look in the eye:
> no work today, buddy, no work...

The problems of staying alive and supporting a family in difficult times were bound to affect Kalar's efforts at writing, and he had the additional difficulty of being far from the main centres of publication and influence. Like most working-class writers he also came up against the harsh fact that his environment, whilst providing material for writing, did not provide the circumstances for it. "Not the work, but the hours, militate against my ever creating as I would like to create -I have always been caught in the trap of long

21

hours and small pay" he wrote to a friend in the early -1930s. There was, too, the irony that although he claimed solidarity with his workmates he didn't share their tastes and values. As a political radical he was bitterly disappointed by the indifference of most of his colleagues to any revolutionary change. People who knew Kalar at this time said that his fellow workers tolerated his politics because they liked him personally, but he grew increasingly cynical and, by the mid-1930s, had virtually stopped writing for publication. He was active in union organising and stood for public office as a candidate for the Farmer-Labour Party, which was active in the Midwestern states, but by the end of the decade had drifted away from both poetry and politics.

As with Herman Spector, the period after 1940 saw Kalar caught up with family life and a routine job, in his case in industrial and personnel relations for a Minnesota paper company. And, again like Spector, he was almost forgotten as a poet when he died in 1972. Kalar's interests, his intelligence, and his skills, had taken him away from the manual jobs he had once gloried in, and the raw edge that had characterised his best poems perhaps had no reason for being applied once he'd lost the anger that came with the injustices of the 1930s.

*Sol Funaroff*

In a memoir of life in Manchester in the 1930s and of his activities with a group performing radical street theatre outside factory gates and elsewhere, the folk-singer Ewan MacColl referred to "a group declamation of a poem called *The Fire Sermon* by Sergei Funarov." The poem was actually called *What the Thunder Said: A Fire Sermon*, and the author was Sol Funaroff, who also wrote under the name Charles Henry Newman. He was born in 1911 and in the 1930s was active in left-wing literary circles in New York, where he was on the editorial staff of *New Theatre* and edited a little magazine, *Dynamo*, as well as the *Dynamo Poets Series*, publishers of Kenneth Fearing's first book. He wrote for major publications, such as *New Republic* and *New Masses*, and was included in the influential anthology, *Proletarian Literature in the United States*.

Some of Funaroff's poems have much in common with those by Spector and Kalar, with their images of unemployed men, homeless old women asleep on park benches, and general social breakdown. His poem *Uprooted* vividly evokes the mood of the times:

> The shadows of silent machines
> spread on the walls of the city.
> Amid uptorn pavement of the broken street
> a blanketed steamroller,
> stranded, waits.
> Hands in pockets, he stands at the corner, waiting,
> or walks, a brooding figure, through the streets.

But Funaroff had a wider range and wrote several long poems which attempted to place Marxist ideas into a framework of modernist verse. *The Spider and the Clock,* the title poem of Funaroff's first book, published in 1938, took its inspiration from a newspaper report about a biologist who was studying the battle of a large spider to harness the moving hands of an alarm clock in its silken web. The metaphorical implications of this for a Marxist poet will be obvious, and Funaroff built up his picture of a society in turmoil admittedly using many standard images - "A torn time-card," "crumbs in the bread box, the landlord at the door" - but also bringing in references to the international situation and the wider crisis of capitalism. And he ends the poem with a series of questions which refer to the inevitability of certain events, including, of course, the triumph of communism:

> Does man walk upward down a hill?
>
> Will the sun
>
>> stand
>>> still?

Funaroff's most ambitious poem was probably *What the Thunder Said: A Fire Sermon*, and it was, in his own words,

> "based on Marxian philosophical concepts. As symbol and as history this event (the Russian Revolution) challenges the fundamentally political and religious attitudes of negation, frustration, the martyrdom of the individual and the decay of the materialistic world which find their most significant poetic expression in T.S.Eliot's *The Waste Land*."

The setting of the poem was a street meeting with a speaker addressing a crowd of workers while a thunderstorm threatens. What Funaroff did was to transform the speech into a poetic form and use the city scenes as "a cinematic language which, as in montage, correlates and fuses the objects as symbols that visualise the changing themes of the speaker." Funaroff had presumably read Mayakovsky and other Russian poets of the Revolution, as well as Eliot, and was clearly at home with the techniques of modernism. Was he totally successful? Perhaps not, though the poem is, if flawed, a powerful document. Our view of it will necessarily be distorted by the passage of time, which allows us to see the slogans as empty and the dreams as destroyed, but much of the energy and narrative force still comes through, and it's easy to imagine Mac-Coll and his friends performing it with gusto;

> In the Smolny
> the decisive delegates,
> drawn faces,
> burnt cigarettes, telephones,
> wires, leaflets, -
> telegraphic congresses:
> and in the chill streets
> armed workers, soldiers,
> add fuel to the street fires.
> Rifles ready. Waiting. Deciding.
> Who are the riders ?

Funaroff's star seemed to shine brightly for a time in the 1930s, but ill-health, which had dogged him for much of his life, took its toll and he died in 1942. His friends got together and brought out a limited edition of his poems under the title, *Exile From a Future Time*, though his earlier volume had probably contained most of his best poems. There is, as far as I know, no record available which shows how Funaroff reacted to the events of the late 1930s and early 1940s, including the Nazi-Soviet Pact, the German invasion of Russia, American entry into the War, etc., so it's impossible to tell if he would have withdrawn from radical politics in the way that Spector and Kalar did. What is certain is that his early death, and the falling away of interest in left-wing poets, consigned Funaroff to the same near-oblivion that the others shared.

Spector, Kalar, and Funaroff can be seen as failures, in more ways than one, and yet their attempts to combine left-wing politics with modernist literary techniques were, I believe, worthwhile and not without interest. And it seems to me that they have all been unjustly neglected and that they deserve to be read now and given their rightful place in the history of 20th Century poetry.

NOTES

*We Gather Strength* was published by the Liberal Press, New York, in 1933. The fourth poet, Edwin Rolfe, was also a communist. Readers might like to refer to my article about him in *Beats Bohemians and Intellectuals*

The easiest-available selection of poems by Spector, Kalar, and Funaroff, is in *Social Writing of the 1930s: Volume 1: Poetry,* edited by Jack Salzman and Leo Zanderer, published by Burt Franklin & Co., New York, 1978. One of the advantages of this anthology is that it sets them in context and alongside other 1930s radicals like Kenneth Patchen, Ben Maddow, Alfred Hayes, Michael Gold, and Norman Macleod.

Herman Spector's poems, together with other writings by him and some useful information, can be found in *Bastard in the Ragged Suit*, edited by Bud Johns and Judith S.Clancy, published by Synergistic Press, San Francisco, 1977.

Joseph Kalar's work has been reprinted in *Joseph A. Kalar: Poet of Protest*, edited by Richard G.Kalar, published by RGK Publications, Blaine, Minnesota, 1985. There is also a great deal of information about Kalar in Douglas Wixson's *Worker-Writer in America,* University of Illinois Press, Urbana, 1994.

Sol Funaroff's work does not appear to have been reprinted in book form in recent years.

Cary Nelson's *Repression and Recovery: Modern American Poetry and the Politics of Cultural Memory 1910-1946* was published by the University of Wisconsin Press, Madison, 1989. Walter Kalaidjian's *American Culture Between the Wars*, Columbia University Press, New York, 1993, is also of interest for attempting to redress the balance between poets taken into the canon and those left out of it.

Alan Wald's *Writing from the left: New Essays on Radical Culture and Politics*, Verso, London, 1994, is similarly useful and informative.

Alan Filreis's *Modernism from Right to Left: Wallace Stevens, the Thirties, and Literary Radicalism*, Cambridge University Press, Cambridge, 1994, develops the idea that "radicals knew and appreciated modernism, more than has been recognised."

Ewan MacColl's *Theatre of Action, Manchester* can be found in *Theatres of the Left 1880-1935: Workers' Theatre Movements in Britain and America* edited by Raphael Samuel, Ewan MacColl, and Stuart Cosgrove, published by Routledge and Kegan Paul, London, 1985.

# WHO WAS ALBERT HALPER?

Writing to Sebastian Sampas in 1941, Jack Kerouac mentioned that he was reading books by "Wolfe, Saroyan, Halper, Dos Passos." With the exception of "Halper" these are names that still mean something and at least some of their books can usually be found in the shops. But who was "Halper"? And why did Kerouac think it important to read him?

Albert Halper was, in the 1930s, considered to be an important American novelist and his name was mentioned alongside the leading writers of the day. Sinclair Lewis, himself a noted novelist, said that Halper ranked with Faulkner, Hemingway, and O'Hara, and added that he had "the skill of Dickens in making beauty out of grime." And yet, despite praise like this (and Lewis wasn't alone in enthusing about Halper's work) Albert Halper had, by the mid 1940s, disappeared from the front rank of American writers. By the 1960s he was almost forgotten, and in recent years his name has only cropped up when academics have written about the radical writers of the Depression era.

Halper was born in Chicago in 1904, the son of Lithuanian Jewish immigrants. He grew up on Chicago's West Side, went to local schools, worked in his father's grocery store, and was an errand boy for a fur and haberdashery business. He left high school in 1921 and got a job with a mail order company but then moved to an electrotype foundry, where he stayed for four years. Halper's work experiences need to be mentioned because they later played an important part in his writing. While working in the foundry he attended evening classes at Northwestern University, taking courses in writing, newspaper reporting, and psychology. He also read writers like Mark Twain, James Joyce, Knut Hamsun, Sherwood Anderson, Theodore Dreiser, F. Scott Fitzgerald, and Ernest Hemingway, and visited art galleries and theatres. He heard jazz in Chicago, listening to musicians such as King Oliver, Bix Beiderbecke, and Charlie Straight.

When he left the foundry Halper worked as a salesman and a clerk, then as a machine operator in a factory. And he spent a year or so with the Post Office. But his thoughts were increasingly inclined towards writing, and he later said: "I always wanted to become a writer, but I could never work myself out of the rut of the dull, monotonous West Side streets and my dreary bread and butter labour." In the autumn of 1928, however, the prestigious *Dial* magazine accepted a couple of short pieces by him and he immediately handed in his notice at the Post Office and moved to New York. His savings lasted only a short time, so he returned to Chicago and got a job in a law office. As soon as he'd saved more money he went back to New York, just in time to try and make it as a writer as the Wall Street Crash pushed America into a major economic slump.

Halper had never been involved with intellectuals and writers in Chicago and had lived the life of a poorly paid worker, gaining experiences which were to prove useful when he began to write novels. As the Depression deepened there was an upsurge of interest in literature which dealt with the lives of ordinary people, whether in work or unemployed. And there was an increase in political activity, with communists and others organising and agitating. Halper had friends in New York who wanted him to use his writing to further left-wing causes but he was wary of getting too involved. He was sympathetic to the plight of the homeless, the unemployed, and striking workers, but saw his role as a writer as a kind of historian of the lives of ordinary people as they were and not as political activists wanted them to be. He didn't think that joining a party or tailoring his writing to a specific programme was likely to help him produce the kind of literature he had in mind. His aim was "to see life clearly, and as whole as may be, and then to tell the truth about it." Obviously, the fact that he wrote about working people did give him credibility in left-wing circles and some of his stories began to appear in magazines like *Pagany, The Menorah Journal,* and *The Midland.* And he got to know writers like Kenneth Fearing, Tess Slesinger, and Charles Reznikoff, and he was introduced to a literary agent named Maxim Lieber, who acted for many left-wing writers. Lieber later turned out to have also been an agent of another sort and caused the FBI to take an interest in Halper.

In his vivid memoir of the 1930s, *Goodbye, Union Square*, Halper paints a fascinating picture of the life of a young, struggling writer. He wrote two novels which his agent was unable to place with publishers, and although he eventually managed to get his stories in well known publications such as *The American Mercury* and *Harper's*, and in one of the *American Caravan* anthologies, it took time for his name to become known. He scuffled, did odd jobs, cut his living expenses to a bare minimum, and generally tried to survive in the harsh atmosphere of New York, with the streets full of the unemployed, the police breaking up demonstrations, and hard times all round.

But, in 1932, his luck began to change when his novel, *Union Square*, was accepted for publication. It came out in 1933, was chosen by The Literary Guild as its March selection, and received some good reviews. The bad reviews tended to come from the communist press, with Mike Gold, the party's literary spokesman, attacking Halper because his novel satirised young communists. Gold thought that too many of its characters represented a "stale Bohemianism" which Halper mistook for "social revolution." The book did indeed have some bohemian types, but it was much more varied than that and was written in a fast, racy style that caught some of the atmosphere of 1930s New York and its turbulent mixture of high hopes and low life.

*Union Square* started Halper's period of fame, and in 1934 a collection of his stories appeared as well as a novel, *The Foundry*. He went back to his Chicago experiences in this, and though the book can be placed in a line of socially conscious writing it did not follow any kind of pattern of politically committed literature. The 1930s saw the rise of "proletarian writing," a term which could be applied to literature about the working class and to literature by working class writers. Halper, because of his background and experiences, could probably claim a closer association with the working-class than many left-wing authors, but he said that he didn't know what "proletarian writing" was and that all he was trying to do was write about the lives of the kind of people he'd known when he was employed in routine jobs. *The Foundry* featured a large cast of characters and even tried to present the point of view of the bosses. What he was aiming for was a composite picture which would show how industrialism affected behaviour and how men and machines inter-related. The book was praised by some reviewers, though the communists again criticised Halper for failing to make his workers heroic and the American Communist Party the beacon to which they should look for guidance. Halper had left America just before *The Foundry* was published and spent some time in London, where he worked on another novel and met various British writers. He then spent a couple of months in Russia and returned to New York in the summer of 1935. His next novel, *The Chute,* came out in 1937, with Halper's stint with a mail-order company providing material for a different look at working lives. The chute, like the foundry, acts as a focus for all the activities of the people concerned, shaping their thoughts, attitudes, relationships, and so on. It is sited in the middle of the floor and goods are collected from storage, packaged, and despatched down the chute for delivery. Speed is central to this business, with the employees here and there, grabbing goods from shelves, wrapping them and desperately trying to keep up with the flow of new orders and the urgings of the supervisors to quicken the pace. Some even wear roller skates so they can get up and down the aisles faster. The chute can be seen as representing the way in which capitalism pushes everyone into more activity to satisfy the demands of consumerism, and the novel is a powerful indictment of how the system destroys individuals. But, as usual, Halper didn't draw any conclusions in terms of the workers revolting or a political theory offering a solution. *The Chute* is a dark novel in which, as someone said, "everyone fails."

It's difficult to know which of Halper's novels were read by Jack Kerouac, though *Sons of the Fathers,* published in 1940, may have interested him. It was something of a family chronicle, describing how the entry of America into the First World War affects its different members and pushes them into activities they might not have experienced otherwise. Kerouac, as we know, tackled the family theme in his first novel, *The Town and The City*, with the Second World War having its impact on relationships. Two more novels, *The Little People* (1942), which was about working in a haberdashery store, and *Only an Inch From Glory* (1943), describing the lives of a group of young bohemians in Greenwich Village, showed that Halper was still active, though neither made any great impression on the critics. Halper himself once said that the 1930s was his key period, and as the war effort dominated everyone's time and energies he seemed to retreat into silence. Nothing was heard from him until 1952, when he edited a collection of stories about Chicago. He did have a couple of plays produced in the mid 1950s, though neither made it to New York. And in 1956, when a new novel, *Atlantic Avenue*, was published, it was clearly aimed at the paperback market for easy to read stories about the sleazy side of urban life. One critic remarked that it was "hardly a successful potboiler," suggesting that Halper's heart hadn't really been in it when he sat down to write the book and it therefore didn't work either as a serious novel or as pulp fiction.

Another long silence ensued until 1966, when his last novel, *The Fourth Horseman of Miami Beach*, appeared to no great acclaim. Halper's final book, *Goodbye, Union Square,* was published in 1970, and at least took his career out on a reasonably high note, being a well written and evocative account of his experiences in the 1930s and, to some extent, the 1940s. It is slightly affected by Halper's need to distance himself from any real involvement with radical movements and ideas, and he seems to be trying too hard to show that he was always wise to what the communists were up to. It's easy to understand why Halper felt some bitterness towards the communists, and especially Maxim Lieber, his one-time literary agent. In 1948 he was visited by the FBI, who questioned him closely about his links to Lieber and the extent of his involvement with radical causes. They knew that he had visited Russia and had been published in *New Masses* and other left-wing magazines. But what particularly interested them was that Halper's signature was on documents relating to an organisation called The American Feature Writers Syndicate. This was, according to the FBI, a front for communist espionage activities. Halper denied any knowledge of the organisation and didn't know how his signature had got on the document, though in his memoirs he claimed to recall acting as a witness for a contract that Lieber was drawing up for another writer. Halper suspected that this may, in fact, have been the document the FBI referred to, and that Lieber had lied to him and tricked him into signing it.

*Goodbye, Union Square* took its place alongside other memoirs by writers who had lived through the social, political, and literary up-heavals of the 1930s, and were anxious to set down their versions of those years. But little was heard of Albert Halper after it appeared and he died in obscurity in 1984.

It's interesting that Kerouac thought of him as sufficiently important in 1941 to want to read his books. Kerouac did have some woolly left-wing ideas when he was young, as he said in *Vanity Of*

*Duluoz* "in those days we were all pro-Lenin, or pro-whatever Communists") and it may be that Halper's social commentary in novels like *The Foundry* and *The Chute* caught his imagination and that he liked the way in which the books dealt with the everyday lives of ordinary people. He may also have been impressed by the sheer energy of Halper's early writing. His books sizzle with life, even if they are sometimes a bit rough and ready, and are full of vivid descriptive passages. And the dialogue in them is always lively and convincing in its recreation of the kind of language heard in a factory or around the warehouses of a mail-order company. Writing about *The Chute,* one critic said "talk is often slangy, raw, obscene, a tissue of clichés and shop talk, of quirks and verbal mannerisms." Halper was, additionally, a very autobiographical writer, with a remarkable memory for what he'd seen, heard, and experienced many years before, something that Kerouac himself ("The Great Rememberer," as Allen Ginsberg called him) was noted for. It may have been that Kerouac was simply reading Halper because his was a name that was well known at the time, but I think there may have been more to it than that. Albert Halper, in the novels he published between 1933 and 1943, created a body of work that described and commented on his America, and I'd guess that Kerouac responded to that and found something of value in it.

## ALBERT HALPER A CHECKLIST

A brief listing of his major books, not meant to be comprehensive at all. As far as we know all Albert Halper's books are out of print.

*Union Square* published in 1933 by The Viking Press of New York. The copy I refer to here is a Belmont paperback published in 1961.

*Only An Inch From Glory* published in 1943, the copy I have is a Belmont paperback published in 1963.

*Atlantic Avenue* published in 1956. The copy I have is a 1966 Award Books USA paperback.

*The Little People* was published in 1942 by Harpers & Brothers.

*Sons of The Fathers* was published in 1940 by Viking.

*The Chute* was published by Viking in 1937.

*The Foundry* was published by Viking in 1934.

*Goodbye, Union Square* was published in 1970 by Quadrangle.

*The Fourth Horseman of Miami Beach* was published in 1966 by Norton.

NOTE

The checklist was added to the essay by the editor of *Beat Scene*. I have included it as it may be useful.

# WILLIAM HERRICK AND THE SPANISH CIVIL WAR

William Herrick is an American writer, author of ten novels and an autobiography, and unfortunately too little known in this country. Some of his books have been published here, but he's rarely mentioned when contemporary American writing is discussed, probably because he doesn't fit into any kind of neat category and can't be lumped in with younger, more fashionable novelists. And I suspect that the political content of much of Herrick's work isn't to the taste of British readers. His concerns are no doubt seen as dated or irrelevant, though nothing could be further from the truth. What Herrick writes about in many of his books are the politics that shaped the modern world, and no amount of talk about the end of history, nor interest in matters meant to divert attention from what really counts, can alter this fact.

He was born in 1915, the son of Jewish parents who had come to the United States from Byelorussia (now Belarus) and settled in Trenton, New Jersey. He grew up in an atmosphere of political commitment and debate, and opens his autobiography with the following words:

> "I was born too late to be a Wobbly, one of the I Won't Work guys, the Industrial Workers of the World. Too bad. Over my crib hung a piece of tin embossed with the stern physiognomies of Vladimir Ilich Lenin and Leon Trotsky. It hung on one wall or another until I was in my teens. Finally, it was replaced by another piece of tin, this one stamped with the benign image of Joseph Stalin."

Herrick's father had a wallpaper shop and also worked as a wallpaper hanger, but he died when he was only thirty-six and Herrick was brought up by his mother and various relatives. He records that his mother went to work as a seamstress when she was ten and stopped at the age of sixty-nine. But she was also a woman who was active in the Yiddish art world. Herrick says: "She was sought after by the leading Yiddish poets and actors of the time to read their poems, to sing their songs." I don't want to provide too much information about Herrick's childhood, because it's much better to read the vivid details in his autobiography, but it's worth referring to the kind of environment he grew up in. He recalls a neighbourhood where political activity was central to life, and describes being taken to meetings to listen to his uncles and others argue about socialism, communism, and anarchism. His mother was a charter member of the American Communist Party. And he mentions that, even forty years after those days, a family funeral was likely to turn into a political battleground as arguments raged about which ideology the dead person really believed in.

By the time he was thirteen Herrick was going to Young Pioneer meetings and reading widely. John Reed's *Ten Days That Shook The World* is in the list he provides, but so is *Anna Karenina* and the Nick Carter detective novels. There were literary types around his family, too, though at the time Herrick didn't know about them. His cousin had a friend, "a tough-speaking guy from Brooklyn, a know-it-all named Henry," who later wrote a book called *Tropic of Cancer* and was, of course, Henry Miller.

Herrick and his mother had moved to New York, and when he left school in 1932 the Depression was at its height and jobs hard to come by. He spent some time in a utopian colony in Michigan, then drifted from place to place joining picket lines and protests wherever he found them. And he continued to read - Melville, Tolstoy, Dostoevsky. He is not starry-eyed about being on the road, and mockingly says:

> "In the seventies I met a forty year-old, over-moneyed, under-dressed hippie who, when he learned I had been on the road in the thirties, breathlessly asked me what songs we had sung. He was certain every hobo camp, every Hooverville, sported at least one Woody Guthrie. When I told him that not once had I encountered a wandering minstrel, his face deflated. How terribly disappointing. There were no choral societies, barber-shop quartets, or wandering minstrels like Guthrie singing working class songs on the road. Once in a while you'd see a guy playing a uke or banjo on some street corner, his hat at his feet, hoping for a couple of pennies. Buddy, can you spare a dime? Life is just a bowl of cherries. Three little words, I love you. Later, you might run into him at the Hooverville out of town."

Thoroughly involved with the communists, Herrick helped smash up Trotskyist meetings and then went south, to Georgia, to try to organise the black sharecroppers. When a secret meeting was broken up by local police and racists he was lucky to escape with his life. In later years he realised what he had actually been doing and he quotes from a historian who says that the Communist Party was "recklessly pushing oppressed black people into a premature confrontation with white planters. The result would be the shedding of black blood in a hopeless cause so that Communists could make propaganda from it."

The Party line changed in the mid-Thirties and the Popular Front came in. In retrospect Herrick sees it as "an ingenious scam." The Civil War broke out in Spain and Herrick, caught up in the excitement and enthusiasm for the Loyalist cause and fully believing everything he read in the Party papers, volunteered to join the International Brigades.

Herrick's experiences in Spain are the most colourful parts of his autobiography. Some might also say that they are the most contentious. He came back from Spain disillusioned with the role of the communists and the incompetence of many officers who had been appointed simply because they were politically acceptable and not because they had any military skills. The story of Oliver Law is an example. He was a black American who was given a senior position so that the communists could exploit it for propaganda purposes. But he was hopelessly inadequate in the field and caused the deaths of many of the men under his command. When he was killed in action the Party press had him dying a hero's death when leading an attack, but Herrick suggests that he was deliberately shot by some of his own troops. It's only fair to say that Herrick's account has been challenged by International Brigaders who were actually with Law when he died, and that Herrick himself only got his information from second or third-hand sources. The point is, though, that Law wasn't a good officer, though he seems to have been a courageous soldier when not in command, and that his promotion was a matter of Party policy rather than making sense from a military standpoint.

It slowly began to dawn on Herrick that anyone who even mildly disagreed with Party ideas was likely to be treated badly, even to the extent of disappearing in mysterious circumstances. He cites the case of Marvin Stern who had a good combat record but was inclined to question the capabilities of the leadership of the American section of the International Brigades. Stern was taken from the front line and his friends were warned not to ask questions about what had happened to him. When Herrick approached a high-ranking Party official who was visiting Spain and asked him to find out about Stern he was told to be careful. The official, known to have been Stern's friend in the USA, said: "In Party matters friendship doesn't count, the Party come first - and don't you forget it." Herrick was vehemently anti-Communist in later years, and felt particularly bitter about some of his old comrades in the Abraham Lincoln Battalion, but information that has recently come to light as the archives in Moscow are opened up to scholars does perhaps lend weight to the suggestion that troublesome members of the International Brigades often tended to die or disappear in curious ways. The Communist Party dominated the Brigades and ruthlessly suppressed any opposition.

Herrick was wounded and, whilst recovering, had an affair with a nurse who was married to Laszlo Rajk, then a top communist official in Spain and later active in the Hungarian government until he was purged and then executed in the early 50s. Because of this liaison, and probably because the woman reported him as critical of the Party and the Soviet Union and possibly even sympathetic to the POUM militia, Herrick came under suspicion and was questioned about his loyalty. He was taken to watch the execution of some Spaniards who were members of non-communist left organisations, and had no doubt that it was meant as a warning to him. He eventually left Spain because his wound (a bullet was lodged in his spine) needed special treatment, and on his return to New York was given a job with the communist-controlled Furriers Union. But in 1939 the Nazi-Soviet pact finally pushed him into leaving the Party and he was fired from his job. He trained as a court reporter and made a living that way, and got around to publishing his first novel in 1967.

I've spent a little time giving a rough outline of Herrick's life because the details are important to his writing. He has, in several of his books, used his experiences, and those of his friends, as a basis for what he has written. In *The Itinerant* (1967) the hero, Zeke Gurovich, grows up in the slums, meets artists and revolutionaries, visits a utopian commune, knocks around the country during the worst of the Depression, organises blacks in the southern states, goes to Spain, serves in the American Army during the Second

World War, and finally comes to terms with life and the failure of his dreams. Put this way the novel sounds like a lightly-fictionalised version of his autobiography, though Herrick was medically unfit for service in the American Army. But he introduces a rich cast of minor characters into the novel, has a love theme running throughout the story, and uses dialogue and description in a way that allows him to colour his writing and keep the story line constantly moving. Zeke's activities in Spain are much more varied than Herrick's, and the book as a whole has a panoramic feeling that only fiction can truly present.

Another Herrick novel, *Hermanos!* (1969) is probably his best known and is, as the title suggests, about the Spanish Civil War. But the hero of the book is not an autobiographical figure in the way that Zeke in *The Itinerant* often appeared to be. Jake Starr is a hard-line Party activist, rushing around organising strikes, going to meetings, giving speeches, enrolling volunteers for Spain. The background, as so often in Herrick's writing, brings in real events, as when he refers to a group of Communist Party members boarding a ship in New York harbour and ripping down a Nazi flag. You can find a factual account of this incident in Bill Bailey's *The Kid From Hoboken* (Bailey was one of the people involved and later fought in Spain) and a fictional one In Irwin Shaw's short-story, *Sailor Off The Bremen.* And it's easy to recognise the real-life basis for a character like Joe Garms in *Hermanos!* He was Joe Gordon, one of Herrick's friends In Spain and after.

Starr is ordered to go to Europe to help with getting volunteers into Spain and spends some time in Paris where he has an affair with an English woman whose husband is a Professor who has a great deal of influence in Communist Party circles. Starr moves to Spain, is wounded in action, and is later incorporated into the secret police and is responsible for hunting down and executing alleged enemies of the Republic. These are not just fascists, but socialists, anarchists, and anyone else seen as a threat to communist domination of the Loyalist war effort. This isn't pure invention on Herrick's part, as historians have documented how the communists did operate such a policy. In one key scene in *Hermanos!* Starr executes an anarchist who has cropped up earlier in the book and is a kind of spokesman for the anti-Communist left. Before Starr shoots the man they debate their respective philosophies, with the anarchist pointing out that Starr's cause is doomed to failure because of the perversions of the truth practised in its name.

Throughout *Hermanos!* a second story, that of Joe Garms and the rank-and-file in the front line, tells how they fight and die and are constantly let down by bad planning and poor leadership. Their story is sometimes in the form of letters from Garms to Starr and sometimes in straight narrative accounts of the fighting. Garms is wounded and evacuated to France, along with a man called Horton who is the nearest to Herrick in terms of autobiography, though he figures as only a minor character. And then the Republic begins to fall apart as the war comes to an end. Starr, by now distrusted by the Party because he has begun to express doubts about communist policy and has helped dissidents to escape, is finally hunted down by the secret police and killed.

*Hermanos!* is probably Herrick's finest work and offers a balanced portrait of individuals and events. Numerous subsidiary characters come into it, and their lives add up to a picture not only of Spain in the 1930s but the whole world that was represented there as volunteers poured in from the international communist movement. It's well known that many of the people who survived Spain became leaders in the various communist governments established in Hungary, Poland, East Germany, and elsewhere, in the post-1945 period. And the countries that didn't fall under communist control but which had large communist parties (France and Italy are two examples) also saw Spanish Civil War veterans in important positions. Herrick is good at showing how Spain was, for many of them, a rehearsal for what came later. And he expresses clearly how cynical they could be about why they were in Spain. When Starr voices his concern about the tactics used to fight the fascists, a Russian officer tells him: "This Spain is only a game. What do we care what happens here. What is important are the lessons we learn to take home to the Red Army...."

Herrick used Spain in at least three other novels, *Shadows and Wolves* (1980), *Love and Terror* (1981) and *Kill Memory* (1983), though in varying ways. *Shadows and Wolves* is set in post-Franco Spain and concerns the conflict between an elderly Falangist general who may have been involved in the murder of the poet, Federico Garcia Lorca, and his son, who is working with an underground organisation planning strikes and other protests against the government. It neatly exploits the situation to comment on how things change, and to show how the different generations may arrive at an understanding about the events of the 1930s.

*Love and Terror* is similarly interested in the clash of generations, though in this case it is between old and young revolutionaries. A group of German and Arab terrorists hi-jack an Israeli jet and hold the passengers and crew to ransom. On board the jet are three elderly Jewish left-wingers, Avram ben Itzchak, Clara Z., and David Grad. Itzchak was an early member of the Polish Communist Party, fought in Spain, and after various other adventures, including being an assassin for the Party, had a place in the post 1945 government in Poland. He was forced to leave the country when anti-Semitism reared its ugly head in the 1960s. Clara Z. was also born in Poland, joined the Party, went to Spain as a nurse, and worked for the Polish government in exile in England, though she was acting as a communist spy at the same time. Later in the Second World War she was in Hamburg, again spying for the Party. Like Itzchak she was forced to leave Poland because of anti-Semitism. David Grad, an American, served in Spain and in the Second World War and was a union organiser in the 40s and 50s. He seems to have been based on a man named Robert Gladnik who is mentioned in Herrick's autobiography. It's wise, though, to remember that Herrick is writing fiction. He based the character of Clara Z. on someone referred to briefly in a letter from a friend, and "gave her a full life," as he put it.

Intertwined with their stories are those of the terrorists, particularly Viktor and Gabriele, two young middle-class Germans at war with their society. Again, Herrick skilfully plays off their experiences and ideas against those of the older revolutionaries, and raises the question of how much the young terrorists are the children of the older activists. Is there a line that can be followed between them? It's interesting that Herrick appears to suggest that, although the elderly Europeans have a kind of understanding, if not sympathy, for the terrorists, the American looks on them with contempt. But Grad had never been as involved in the dark side of communist activities and Clara describes him as "very sentimental."

Another old revolutionary is at the centre of *Kill Memory*, as Boishke, living alone in Paris, reflects on her life, past and present, and her time in Spain where she met a wounded American. In his autobiography Herrick says that the woman was partly based on the Boishke he had an affair with, though in actual fact he never did find out what happened to her after Spain. When her husband, Laszlo Rajk, was purged in the 1950s the newspapers referred to someone called Julia as his wife, but Herrick didn't know if it was the same woman. So the character in *Kill Memory* is largely a product of his imagination though with some historical background to give his story a feeling of reality. Novelists often base characters on real people, but it's a mistake to assume that fiction is fact.

It may seem that Herrick has over-used the same material, but he has, rather, exploited it adroitly. The point is that the material lends itself to so much interpretation that it provides for endless variations on the basic theme of how and why people allow their humanity to be taken over by ideology, and what it does to them. The problems he deals with are just as relevant today as they were in the 1930s, even if we glibly believe that we have somehow exhausted our capacity to be taken in by seemingly perfect solutions for solving all the problems of mankind. A glance at the newspapers will tell us that people still lie and murder for some cause or another. And attempt to excuse and explain it all by saying that the end justifies the means.


NOTES

Herrick's *Jumping The Line:The Adventures and Misadventures of an American Radical* was published by the University of Wisconsin Press, Madison, 1998. *The Itinerant* was published by Weidenfeld and Nicolson, London, 1957, and *Hermanos!* by Weidenfeid and Nicolson, 1969. *Shadows and Wolves* (1980), *Love and Terror* (1981) and *Kill Memory* (1963) were all published by New Directions, New York.

Bill Bailey's *The Kid From Hoboken* was published by Bailey himself in San Francisco, 1993, with funds for publication raised by friends in the radical movement. Irwin Shaw's *Sailor Off The Bremen* was first published in *The New Yorker* in the 1930s, and in his collection *Sailor Off The Bremen and Other Stories*, Random House, New York, 1939. It has been reprinted in other Shaw collections, including *Mixed Company*, New English Library, London, 1977.

The literature concerning the Spanish Civil War is voluminous, but of particular interest in relation to Herrick's views are Cecil Elby's *Between the Bullet and the Lie: American Volunteers In the Spanish Civil War*, Holt, Rinehart and Winston, New York, 1969, and Peter N. Carroll's *The Odyssey of the Abraham Lincoln Brigade: Americans in the Spanish Civil War*, Stanford University Press, Stanford, 1994.

# BEN MADDOW

Some years ago I interviewed Allen Ginsberg and asked him about possible early influences. He'd grown up in a household where his mother was a member of the American Communist Party, and his father, a published poet, had leanings towards socialism, so it was only reasonable to assume that left-wing literary magazines would be available for him to look at. I knew that his father had been published in anthologies like *May Days* and *Unrest,* as well as in Louis Untermeyer's *Modern American Poetry,* which also featured Arturo Giovannitti, Lola Ridge, Maxwell Bodenheim, and others with socialist sympathies. Ginsberg acknowledged that he'd read old copies of *The Masses* (a prominent radical magazine suppressed by the government during the First World War, and later followed by *New Masses,* which was heavily dominated by the Communist Party), and then remarked that the poem from the Thirties that had impressed him and influenced the writing of his famous poem, *Howl*, was Ben Maddow's *The City.*

I happened to have a copy of Maddow's poem, and I also knew his name from his work in Hollywood in the post-war period. I went back to *The City* and read it again, and I could see how it might have shaped Ginsberg's thinking in some ways. Maddow's vision of the modem city as a monster consuming its inhabitants is not dissimilar to Ginsberg's, and the effect is built up through a series of powerful stanzas which push the poem along with the same kind of rhythmic impetus that *Howl* displays:

> Children of the cold sun and the broken horizon
> O secret faces, multitudes, eyes of inscrutable grief,
> great breath of millions, in unknown crowds or alone,
> rooms of dreamers above the cement abyss, - and I,
> who all night restive in the unsleeping rain,
> awoke and saw the windows covered with tears.

Maddow is more directly political than Ginsberg, in the sense of pointing the finger of blame, and whereas *Howl* largely charts the activities of specific people known to Ginsberg, *The City* aims for broader statements:

> Here the strict labour of the many must support
> the monotony of the useless; and luxury is got

with smiles, false kindness, marriage, or embezzlement;
he who can feign desire, praise poison, or hang by his teeth,
lives well, accumulates the powerful bond,
receives inhuman honour, - but the kind man is strangled.

I don't want to enter into a detailed analysis of *The City* and its links to *Howl,* and in any case it is possible to point to other Maddow poems - *Acts of God* and *Images of Poverty,* for example - as possibly influencing Ginsberg in terms of technique. The long lines and packed units are from a tradition that, in America, derives from Whitman and goes through populist poets like Carl Sandburg, Arturo Giovannitti, and Michael Gold, and Ginsberg has always been seen as working in that way. Insofar as Maddow is concerned, you can observe how, in short, pictorial phrases packed closely together, he constructs his vision of the world:

Sleep on the way home 5 p.m., and each one shaken to a stifled flat. Sleep. The ads murmur buy me, buy me. Hands hanging in a net of veins; the sweated collar; feet unseen; heart sodden with a full week's overtime. Heavy, hungry. Light scuds on the concrete. Our sleep is shaken like the shadow of vibrating chain. Another hour toward another hour, another hour toward.

It is powerful stuff, mostly forgotten now but still capable of evoking a picture of a riven, discontented society. And Maddow himself, unknown to all but a few specialists in American radical writing and those with an interest in Hollywood screenwriters and politics, deserves to be remembered. His career, though sliding toward a sad ending, says a great deal about his times.

Maddow was born in 1909 in New Jersey, his parents being immigrant Jews from the Ukraine. His father had socialist ideals which influenced the son, but the family had to split up when their shop failed and Maddow's father went to work on a farm. Maddow lived with his mother in Passaic and New York City. He had ambitions to enter the medical profession, but came up against the system which restricted the number of Jews who could enrol on certain courses. He switched to biophysics and graduated from Columbia University in 1930. The Depression had hit hard by then and Maddow was unemployed for two years before working as a hospital orderly and then as a case worker for the Emergency Relief Bureau for another three. He later recalled how his experience of unemployment had affected him: "You have no idea, unless you have experienced it yourself, how it is to be out of work for two years, to have this big gap of empty time which makes you feel as if your life is being wasted."

He had always had a strong interest in literature and started writing poems and short stories, though he published them under the name of David Wolff. He did this, he said, because he didn't want his colleagues at the Bureau to "think him uppity." Known radicals were often excluded from government jobs. I've already noted that Maddow's poems were heavily political, and most of them revolved around images of the Depression, of broken and stunted lives, and of injustices. There was, perhaps inevitably, a great deal of personal need in the poems, even if they weren't directly auto-biographical, and one critic, looking at Maddow's work some years later, thought that they "suggest an almost frantic need for a way up and out, for a personal vitality, for a career or commitment that would suffice. Emotional, concentrated, biting, his poetry is some-times almost too private." The same critic also said: "Maddow's poems have a common pattern, moving in a rather simple dialectic from depressing moments (sometimes juxtaposed to scenes from the life of the rich) to points of strong affirmation." Maddow himself, interviewed several decades later, said that "there was a tre-mendous amount of morbidity and inner depression from your ex-periences. Because you didn't know quite where you were going when you got out of college. There were no jobs and it was very tough on you spiritually."

Maddow was publishing in *New Masses, Dynamo,* and *Partisan Review*, and was included in the 1935 anthology, *Proletarian Lit-erature in the United States.* All these appearances were as David Wolff, and he used that name when he began to work with a num-ber of left-wing documentary film-makers. Maddow answered an advertisement for someone to write the commentary for a short film, and was introduced to activists connected with Nykino, which was a split-off from the Workers Film and Photo League, a communist-dominated organisation which made short documenta-ries about strikes and such issues, and also arranged showing of imported radical films. Some of its members were unhappy with the way it was run so formed Nykino, their aim being to continue making documentaries but to improve their quality. After a brief time with Nykino, Maddow moved to Frontier Films, where he worked on several films which are now viewed as classics of 1930s American documentary film-making. He wrote the commentary for *Heart of Spain, China Strikes Back, United Action,* and others, and made some highly significant advances in how these things were done. In his own words:

> "As anybody who knows the history of the field can tell you, I invented a way of using narration in film which suited my purposes very well and has influenced other people - which was to construct the narration like poetry, in which every word modifies the image. I worked out a ratio of two words to a second, which worked so perfectly. In those days you ran the film as you were recording the narration, so you had this very, very close connection between the image and the writing. In that sense, I was not a writer, but a poet and a filmmaker. The narration really meant carpentering phrases so they fit the rhythm of the film."

Maddow's recollections of the politics of the group he worked with were that "it was left-labour. You might say the group followed the Communist line, but the Communist line at that time was very Popular Front." I mention this because it is important in terms of later events in Maddow's life. He also recalled knowing "a political circle of various shades of opinion. I also knew a circle of poets that included Muriel Rukeyser, Maxwell Bodenheim, and Kenneth Fearing. We'd often read our poetry (publicly). Bodenheim always read with his back to the audience and his face to the poets."

During the Second World War Maddow served in the Army, making documentary films, and on his release was offered work in Hollywood. He joined another left-winger, Walter Bernstein, to write the script for a thriller, *Kiss the Blood off My Hands,* which now is listed in books about film-noir. He also worked on *The Man from Colorado* and wrote the screenplay for an adaptation of William Faulkner's novel, *Intruder In the Dust.* He was still writing poetry - there is a story that, to the amazement of everyone in Hollywood, he once turned down a lucrative offer to write a script because he said he was too busy working on a long poem - and he also finished a novel, *44 Gravel Street,* based on his social work experiences. In 1950, Maddow was hired to co-write, with John Huston, the screenplay for *The Asphalt Jungle,* another film which appears in studies of film-noir. Although he seems to have worked regularly in Hollywood in the late-1940s he claimed that he had very little affinity with the system there and kept to himself, or at least restricted his socialising to fellow left-wingers. He said of the MGM studio: "There was a writers' table, which I was appalled by, because they discussed nothing but agents and contracts - don't forget that I grew up where intellectuals got together and fiercely argued some great point, and there was nothing of that there."

What is interesting is that very few people in Hollywood knew anything about Maddow's involvements with left-wing documentaries and radical poetry in the 1930s. But his past was about to catch up with him. In 1952 he was working on scripts for two films, *High Noon* and *The Wild Ones*, which were to become classics of their kind, but was suddenly informed that he was being dropped from both. He wasn't surprised, because other left-wingers had already been blacklisted, and he knew his turn would come. Asked about the blacklist many years later, Maddow said that he didn't think it had much to do with eliminating left-wing propaganda from films - there was little chance to put any in even if you wanted to, in Maddow's opinion - and that it was just a means of cutting off funds from the Communist Party. Its Hollywood supporters were well-paid enough to have poured money into its coffers, and the authorities wanted to stop this. Maddow felt that much of the left-wing activity in Hollywood was simply "a sop to the conscience" of those who felt guilty about earning high salaries for relatively little work.

Like many other blacklisted screenwriters, Maddow survived by writing scripts under assumed names and making uncredited contributions to a variety of films. Amongst those he was involved with, in one way or another, were *Johnny Guitar, Men in War,* and *God's Little Acre.* There are passages in the latter which describe how life in a mill town is affected by the closure of the factory which could almost be from a Maddow documentary narration. He seems to have worked steadily throughout the 1950s, despite being on the blacklist, so what happened next has a curious side to it, one that can perhaps only be explained in terms of personal psychology.

Around 1958 Maddow testified before the House Un-American Activities Committee, naming at least some names in return for clearance so that he could work openly in Hollywood again. When asked about this in interviews, he was vague and sometimes unresponsive, at first denying that he'd testified and claiming that his agent had paid a Republican congressman with connections to the Committee to have his name removed from the blacklist. He later admitted that he'd signed "some sort of statement," but that he didn't remember what was in it. He was devious about what had happened, and other blacklisted film people were in no doubt that he had named names of former associates. Leo Hurwitz, a leading documentary film-maker of the 1930s, claimed he had evidence that Maddow had named him. And Walter Bernstein, in his memoir of the blacklist, *Inside Out,* tells of meeting Maddow in the late 1950s and being given the reason why he'd decided to name names.

According to Bernstein, "it had nothing to do with money or politics or being afraid or not able to work. He simply could no longer stand living in the shadows. Something had broken in him." Maddow explained how, when there was a screening of a completed film for all the studio heads, he had to wait until the lights went out and then slip into the cinema. Bernstein was horrified when he heard this:

> "Maddow had not been forced to do what he did. He had been working, being well paid, surviving the blacklist better than most. He had gone through the worst of it. But there are no gradations of betrayal. He had sold his friends so he could come out of the dark. Now he stood in the light and could put his name to his work, but he had sold his name as well as his friends. All I could feel was sadness."

Maddow returned to working openly in Hollywood, though ironically he asked for his name to be removed from the credits of Elia Kazan's *Wild River* (a film about the 1930s and the New Deal) because he was dissatisfied with the re-written script. He then wrote *The Unforgiven* for John Huston, and made a bleak little film, *The Savage Eye*, which was a dramatised documentary look at the seedy side of Los Angeles. He also worked on *The Balcony* (from the Genet play), *The Way West*, and *The Mephisto Waltz,* but by 1970 he had effectively retired from films and was concentrating on writing fiction and books about photography

The reasons why people co-operated with investigating Committees were many and complex, and in Maddow's case maybe Walter

Bernstein got it right when he said that "something had broken in him." Maddow said that, around the time concerned, he was in low spirits and in analysis. But that he had testified shocked his friends, who had seen him as a talented, likeable left-winger with a good record as a poet, documentary film-maker, and Hollywood screenwriter. Perhaps going to Hollywood was his big mistake? Did he come to rely on the money and the boosts to the ego that seeing his name on successful films could bring? The sad thing is that had he held on for another year or two he might, like Walter Bernstein, have been able to work under his own name. The black-list was breaking down by 1960 and Ben Maddow should have been able to survive until then.

Maddow's career from the heady days of 30s radicalism to the Hollywood highlights of the 40s, the blacklisting of the 50s, and the low-key return to feature films in the 60s, is fascinating for what it says about the times he lived through. His early poetry is still worth reading, and not only because of its historical interest. It can still be relevant with its comments on social evils and injustices. And his contribution to documentary film-making ought to be acknowledged. He was not a prolific screenwriter, but he produced some scripts that deserve recognition. As for his human failings, it's best to be charitable by trying to understand the pressures he was under in difficult circumstances.

## NOTES

The best source for Maddow's poetry is *Social Writing of the 1930s: Poetry*, edited by Jack Salzman and Leo Zanderer, published by Burt Franklin & Co.Inc., New York, 1978.

Information about his work with documentary film-makers can be found in William Alexander's *Film on the Left: American Documentary Film from 1931 to 1942* published by Princeton University Press, Princeton, 1981.

A long, informative interview with Maddow can be found in *Backstory 2: interviews with Screenwriters of the 1940s and 1950s* by Pat McGilligan published by California University Press, Berkeley, 1991.

The screenplay, by Maddow and John Huston, for *The Asphalt Jungle* was published by Southern Illinois University Press, Carbondale, 1980.

Walter Bernstein's *Inside Out: A Memoir of the Blacklist* was published by Alfred A. Knopf, New York, 1996.

For general information about the blacklist, including references to Maddow, see Victor S Navasky's *Naming Names*, Viking Press, New York, 1980, and *The Inquisition in Hollywood:Politics In the Film Community 1930-1950* by Larry Ceplair and Steven England, Anchor Press, Doubleday, New York, 1980.

# REBEL VOICES

The Wobblies (members of The Industrial Workers of the World) were noted for their use of poetry and song to promote radical ideas, publicise strikes and other protests and generally present the case for what was, for a time at least, a dynamic and imaginative organisation. Much of the work produced by Wobbly activists was designed for immediate use and was deliberately kept clear and direct so that the message would be understood by those it was aimed at. I'm not intending any criticism by saying this. It seems to me that there is a place for quick and contemporary comment in poetry and for the adaptation of well-known tunes for social commentary. There certainly was in the hey-day of the Wobblies, which was before radio came into use and when people were still inclined to gather together to sing and sometimes recite poetry. The Wobblies were adept at taking hymns, music hall songs, and traditional ballads, and changing the words so that they commented on the class war, social injustice, and specific events such as strikes and free-speech fights. A look at *Songs of the Workers*, or *The Little Red Songbook* as it's often known, will show that Joe Hill, one of the most celebrated Wobbly songwriters, used religious tunes like *There Is Power in the Blood* and *Sweet Bye and Bye* and gave them new words. In his version, *Sweet Bye and Bye* became the wonderful *The Preacher and the Slave*, with its mocking line, "You'll get pie in the sky when you die." Hill wasn't the only Wobbly to do this, of course, and *The Little Red Songbook* has many other examples.

Some of the Wobbly songs and poems were by people who wrote only a few such things, saw them perhaps published in a Wobbly paper, and then moved on. A few are remembered by name, though little is now known about them, but many of the poets and songwriters simply have the "Anonymous" tag to mark their contributions to radical writing. *My Wandering Boy*, set to the tune of the popular song, *Where is my Wandering Boy Tonight?* dates from around 1907 and was one of four songs printed on coloured card by the I.W.W., but no-one could recall who wrote it. And the famous, *Hallelujah, on the bum*, has always had disputed authorship. It was around in the 1890s but a one-time Wobbly, Harry McClintock, later claimed copyright of the words, if not the tune (derived from the hymn, *Hallelujah, Thine the Glory*), and re-corded the song in the 1920s when he was working as a singer and musician for a San Francisco radio station. McClintock, like many of the old-time Wobblies, was a colourful and energetic character, and had been a railroad worker, a mule-skinner in the Spanish-American War in Cuba (which is where he may have first heard American soldiers singing a parody of *Hallelujah, Thine the Glory*), and an I.W.W. organiser. He'd also spent time in China, South Africa, Australia, Argentina, and Britain, working his way all the time, and became a popular figure on radio in the 1920s. When the Depression affected his earnings he went to Hollywood and appeared in a few Gene Autry Westerns. He also wrote articles and stories for pulp magazines. McClintock eventually returned to San Francisco, where he died in 1957, and it's amusing to think that he was around when the Beats were surprising everyone with their supposed radicalism. McClintock's experiences suggest that he was a far more adventurous person than most of the poets and hangers-on of the Beat Generation.

I've diverted from my original intention by talking about someone like McClintock and the grass-roots side of I.W.W. music and po-etry. What I really want to do is look at some forgotten work which can probably be placed in a more orthodox framework than adaptations of hymns and popular songs. There were plenty of writers belonging to or associated with the I.W.W. who wrote po-ems and other material using the standard forms of the day, but many of them were hardly prolific. The three writers I'll deal with did, however, produce some work which did point to them having literary intentions beyond the immediate. Ralph Chaplin, Charles Ashleigh, and Arturo Giovannitti, are not usually referred to in literary histories, and it's doubtful if they're much read now, but they each wrote some things that deserve to be acknowledged.

Ralph Chaplin was born in Kansas in 1887 and grew up in Chi-cago. He got to know Big Bill Haywood, one of the leading lights of the I.W.W., in 1907 and joined the organisation in 1911. Prior to that he'd been in Mexico during the Revolution and had reported on strikes in America for radical publications. He was editor of *Solidarity*, the Wobbly paper, and was rounded up with hundreds of other activists when the Government decided to break the I.W.W. by accusing it of opposing American entry into the First

World War, campaigning against conscription, and advocating sabotage and other criminal acts. Chaplin was sentenced to twenty years in prison but was released in 1923 when the wartime and post-war anti-radical hysteria had died down and the imprisoned Wobblies were offered amnesties. Chaplin's autobiography, *Wobbly*, is a well-written account of his experiences. He stayed with the I.W.W. after his release from prison, working to have other radicals freed, and editing *The Industrial Worker*. He finally left in 1936, by which time the I.W.W. was a shadow of its former self, but remained active in labour journalism, though he lost one job when he clashed with communists. Quite a few Wobblies had joined the American Communist Party, swayed by the impact of the Russian Revolution and what seemed to be a tightly organised and disciplined policy for bringing about change in America, but Chaplin and others remained suspicious of communist motives.

Chaplin had always thought of himself as an artist and poet and his work appeared in well-known literary magazines as well as in Wobbly publications. I have an anthology, *May Days,* published in 1925 and featuring poetry from *The Masses* and its successor, *The Liberator*. The contents pages are an astonishing display of what might be called the radical bohemian poets active in America at that time. Chaplin's name crops up several times, alongside Carl Sandburg, Maxwell Bodenheim, Floyd Dell, e.e. Cummings, Claude McKay, and many more.

In 1922, when Chaplin was still in prison, a small collection of his poems appeared under the title, *Bars and Shadows*. They were described as "prison poems" written either while Chaplin was on trial or serving his sentence, and most of them do relate to those experiences. It has to be said that, on the evidence of these poems and others in Wobbly publications, Chaplin seemed unaware of or uninterested in modernist developments in literature. This could be because he thought that using traditional forms was the best way to reach the audience he had in mind. I'm never sure about this, and it can be seen as suggesting that the audience hasn't the intelligence to appreciate anything different or difficult. On the other hand, it can be argued that most people probably do prefer poetry that rhymes and says simple things. Chaplin's poem to his son would likely appeal to a lot of people:

I cannot lose the thought of you,

It haunts me like a little song,
It blends with all I see or do
Each day, the whole day long.

And so on for several similar verses which would probably be
viewed as sentimental, even trite, by many contemporary readers
of poetry. But I don't want to waste time by attacking Chaplin for
what he didn't do. Some of his poems made good points, as in *The
West is Dead*, which laments the passing of the open spaces of the
American West, "fenced and settled far and near." The "blanket-
stiff" the wandering Wobbly who followed the harvests and didn't
adhere to fixed times and places, is on the way out:

Now dismal cities rise instead
And freedom is not there nor here
What path is left for you to tread?

In another poem, *Salaam!*, the lines spit with bitterness and anger
at the way in which people allow themselves to be manipulated by
leaders of one kind or another:

I will not bow with that mad horde
And passively obey.
I will not think their sordid thoughts
Nor say the things they say,
Nor wear their shameful uniforms,
Nor branded be as they.

If some of Chaplin's poems now seem naive to our jaded and supposedly sophisticated tastes then it's perhaps because we've lost the
things - belief, hope, optimism - that kept him alive.

Sentenced along with Chaplin was Charles Ashleigh, another poet
whose work was in the *May Days* anthology. Ashleigh was born in
London in 1892 and moved to America in 1910. His autobiographical novel, *Rambling Kid,* gives a lively picture of his early
days in England and his wanderings in the United States, where his
awareness of radical politics, literature, and the I.W.W. developed.
In the following passage, "Joe" (the character based on Ashleigh)
remembers discovering various writers:

"Joe couldn't stand Emerson at any price. He rather liked Tho-
reau. As for the poets, Longfellow and Whittier bored him; but
it was a great day for him when Beasley lent him Whitman.
Here was poetry he could understand. It was about ordinary
people's lives, for the most part, and it was not finicky like so

much verse. The long unrhymed lines did not annoy him like
more formal verse did. He had a good time with old Walt."

Ashleigh had spent some time in South America and spoke fluent
Spanish. He published poems in *The Masses* and *The Liberator*
and in Margaret Andersen's *The Little Review,* one of the leading
literary magazines of the period. He knew Greenwich Village bohemians like Eugene O'Neill but also worked hard for the I.W.W.
and was particularly active in the organising drives in the wheat
fields. *Rambling Kid* gives a good picture of the kind of life led by
many Wobblies, but it may be useful to point out that its overall
political opinions may have been affected by the fact that Ashleigh
had linked up with the communists while in prison. He was de-
ported from America in 1923 and became a member of the British
Communist Party on his return to London, so by the time his novel
was published in 1930 he would have been inclined to follow the
communist line that the I.W.W. failed because of its lack of organisation and specific political and economic theories. But the
book does show how the First World War divided the Wobblies
and the sometimes near-criminal activities of individuals left the
I.W.W. open to attack by the authorities.

The handful of Ashleigh's poems that have survived indicate that
he was, like Chaplin, a conventional poet in terms of technique,
and unlike the character in the novel doesn't appear to have been
influenced by Whitman's free verse. In *Vespers,* written during his
prison years, he creates a mood of peace:

> The sun goes down, and on the grass
> With silent feet the shadows pass.
> The trees stand still in fragrant prayer:
> Cool as a pearl is the twilight air;
> Cool as God's breath, at the close of day,
> On my heated soul the mild winds play.

The poem ends with him returning to his cell almost refreshed by
this brief encounter with nature, something that more than one of
Chaplin's poems also refer to. But what are possibly the most striking of Ashleigh's lines are in *Everett, November Fifth,* a poem
which refers to the deaths of several Wobblies during a free-speech
fight in Everett, a town in Washington on the West Coast of America:

> Song on his lips, he came;

Song on his lips, he went;
This be the token we bear of him,
Soldier of Discontent!

Ashleigh was still alive in the 1960s, a member of the British Communist Party, and, he said, "a worker in the cause of British-Soviet friendship," as well as a contributor to *The Daily Worker*. But his reputation in radical literature rests firmly on the work he produced during and about his days as a Wobbly.

Arturo Giovannitti wasn't among the I.W.W. members caught up in the great Chicago trial that saw Chaplin and Ashleigh imprisoned, but he had known the inside of prison in 1912 when he was arrested and charged with murder during the textile strike in Lawrence, Massachusetts, A young striker was killed during a demonstration, most probably by a police bullet, and Giovannitti and fellow strike leader, Joe Ettor, were arrested and charged because they were held responsible for the demonstration, despite not being present at it. The arrests were clearly meant to break the strike by destroying the leadership. Giovannitti and Ettor spent a year in prison but were eventually found not guilty by a jury.

Giovannitti was born in Italy in 1884, emigrated to Canada when he was a teenager, and moved to New York in 1904. He was a socialist at first but soon converted to revolutionary syndicalism and, in 1911, was the editor of an Italian-language newspaper published by the I.W.W. Following his arrest and trial in Lawrence he continued to associate with the Wobblies and also became part of the Greenwich Village bohemia of those days, mixing with John Reed, Max Eastman, Floyd Dell, and Michael Gold, among others. His poetry appeared in *The Masses, The Liberator,* and *Atlantic Monthly*, usually known as a conservative publication. In the 1920s he was involved with the mainstream labour movement and was active in cultural circles, but after 1930 or so he more or less disappeared into union bureaucracy and was secretary of a Labour Education Bureau.

As a poet Giovannitti was far more interesting than Chaplin and Ashleigh. Some commentators have noted that he always maintained "a certain religious temperament, which manifested itself particularly in his poetry," and it may be that the long-lined declamatory style he favoured did reflect some biblical influence. But another source could have been Walt Whitman. Giovannitti wouldn't have been alone in being influenced by Whitman and poets like Carl Sandburg, Vachel Lindsay, and Michael Gold, all followed the populist line pioneered by him. There were, it's true, even earlier examples of poets using a long-lined style derived from the Bible. Christopher Smart springs to mind, though it's difficult to say if Giovannitti had read his work.

The poem by Giovannitti which attracted attention, not just in radical circles but in the wider literary context, was *The Walker*, a long meditation on prison life which Louis Untermeyer, who included it in his *Modern American Poetry* anthology, described as "remarkable, not only as art-work, but as a document; it is a twentieth-century *Ballad of Reading Gaol*, but with an intensity and social power of which Wilde was incapable."

It's difficult to extract from *The Walker* to illustrate its power because to do so reduces the effect of the language and the rhythm, but the opening lines may give an indication of how the poem works:

> I hear footsteps over my head all night.
> They come and they go. Again they come and they go all night.
> They come one eternity in four paces and they go
> one eternity in four paces, and between the
> coming and the going there is Silence and the
> Night and the Infinite.

*The Walker* was printed in full in the *Atlantic Monthly* and so reached a wider audience than that which read radical magazines. There were other Giovannitti poems in the same style. *When the cock crows* is a hymn of praise to Frank Little, a Wobbly organiser who was lynched in Butte, Montana, after making a speech opposing involvement in the First World War. And *The Senate of the Dead* is a long poem in which a group of dead revolutionary heroes are assembled to assess the admission of Karl Liebnecht to their company. Spartacus, Louise Michel, Marat, John Brown, and Francisco Ferrer, all appear, and the list may well have something to say about Giovannitti's own concerns. But it's a powerful piece, even if, as with Chaplin and Ashleigh, the sentiments expressed seem naive to our cynical and irony-laden eyes.

Giovannitti's poems have lasted better as poems, as opposed to political statements or personal reflections, than either Chaplin's or Ashleigh's. They can be seen as of their time and place but they still read powerfully, perhaps because of their long-lined sweeping movement. As an aside, it always struck me that Allen Ginsberg's poetic approach, especially in *Howl*, may have been affected by Giovannitti, whose work was in the left-wing magazines that Ginsberg read in his youth. He never mentioned Giovannitti when asked about influences, usually preferring to refer to Smart, Whitman, and sometimes Ben Maddow, who himself may have known Giovannitti's work. But when I asked Ginsberg about Giovannitti he certainly knew his work and quoted from one of his poems.

I've not tried to be complete in this short survey of the work of the three poets concerned. Each of them led a rich and varied enough life to warrant an individual article, but it may have been useful to set them in context by dealing with them together. My main aim has been to draw attention to their existence. Most literary histories ignore writers like these, seeing their work as limited in scope and achievement, though many other minor poets are written about at undue length. But it's perhaps worth quoting Ralph Chaplin on the subject of being a poet. His comments may be slightly defensive, because I think he did see himself as a poet, but they may also indicate why he never became accepted in literary circles:

> "Above all things, I don't want anyone to try to make me out a 'poet' - because I'm not. I don't think much of these aesthetic creatures who condescend to stoop to our level that we may have the blessings of culture. We'll manage to make our own - do it our own way, and stagger through somehow. These are tremendous times, and sooner or later someone will come along big enough to sound the right note, and it will be a rebel note."

Chaplin knew his limitations as a poet and it's more than likely that his autobiography, *Wobbly*, will be his lasting literary legacy, just as Ashleigh's autobiographical novel, *Rambling Kid,* will be his, assuming even those books are remembered. Giovannitti may have a greater claim to poetic fame, though I wouldn't place any faith in the possibility of most academics and literary critics doing much to ensure that his claim is acknowledged. It's easier to play it safe and stick to talking and writing about the known and accepted than to attempt to revive the work of the unfairly forgotten.

NOTES:

Obviously, a lot of the literature referred to is difficult to find. I used the following books when writing this piece: *Wobbly* by Ralph Chaplin, published by the University of Chicago Press, 1948, reprinted by Da Capo, New York, 1972. *Bars and Shadows* by Ralph Chaplin, published by Allen and Unwin, 1922. *Rambling Kid* by Charles Ashleigh, published by Faber, London, 1930. *Poems* by Arturo Giovannitti, published by El Corno Emplumado, Mexico, 1965.

*Rebel Voices: An I.W.W. Anthology*, edited by Joyce L. Kornbluh, published by the University of Michigan Press, Ann Arbor, 1954, is an invaluable collection of songs, poetry, and prose, which shows how humorous and pointed the Wobblies (including all those anonymous and forgotten writers) could be. *May Days*, edited by Genevieve Taggard, published by Boni and Liveright, New York, 1925, sets Chaplin, Ashleigh, and Giovannitti in context. *Modern American Poetry*, edited by Louis Untermeyer, published by Cape, London, 1932 (revised edition) is also useful. It has work by many now-forgotten poets and, like *May Days*, gives a context for the Wobbly writers.

Two of the most readable histories of the Wobblies are *We Shall Be All* by Melvyn Dubofsky, published by Quadrangle Books, New York, 1969, and *The Wobblies* by Patrick Renshaw, published by Eyre and Spottiswood, London, 1967.

*Songs of the Workers* or *The Little Red Songbook* has been circulated by the I.W.W. in a variety of editions over the years. The one I have to hand was published in 1955 to mark the 50th anniversary of the founding of the I.W.W.

There are few academic studies of Wobbly and other radical poets. One exception is Cary Nelson's *Repression and Recovery: Modern American Poetry and the Politics of Cultural Memory 1910-1945*, published by Wisconsin University Press, Madison, 1989. Chaplin and Giovannitti are mentioned in this book.

I referred to Giovannitti's poem, *When the Cock Crows*, and Frank Little, the Wobbly lynched in Butte. Readers with a taste for literary curiosities might like to look at Zane Grey's *The Desert of Wheat*, which was published in New York in 1919 (my English edition, published by Hodder and Stoughton is undated). Grey was a popular author of Western novels but this book is set during the First World War and is about defeating the Wobbly "threat" in the wheat fields. The I.W.W. is referred to as "Imperial Wilhelm's Warriors" because strikes are seen as working against the war effort and, it is suggested, are financed by German money. A lynching takes place in the novel and is based on what happened to Frank Little. Grey gloatingly describes the actions of the vigilantes and expresses his approval of them.

## JOHN HERRMANN: WRITER AND SPY

In recent years information from FBI and KGB files has confirmed what had long been suspected, that in the 1930s and 1940s an extensive communist spy network operated in the United States. It's now almost certain that Alger Hiss, who for a long time proclaimed his innocence after being identified by Whittaker Chambers and convicted of perjury in 1950, had been involved in passing Government documents to Soviet agents. The whole complicated Hiss/Chambers controversy, which became a cause-célèbre for many American liberals and left-wingers, is not relevant here but it is necessary to mention it if one wants to understand how John Herrmann, a minor novelist and short-story writer, got caught up in the murky world of espionage.

Herrmann was born in 1900 in Lansing, Michigan, the son of a reasonably prosperous businessman. He grew up in Michigan and, according to biographical notes in a 1930s magazine, 'when he was 15, and every summer thereafter, he went on the road as a travelling salesman, selling everything from books to jewellery. He spent several summers peddling garden seeds through the mining mountain country of Kentucky and West Virginia.' When Herrmann left high school he went to Washington to study law but gave up to become a correspondent covering political matters for a Detroit newspaper. He then moved to New York, ostensibly to renew his studies, but got another job as a salesman. Much of this activity was dealt with in a fairly direct way in Herrmann's first novel, *What Happens,* published in Paris in 1926. Likewise, the novel tells how its hero quits his job and enrols at the University of Michigan, which is what Herrmann did. In real life he demonstrated that he had no taste for the routines of a Mid-Western campus, and he dropped out and went to Europe, studying art history in Munich for a couple of years.

By 1924 Herrmann was in Paris, where he took up with writers and drinkers like Robert McAlmon and Nathan Asch and met the novelist Josephine Herbst, who he later married. Herrmann was by now seriously interested in writing, though it seems that he enjoyed socialising too much to settle down to lengthy spells at the typewriter. He was also still under the influence of his family, despite his travels, depending on them for money and always reminded that they would prefer him to join the family business rather than mix with writers and artists. When Herrmann left France in October 1924 he had a novel, *What Happens,* accepted for publication by McAlmon's Contact Editions and was also set to appear in an anthology, *The Contact Collection of Contemporary Writers,* alongside James Joyce, Hemingway, Pound, Gertrude Stein, and other moderns.

Back in America, Herrmann had trouble with his parents, married Josephine Herbst against their wishes (she was several years older than Herrmann), and wrote and drank. *What Happens* ran into trouble with the American Customs when it was published and copies were shipped to New York, though it's difficult now to understand why the authorities objected to it. It does deal with adolescent worries about sex and hints at fumblings on settees and back seats of cars, but it's hardly explicit and tends to the naive. The subject-matter may have aroused the curiosity of the censors, and the fact that it was published in Paris probably counted against it, but it's unlikely that the few who got to read the book would have seen it as anything more than a shaky attempt to capture the mood of certain aspects of growing up. It's easy to see why Robert McAlmon thought it worth publishing, its mixture of almost flat, simple writing and innocent curiosity being similar to his own novels and stories about life in the Mid-West.

Herrmann and Herbst lived in New York for a time, though he worked as a salesman again and was often on the road, a life he enjoyed. But he was writing and a novelette, *Engagement,* appeared in the prestigious *American Caravan* in 1928, with other work in leading little magazines, such as *transition, This Quarter, The Little Review,* and *The New Masses.* The novelette, like *What Happens,* drew on Herrmann's Mid-West background to tell the story of Ruth Mason, who 'was willing to marry George Harvey who was slow and steady and not particularly brilliant because she had been disappointed in a love affair she had been having with Harold Riley, who was not stupid or slow at all.' The style was typical and pointed to Herrmann's liking for Hemingway's prose, while the subject-matter explored what seemed to be a fascination Herrmann had with relationships, or the lack of them, between men and women, and how when people get what they want they often don't want it.

Herrmann's work was never directly political, though it did frequently touch on the underlying unease and mistrust in much middle-class life. And stories like 'Pennsylvania Idyll' (written with Josephine Herbst and an amusing account of local people helping themselves when some lorries loaded with beer run into a river) and 'The Gale of August 20th' (a convincing account of a lone sailor weathering a storm) didn't indicate any conversion to left-wing ideas as the 1920s ended. But in 1930 the couple went to Kharkov for the Second International Congress of Revolutionary Writers and began to experience a change in their view of the world. When they returned to America and their home in Connecticut they found that banks were foreclosing on farms and the local farmers were organising to oppose evictions. Also, many of their friends in writing and intellectual circles were increasingly involved with politics. Herrmann was carried away with enthusiasm for communism and Russia, remarking that he thought 'the rest of the world dead compared to it.' He began to give lectures about Russia and allied himself with the League of Professional Groups for Foster and Ford, the communist candidates in the forthcoming election. And he marched in the May Day parade in New York. Malcolm Cowley recalled meeting Herrmann that day: 'Arriving early I ran into John Herrmann, one of the Paris crowd; he now looked pale, shabby, and, I thought, exalted. He invited me to join a delegation of writers from *The New Masses* and the John Reed Club.'

1932 was also the year when Herrmann's literary star was at its brightest. His second novel, *Summer is Ended,* was published, and he was declared a joint winner, with Thomas Wolfe, in the *Scribner's* magazine short novel contest. *Summer is Ended* again looked at the lives of middle-class people who aimed for one thing and usually got another: 'Charlotte Dale had felt from her high school days that what she wanted most in life was a home and children, quite a few children, and for their father she wanted Carl Yeoman'. Carl, for his part, wants to marry Charlotte, but he doesn't want children and he has ambitions to be a crack newspaperman. They do marry, after various misadventures which link them to other partners, but at the end of the novel Carl is seriously thinking about giving up journalism and joining the family business and Charlotte has been told that it's unlikely that she will ever be able to have children. Tighter and less sentimental than *What Happens*, the novel still reads well even if its basic style would not find favour today, the Hemingway-esque terseness no longer being in fashion.

Herrmann's prize-winning story, 'The Big Short Trip', is his finest piece of writing and something of a minor masterpiece of Depression literature. The story concerns an elderly salesman making his last trip through the Mid-West and registering the effects of the Depression as he visits towns where shops have closed or are cutting down on their orders. It succeeds because of the way in which it allows details to accumulate, with a remark here about a reduction in advertising, a comment there about salaries being cut, a reference to credit limits having to be restricted, and a brittleness in the relations between buyers and the salesman that captures the nervousness everyone feels about the economy of the country. Herrmann's dialogue is at its best, the colloquial tone and snappy exchanges matching the mood and the uncertainty.

Herrmann and Herbst went to Iowa in 1932 to cover farm strikes, but their marriage was foundering and Herrmann was soon on his own and increasingly involved with political work in farming communities. The American Communist Party was, at that time, trying hard to develop its influence amongst farmers and forge farmer-labour alliances, with Harold Ware (the son of Ella Reeve Bloor, a leading figure in communist circles) particularly active. Ware had spent much of the 1920s in Russia and was an expert farm economist and engineer. Herrmann met him and was drawn into his circle and, in 1934, was invited by Ware to work for him in Washington, where he was a senior member of the Agricultural Adjustment Agency, a branch of Roosevelt's New Deal programme. It is at this point that John Herrmann's activities begin to touch on matters which were, some years later, to be a highlight of Cold War politics.

There is no doubt that the Ware group was involved in espionage, even if many of the documents they copied and passed to Communist Party officials were often economic and technical papers not likely to put the security of the country at risk. Whittaker Chambers, who worked as an underground agent for the American Communist Party, later testified to having taken part in these activities, as did others who had been involved. Josephine Herbst, although never active herself in spying, said that she knew there were 'certain documents that had been taken from Government offices by members of the 'cell' for transmission to New York. And she pointed out that Herrmann introduced Alger Hiss to Whittaker Chambers and that 'Chambers and John regarded Hiss as an important prospect to solicit for the purpose of getting papers.' The Ware group was primarily based in the Agriculture Department, but Hiss left it in 1934 and took an important position with a committee investigating the impact of foreign and domestic munitions makers on American policy before and during the First World War. This gave him access to all kinds of classified information from the State, War, and Navy Departments, hence Herrmann's desire to cultivate Hiss and put him in touch with Chambers.

Harold Ware was killed in a road accident in 1935, and though Herrmann attempted to take over running the group it seems that he wasn't too successful and was soon replaced. He continued to be active, working with farmers and transport workers, and he also wrote. His stories were in *Esquire* and *Scribner's* in the mid-1930s, and one of them, 'Two Days from the South', was set in Kansas and was about the effects of the Depression and the dust-storms on the farmers of the region. It is only lightly political and focuses more on local matters, with hints of wider concerns, but it is vividly told. Herrmann also managed to finish another novel, *The Salesman,* which was published in 1939 though it made little impact. During the Second World War he served in the Coast Guard, and he later tried to make a living as a cabinet-maker. And, as always, he drank heavily.

When the Cold War began to build up in the post-1945 period the activities of the Ware group became the subject of investigation by the FBI. Whittaker Chambers had given the authorities information about Alger Hiss and others, including Herrmann, and the FBI started to track down the various individuals concerned. Herrmann quietly left for Mexico, a move which could be seen as a near-admission of having something to hide. He was contacted by FBI agents but refused to cooperate, and it's likely that they were more interested in obtaining facts about Hiss than in prosecuting someone who had been a relatively minor figure in the spy ring. The FBI also interviewed Josephine Herbst and she was evasive and offered little concrete information about either Hiss or Herrmann.

John Herrmann doesn't appear to have done much in the 1950s and he died of a heart attack in Guadalajara in 1959. He was not alone in making the transition from 1920s expatriate to 1930s radical, but it's unlikely that any of his contemporaries also became spies. Their discontent was expressed in writing, but Herrmann felt the need to take his a step further by engaging in activities which brought him into contact with the communist spy system in America. And it's ironic that he'll probably be remembered for this rather than his literary works.

# LEFT IN LOS ANGELES

Histories of poetry often tend to stick to well-worn ideas. One group or style succeeds another as signposts are erected to guide newcomers through the various developments and certain individuals are singled out for special attention because they seem to represent a shift of emphasis or a change of mood. The problem is, of course, that along the way a lot of talented people are overlooked and any group that doesn't fit tidily into the accepted pattern is forgotten. It's unlikely, for example, that many readers of 20th Century poetry have come across the poets who clustered around *Coastlines* and *The California Quarterly*, two magazines published in Los Angeles in the 1950s and yet, in retrospect, they had (and have) much to offer. But because the focus of American poetry in the Fifties has usually concentrated on San Francisco and New York, with additional nods in the direction of Black Mountain College, the Los Angeles poets have been neglected. And there may be a degree of prejudice involved, with Los Angeles not seen as a place conducive to poetry. Films, yes, and TV and popular music, but not poetry other than in the case of Charles Bukowski and he was a maverick who was expected to act outside the usual channels.

What is interesting about the Los Angeles group, if it can be called that, is that many of the poets, and the prose writers and artists who also contributed to the magazines, were left-liberal in their politics, and that at a time when it wasn't always safe to be so. The FBI certainly knew of their activities and two of the poets were called before the House Un-American Activities Committee and lost their jobs as a result. A third poet would have made an appearance had he not died, possibly because of the pressure he was under. Others felt the weight of suspicion and were careful about what they said.

It has to be acknowledged that not all of the poets were active left-wingers, but it is probably true to say they mostly shared a common view of what poetry could and should do. A statement by Gene Frumkin, one of the editors of *Coastlines*, perhaps sums up the prevailing ethos:

"As a literary magazine, our first duty is toward the things of the world, for without these there is no literature, no art just desolation. Among these things are the timeless human problems, public and private. We must try to see them honestly, from the inside, in the material we publish and in our own commentaries. We must try to see them freshly too, for otherwise we cannot see them honestly. But originality should not be our only value; it dare not be accepted as an abstract value cut off from the world's images."

And it's relevant, too, to quote from an editorial statement in the first issue of *The California Quarterly*.

"*The California Quarterly* is founded on the conviction that more good writing will come out of the nineteen-fifties than is likely to achieve publication...Contemporary writing is threatened equally by censorship and by obscurantism...We hope to encourage writing that faces up to its time - writers who recognise their responsibility to deal with reality in communicable terms...If we have a claim to newness, it is this moderate position in an immoderate time."

As can be seen from the two statements, there were at least some similarities in the reasons given for starting each publication.

One of the guiding lights behind the founding of *The California Quarterly* in 1951 was Philip Stevenson, a blacklisted Hollywood writer. Stevenson and his wife had written a play, *Counter-Attack*, adapted from a Russian story about a soldier trapped in a town occupied by the Germans. It was made into a film in 1945 and the couple stayed in Hollywood, with Stevenson achieving some success as a screenwriter. But he was eventually blacklisted, though he continued to produce scripts under pseudonyms. And he wrote an ambitious series of novels which dealt with a Mexican-American community and the effects of a strike. These were published as by Lars Lawrence because publishers were afraid to allow Stevenson to use his own name. Even so, they sold only in small quantities due to a lack of reviews.

Stevenson wanted a magazine that would provide a platform for committed writers, including many who, like himself, had fallen foul of the blacklist, and he was joined by Thomas McGrath and Sanora Babb in getting *The California Quarterly* off the ground. I'll say more about McGrath in a moment but Babb, a novelist and short-story writer, had worked at various jobs, including union organising, and had been connected with an earlier left-wing Hollywood magazine, *The Clipper.*

It's not my intention to provide a complete history of either *The California Quarterly* or *Coastlines,* and I'm more concerned to show that they existed despite having been ignored by literary historians. And I'm concerned to throw a little light on at least some of the poets they printed. Looking at a related publication, the first (and only) issue of *Poetry Los Angeles*, inclines me to the view that only Thomas McGrath continues to be known, and I suspect that even he has a reputation limited mostly to readers familiar with left-wing poetry. E.P. Thompson acknowledged that McGrath was neglected but said: "Yet McGrath's poetry will be remembered in one hundred years when many more fashionable voices have been forgotten. Here is a poet addressing not poets only but speaking in a public voice to a public which has not yet learned to listen to him." I'm not sure that the "public" will ever listen to McGrath, any more than it listens to other poets, but that doesn't alter the fact of his importance. He was a major voice in American poetry but his un-apologetic left-wing views certainly kept him from becoming better-known.

McGrath was born in 1916, grew up on a farm, went to university and was awarded a Rhodes Scholarship. The Second World War stopped him taking up the Scholarship so he taught, did various jobs, and spent some years in the army. He was also active in communist agitation on the New York waterfront. He took up the Scholarship in the late Forties and also lived in France, where he wrote a novel, *This Coffin Has No Handles,* dealing with the struggles against corrupt union leaders and ruthless bosses in New York. He moved to Los Angeles in 1950 and taught at Los Angeles State College but lost his job when he was called before the House Un-American Activities Committee and declined to answer questions about his political activities.

It has been said of McGrath that he "stood at the centre of the community of poets in Los Angeles in the 1950s," and it's true that he seems to have been something of an inspiration to many younger poets. He also created a large body of work of his own. His major accomplishment, written over a period of time, was the long poem, *Letter to an Imaginary Friend*, which E.P. Thompson said could be "justly compared" to Wordsworth's *The Prelude*:

"There is the same autobiographical structure (and the same indefiniteness as to biographic detail); the same recovery of childhood experience, seen through both the child's eye and the adult poet; the same central concern with political experience; the same strenuous attempt to settle mythological accounts with the poet's own time."

And the critic, Terrence Des Pres, described it as a "Poem of witness to the radical spirit 'the generous wish,' as McGrath calls it - of American populist tradition." This is not the place to look closely at *Letter to an Imaginary Friend*, but it's worth noting that the impulse to write it stemmed from the time when McGrath was blacklisted but mixing with the poets in Los Angeles:

"I'll tell you how it started. Some of us used to go to each other's places. Don Gordon, Ed Rolfe, Naomi Replansky. We'd read poems to each other. They'd normally be torn to shreds. Don asked me, 'What are you doing now? Do you have any plans?' I told him, 'I have this notion for this poem. It's very long. As much as fifteen pages. I'm kind of worried about starting the poem.' He said, 'Go home and sit down and write the first line that comes into your head. And go on.' I did that. I didn't know what to write, so I wrote, 'I'm sitting here at 2716 Marsh Street writing, turning east with the world. Dreaming of laughter and indifference.' 2716 Marsh Street is where I lived. Then I began to have these tremendous rushes, and I wrote the poem from morning until night, about fifty odd pages, then I stopped. I didn't know how long it was. I thought that was the end of it. It wasn't the end...."

The three poets mentioned by McGrath in that passage were all linked to the Los Angeles poetry world and were published in *The California Quarterly* and *Coastlines*. Don Gordon, like McGrath, was blacklisted from his work as a reader for various film studios because of his refusal to answer questions when called before the House Un-American Activities Committee. Less obviously political in his poems than McGrath, he nonetheless engaged with the social situation, with his poems hinting at the state of mind that created, or was caused by, political paranoia and suspicion:

They need an enemy to tear apart
in the mad season
When the air is burning and the cloud
signals unbearable change.

70

The dissenter is born alive on the edges
of the weather.

I've written about Edwin Rolfe elsewhere (see the essay in *Beats, Bohemians and Intellectuals*) so won't say too much here. A veteran of the Spanish Civil War he'd moved to Los Angeles, hoping to find work in the film industry, but his communist affiliations meant that he was viewed with suspicion. He would have appeared before the Committee but died from a heart attack in 1954. Naomi Replansky, born in 1918, did a variety of jobs as well as writing. I don't think she was an active left-winger, but her short poem, "Epitaph:1945," identifies where her sympathies lay:

> My spoon was lifted when the bomb came down
> That left no face, no hand, no spoon to hold.
> One hundred thousand died in my hometown.
> This came to pass before my soup was cold.

*The California Quarterly* published a wide variety of writers, among them British left-wingers like Randall Swingler, Jack Beeching, Maurice Carpenter, and Ewart Milne. Most of them are forgotten now, though Swingler has had some attention thanks to Andy Croft's sterling work. They appeared alongside American radicals Ben Field, Dalton Trumbo, and Albert Maltz. The latter pair were members of the Hollywood Ten and had served prison sentences for refusing to co-operate with the Committee. The magazine wasn't just devoted to poetry and mixed fiction, articles, and art work with the poems, with most of it having a left-liberal approach.

When *The California Quarterly* closed down in 1956 its role as an outlet for the kind of poets I've referred to was taken over by *Coastlines,* a journal started in 1955 with the encouragement of Thomas McGrath. It's significant that the editors, Mel Weisburd and Gene Frumkin, had been students of McGrath's before he was dismissed from his teaching post. Neither claimed to be as radical as McGrath, nor did they experience problems relating to their jobs (Weisburd was an expert in air pollution control and Frumkin editor of a trade newspaper), but they had liberal views and were not afraid to publish McGrath, Gordon, and Rolfe, along with William Pillin who had been a member of the Dynamo Group in New York in the 1930s. They also gave space to John Beecher. He had lost his job at San Francisco State College in 1950 when he refused to sign a loyalty oath. His work was described by Thomas McGrath as "a holy rage at the enemy at home and a mine of tenderness for the insulted and injured, the jailed and blacklisted." Written in a direct way, and with some Walt Whitman-like overtones, Beecher's poems used the rhythms of the spoken voice to determine line lengths, and they chronicled the struggles of workers and blacks, as well as providing a kind of alternative history of America. The following extract is from an early poem, written in the 1930s, but gives an indication of how Beecher liked to let situations speak for themselves:

> he fell off his crane
> and his head hit the steel floor and broke like an egg
> he lived a couple of hours with his brains bubbling out
> and then he died
> and the safety clerk made out a report saying
> it was carelessness
> and the craneman should have known better
> from twenty years experience
> than not to watch his step
> and slip in some grease on top of his crane
> and then the safety clerk told the superintendent
> he'd ought to fix that guardrail

Beecher was still writing radical poetry in the 1950s and it's easy to understand why he received little acknowledgement from academic circles or the literary establishment. Neither the style or the content of his work would have appealed to those who see themselves as arbiters of what is good or relevant, and the political atmosphere of the period would have worked against Beecher getting favourably reviewed or even reviewed at all. Ignoring the possibilities of alternative approaches is often a way for those in control to convince themselves that they are right.

*Coastlines* lasted until 1964 and so was able to "filter the literary experiments and social humanism" of earlier decades "through the lens of the fifties and to look toward the future." There was a general upsurge in literary activity in the 1950s, with groups like the Beats, the New York poets, the Black Mountain School, and the poets of the San Francisco Renaissance, breaking into print. And *Coastlines* inevitably reflected some of this activity and published poets like Allen Ginsberg and Gregory Corso. But the editors were never over-awed by the Beats and there was a certain amount of friction between them and the Beat group that gathered around Lawrence Lipton (an old radical who re-surfaced in the Fifties) in the Venice West district of Los Angeles. Thomas McGrath expressed doubts about the quality of much Beat writing, and William Pillin said that "the poets of Los Angeles are moved by the same psychic motivations as the poets of San Francisco, but perhaps in a manner less calculated to provoke a journalistic sensation." It should be noted that the arguments the *Coastlines* editors had with Lawrence Lipton didn't stop them using his work and his witty poem, "I was a Poet for the FBI," appeared in the magazine. And poets like Curtis Zahn and Charles Bukowski, who didn't slot easily into any kind of category, also found a home in *Coastlines*. Their work, if not political in the way that McGrath's was, could still be seen as descended from a strain of American poetry that asked questions about the status quo.

The aim of this piece has been to draw attention to the two magazines and some of the poets they published. I also wanted to show how, even in bad times, it's possible to sustain some sort of opposition. It would be foolish to pretend that what happened in the United States during the McCarthy years was repression of a kind experienced by dissident writers in Russia and Eastern Europe. There were casualties, it's true, but most of the Americans survived, found other jobs, and often got their work published, even if major publishers and leading magazines refused to consider it. Small presses and little magazines came to the rescue, as we've seen from this brief study of *The California Quarterly* and *Coastlines*. But it still required a degree of courage to carry on writing socially-conscious poetry in an atmosphere when even the mildest form of protest could attract the attention of the police and employers. And "guilt by association" could be used as a stick to threaten those who weren't radicals but mixed with them. Ann Stanford, who had poems in *Coastlines,* was asked to participate in a reading in 1955 and recorded in her diary: "I had some hesitation when they asked me to submit something because of the blacklisting of people who even associate with people who are suspected of leftist leanings, and Tom McGrath and his wife always participate so prominently in these affairs." She was worried that her architect husband might not get government jobs if she was seen as a leftist sympathiser. It was a sad situation and W.B. Price, whose father was blacklisted, remembered "how courageous poets like Tom

McGrath were in the face of it."

Readers wanting more information are referred to *Poets of the Non-Existent City. Los Angeles in the McCarthy Era,* edited by Estelle Gershgoren Novak, published by the University of New Mexico Press, 2002. This is a well-documented anthology of some of the poets published in *The California Quarterly* and *Coastlines*.

# WALTER LOWENFELS

On 23rd July, 1953, FBI agents raided the home of Walter Lowenfels and arrested him for "conspiring to teach and advocate the overthrow of the government by force and violence," a charge covered by the Smith Act which was used to harass members of the American Communist Party. "Eight men pointing revolvers converged on my typewriter as if it were a machine-gun emplacement," Lowenfels later wrote, and he was put on trial though the case against him was eventually dropped for lack of evidence. During this period he wryly commented that a large part of his adult life had "been spent trying to overthrow not only the government but the universe," a somewhat curious remark from a man who had been a full-time employee of the Party for around sixteen years and so might have been expected to have had a more prosaic view of the aims of the revolution. But Lowenfels was no ordinary communist and his background also included spells as a businessman and years in Paris during the great days of the expatriates. And he had achieved some fame as an avant-garde poet before taking up the communist cause.

Lowenfels was born in 1897 into a prosperous German-Jewish family of butter merchants. He was an inattentive student and did so badly at school that he failed to qualify for college entrance and was taken into the family business. When America entered the First World War in 1917 he enthusiastically enlisted but never actually left the United States, being as inefficient a soldier as he had been a student. His own later explanation for joining up was that he was "illiterate about war and peace and politics" in those days. Between 1919 and 1926 he worked for his father, becoming "very good in butter," but he was also beginning to take an interest in the arts. He wrote poetry, and began to pick up a few ideas from the modernist poets active in the 1920s. His first book appeared In 1925 and included a poem called *From an Exposition of Power and Industrial Machinery*, which was essentially a catalogue of engineering terminology but points to the way Lowenfels was concerned to develop a different kind of language and subject-matter for poetry:

> unit aligning power transmission

non return vertical indicator
pump governing nose
return trap compensating joint
expanding lathe mandrel

make up water
boiler blow down
bleach liquor
stream flow
glass steam trap
air cooled wall for powdered coal

By 1926, Lowenfels had decided that the butter business was hardly the way to proceed as a poet and was planning to go to Paris, where writers like Hemingway, Joyce, Stein, and McAlmon were active and modernist ideas encouraged. His father, annoyed at his wanting to leave the family business, sent him to see a psychiatrist, who suggested that Lowenfels should be sent on a trip, provided it was to Vienna to consult Sigmund Freud about his supposed problems. Lowenfels took the money, sailed for Europe, and made his way to Paris, where he married his fiancée, Lillian Apotheker, the daughter of a Yiddish scholar and humourist who wrote under the name of Hinke Dinke Schlemazel ("limping ne'er-do-well" in English). As Jonathan Cott put it:

"In the late twenties and early thirties, Paris was still the crown of the avant-garde causeway. Little magazines and small presses were springing up everywhere. Mina Loy spoke of the 'crisis of consciousness,' Eugene Jolas of the 'revolution of the word,' Gertrude Stein of the 'actual present,' and Ezra Pound of 'making it new.' Harry Crosby was using found forms and concrete poetry - all relating to sun mythology and imagery. Bob Brown experimented with 'optical' poetry and a tachistoscope-like reading machine. Abraham Lincoln Gillespie wrote 'soundpieces' in a bizarre notation that anticipated the work of Jackson Maclow and John Cage. And the painter De Hirsch Margulies sat on the quays of the Seine and painted pictures in the dark. In fact, the first exhibition of these paintings, which could be seen only in a darkened room, took place in Walter's Paris apartment."

Lowenfels was clearly at home in this kind of atmosphere. With a friend, Michael Fraenkel, he started the Anonymous Movement, advocating total anonymity in the arts. The idea collapsed when he thought the authors of the musical, *Of Thee I Sing*, had stolen material from his own play, *USA with Music* and he launched a plagiarism suit against them, something he clearly couldn't do anonymously. Lowenfels and Fraenkel also started the Carrefour Press, though their plans to publish work by Scott Fitzgerald and Samuel Beckett came to nothing because of lack of funds. Their meeting with Beckett to discuss his work was somewhat bizarre. They expounded their social and artistic theories to the silent Beckett and, eventually, Lowenfels got frustrated and burst out, "You sit there saying nothing while the world is going to pieces. What do you want? What do you want to do?" Beckett crossed his legs and replied, "Walter, all I want to do is sit on my ass and fart and think of Dante."

Lowenfels and Fraenkel also joined forces with Henry Miller and Anaïs Nin to start what was called the 'death school' of writing. "We had the idea that the world was dead," said Lowenfels, "and that the only thing you could do was write poems about it." As part of his contribution to a body of work representing this idea, Lowenfels produced several long poems which celebrated dead writers. The first, "Apollinaire an Elegy," appeared in 1930, the second, "Elegy in the manner of a Requiem in memory of D.H.Lawrence," in 1932, and "The Suicide," which was about Hart Crane, in 1934. It has been said that these pieces are "experimental, yet stately, long modernist reveries," and that they "fuse a slightly formalist rhetoric and form with the oxygen of surrealism." Obviously, a few lines pulled from long poems which depend on their totality for their impact are not the best way of showing what Lowenfels was doing, but they may at least give an idea of his style and use of language:

> His Arc de Triomphe is a structure of the world
> not in the word but in the angels
> and every taxi horn of Paris
> keeps his flame eternally rekindled
> not in the sound but in the angels.
>
> (from *Apollinaire*)


> He moves among the miles
> like Switzerland among the blue bells
> But the edelweiss we picked

among the leaves.
It is turned to day by day.
It yellows slowly. It spreads Its wings.
It folds and unfolds.

(from *D.H.Lawrence*)


The skull sea-washed sprouts anemones
where the black mould eats into the bone.
I saw it down the bottoms
among the tails fin scales
of rise and wash of endless days at sea

(from *Hart Crane*)

Interestingly, Lowenfels stayed in Paris when many other expatriates went back to America as the 1929 Stock Market crash wiped
out family fortunes and their allowances dried up. He had been
making a living as a real-estate agent, renting property to wealthy
Americans and Frenchmen, and managed to carry on doing this
even in the new economic climate. In Henry Miller's *Black Spring*
there is a chapter entitled *"Jabberwhorl Cronstadt,"* which is a
portrait of Lowenfels. The narrator goes to visit Cronstadt and
finds him and his family living in a state of bohemian confusion.
Cronstadt talks non-stop, interrupts his discourse to deal with a
phone call from someone wanting to rent an apartment, and then
carries on talking and drinking. At one point he says: "You think a
poem must have covers around it. The moment you write a thing
the poem ceases. The poem is the present which you can't define.
You live it. Anything is a poem if it has time in it. You don't have
to take a ferry-boat or go to China to write a poem. The finest
poem I ever lived was a kitchen sink." And he passes out and is
put to bed.

Miller's account shows us the bohemian side of Lowenfels, but by
the early-1930s he was becoming more aware of the rise of fascism and other social and political problems. In a memoir published in the 1970s he recalled attending meetings in Paris where
banners saying "Free the Scottsboro Boys," and "Free Ernst
Thaelmann: Unite Against War and Fascism," were displayed. The
Scottsboro Boys were a group of young blacks convicted in Ala-
bama for allegedly raping a white girl, and Thaelmann was the
leader of the German Communist Party and was imprisoned when

Hitler came to power. Lowenfels also started to read Marx and his friendship with Miller and Fraenkel began to weaken. He wrote to them to say: "The insoluble contradictions arising in the social structure are reflected in the personality of the poet. We go to pieces inwardly and, as we sing, toss up brittle pieces of ourselves. And what is it that we have reflected? Nothing more than that Mellon owns all the aluminium in the world and it's killing us."

Lowenfels returned to the United States in 1934 and to the butter business to support his wife and children. But he was by then committed to communist ideas, and a small collection, *Steel, 1937*, published in 1938 pointed to the way in which these ideas were shaping his poetry:

> I don't want to know the name of this town.
> I don't want to know the reasons why
> it spells two more are dead.
> But still I know. From the earth
> In Alcoa from the corpses gas guns
> from the pictures Mellon buys and gives away
> from the dividends that mix with the dead
> the aluminium smells bad.
> The coffee pot spells death.

In an interview published in a newspaper around this time he was quoted as saying of France: "Aragon is making communist poetry at Belleville, the workmen's quarters. All the young men with intelligence enough to be creative are interested in social matters." But his verse didn't find favour in American Communist Party circles, where the Popular Front ideology dictated that modernist verse was elitist, and one critic has suggested that it was considered "far too experimental and surrealist for Party dictates on what was considered poetry for the working class." In 1938 Lowenfels took his family to Philadelphia, where he became a reporter for, and then editor of, the Pennsylvania edition of the *Daily Worker*. His wife became a schoolteacher, a job she would lose when Lowenfels was arrested in the 1950s. It would seem that working full-time for the Party led to Lowenfels abandoning poetry, perhaps because he thought that silence was better than turning out officially-approved verse. Or he may have just thought that he needed to give all his time to Party work. Whatever the reason he certainly gave up poetry, especially of an avant-garde kind, for fourteen or fifteen years. Instead, he produced prose which was suitable for Party papers, as in this excerpt from a report published in the *Daily Worker* in 1947: "Perhaps the most unbelievable part of the coal crisis is that some men, called operators, make money, and spend their winters in fine homes and in Florida, out of what miners go through every day and night in the mines."

It's difficult to know exactly when Lowenfels started to write poetry again on a regular basis. He published pamphlets In 1953 and 1954, one of them, *American Voices*, being an intriguing mixture in which, in the words of Louis Aragon, "the lines of the author alternate with a sort of prose counterpoint made up of letters from readers printed in newspapers all over America." Aragon's words were used as part of the introduction to another pamphlet, *The Prisoners*, which was largely devoted to poems about American Communists who were being hounded by the Government. The following lines, from a poem called *"Letter to Steve Nelson,"* (a veteran of the Spanish Civil War and a leading member of the Party) are fairly typical:

> Let's talk as we used to, Steve
> not as in each other's prison,
> (am I on bail? are you inside?)
> One hardly knows from day to day now
> which of us is where....

Although Lowenfels doesn't seem to have been active as a writer or editor for the communist press after 1954 he remained a Party member, despite the Kruschev revelations about Stalin, the suppression of the Hungarian uprising, and other matters which caused many members to quit. But returning to poetry allowed him to take note of what was happening in literary circles as the Beats, the Black Mountain poets, the New York poets, the writers of the San Francisco Renaissance, and more, began to revive the bohemian and radical traditions in American poetry. Lowenfels rightly saw all this activity as a continuation of the avant-garde tradition he'd been involved in during his Paris years. The social protest aspect of the work of poets like Allen Ginsberg and Lawrence Ferlinghetti naturally interested him, as did the surrealistic leanings of some of the new writers. In 1954, Jonathan Williams, at the instigation of Louis Zukofsky and Kenneth Rexroth, published *Some Deaths*, a selection of poems by Lowenfels, the newer ones of which indicated that he still favoured a modernist approach, with irregular lines and stanzas, prose and poetry sometimes mixed, surrealist flights of fancy alongside direct social observations, and a willingness at all times to take chances. Poets like Allen Ginsberg and Armand Schwerner were impressed by his work, and Lowenfels, in turn, began to relate to many younger writers and regularly attended readings in New York at the Cafe Metro and the Poetry Project at St Mark's.

An idea of how he viewed the new poetry and its links to the past can be gained from an anthology, *Poets of Today: A New American Anthology*, which he edited in 1964. It ranged far and wide in its choice of poets, with older radicals like John Beecher, Don Gordon,and Thomas McGrath, alongside Beats such as Gregory Corso and Lawrence Ferlinghetti, and Spanish Civil War veterans Ray Durem and Alvah Bessie next to Charles Bukowski and Denise Levertov. Lowenfels wasn't afraid to use poems by little-known poets and some by people who probably only wrote poetry occasionally. The overall impression was that most of the poems had a social angle, though not dogmatically so, and the forms were flexible. A similar approach is evident in another anthology, *The Writing on the Wall: 108 American Poems of Protest*, edited by Lowenfels in 1969, which went back in time to find poems by Walt Whitman, Carl Sandburg, and Edwin Markham, to place with those by contemporary writers like Robert Bly, Bob Kaufman, and Leroi Jones. Lowenfels said that many of the newer writers he used were not likely to appear in academic anthologies, and so his collections made (and still make) useful starting places for alternative views of 20th Century American poetry.

It's important to note that Lowenfels saw the various anthologies he edited (and there were several others besides those mentioned) as an integral part of his total output. In response to a suggestion that what was important was his own poetry, he said

> "But I'm concerned with the totality of what I'm doing. To exclude my anthologies is to miss that total creative impact. They're not my words, they're the other guys' words, but I'm making a collage of poems. I am not doing anthologies the way other people do anthologies for schools, literary purposes, academic purposes and so forth. Each of my anthologies is a creative conception."

Joel Lewis was of the opinion that Lowenfels' goal was nothing less than to dissolve the Western notion of 'literature,' reclaim poetry from those who made it "a pedant's game" (in Basil Bunting's trenchant phrase) and replace it with a writing life where there is no difference between poem and non-poem, verse and prose, letter and elegy."

As for Lowenfels' own later work, he was influenced by William Carlos Williams and the Turkish poet, Nazim Hikmet. He had encountered Williams in Paris in the 1920s but had not paid much attention to his writing. It was much later that he read Paterson and recognised that Williams had been making "inventions in rhythms, using documentary material, newspaper quotes, combining prose letters with verse," and generally doing what Lowenfels had gradually worked towards. And Hikmet also used documentary materials, and had the added attraction of being a committed communist. It's also possible to see the influence of someone like Lawrence Ferlinghetti in Lowenfels' new poems:

> And after Governor Faubus led his army against Little Rock
> and General Walker led his troops against the
> Supreme Court and Governor Wallace led his
> bombers against Birmingham
> and after 300 years of If you're white alright, but If you're
> black, step back
> and after 20 millions of us said now, right now and a
> quarter million of us marched on Washington
> and after the secret army of Governor X and Senator Y
> bombed the constitution 41 times in Birmingham
> and nobody was arrested
> we cornered four girl hostages in the basement at Sunday
> School and executed them using the secret dynamite formula.

Although Lowenfels was heavily involved with poetry in the 50s and 60s he also produced a great deal of prose, and in line with his stated aims, switched easily from one to the other, often within the same piece. He wrote a four-part autobiography, put together a large collection of correspondence (he was a great believer in letters as a form of communication), and compiled *The Autobiography of an Empire*, described as "a massive documentary history of the United States as told through visual materials, letters and documents." Much of his work remains unpublished, apart from excerpts in a few little magazines. One small book that did see print, *To An Imaginary Daughter*, published in 1964, is a wonderful series of reflections, comments, anecdotes, reminiscences, and general musings, all of which add up to the kind of volume that often baffles reviewers because it can't easily be pigeonholed. It's autobiography at times, with Lowenfels recalling Bob Brown, "old-time Greenwich Villager, Socialist, cookbook author and collector, bookseller," and experimental poet who, in the period before the First World War, had turned out hundreds of short stories and several novels, including a best-seller, and then given up his career to write poetry. He turned up in Paris in the late-1920s and had several collections published which placed him with the avant-garde, and then quit again. Lowenfels lost track of him until 1955 when he met Brown in New York. Brown was then "in his cookbook period," both writing them and dealing in rare volumes for collectors. Lowenfels also wrote about James Neugass, a poet who did the Paris stint in the early 1930s, served with the International Brigades in the Spanish Civil War, wrote a powerful long poem, *Give Us This Day*, about that experience, and died in 1949 at the early age of forty-four, just before his only novel appeared. Trying to track down Neugass's work some years later, Lowenfels discovered that all his manuscripts had been destroyed when the cellar in which they were stored was flooded. There is, in the lines that Lowenfels wrote about people like Brown and Neugass, a lament for a lost world of radicalism in both politics and literature.

Walter Lowenfels was luckier than Brown and Neugass because his work did receive some attention in the 1950s and 1960s. But his poetry tended to be acknowledged mostly by non-Establishment writers and it was probably his anthologies which gave him a place in literary circles, though I suspect that it was mainly 'underground' audiences which responded most of all to what he was doing. He died in 1976, and within a few years his books were out-of-print. It's only recently that a selection of his poems has become available again.

Lowenfels always thought that there was a continuity in the movement from avant-garde poet to communist activist and then back to poetry again, just as he thought that writing (whether poetry or prose), editing anthologies, and all his other activities, were part of his grand aim to "overthrow the universe." As for his politics, his obvious commitment to communism comes through, but that he that he could be idiosyncratic is perhaps indicated by something that the critic Harold Rosenberg once said. Asked about Lowenfels, Rosenberg replied: "O Walter, he belongs to a party all his own."

## NOTES

The best current source for Lowenfels' poetry is *Reality Prime: Selected Poems*, edited with an introduction by Joel Lewis, published by Talisman House, Jersey City, 1998. Copies of *The Portable Walter From the Prose and Poetry of Walter Lowenfels*, edited by Robert Gover and published by International Publishers, New York, 1968, still turn up in second-hand bookshops. More difficult to find is *Some Deaths*, The Nantahala Foundation, Highlands, North Carolina, 1964. *To An Imaginary Daughter* was published by Horizon Press, New York, 1964.

*Poets of Today: A New American Anthology* was published by International Publishers, New York, 1964, and *The Writing on the Wall 108 American Poems of Protest* by Doubleday, New York, 1969.

Extracts from Lowenfels' *My Many Lives: The Paris Years, 1926-1934* were published in *The Expatriate Review*, New York/ London, issue 1 (Summer, 1971) and issue 2 (Winter/Spring, 1972).

An informative essay/interview, *Walter Lowenfels: The Poet in the Flying Suit*, was included In Jonathan Cott's, *Forever Young*, Random House, New York, 1977.

Information about Lowenfels in Paris can be found in Hugh Ford's *Published in Paris: American and British Writers Printers, and Publishers In Paris, 1920-1939,* Macmillan, New York, 1975.

# WAS KEROUAC A COMMUNIST?

Interviewed, by Yves Le Pellec in 1972, Allen Ginsberg claimed that Jack Kerouac had, when he was young, gone through a brief phase of identifying with communism: "Kerouac had been a communist already. I even think he had been a member of the Party. As a member of the National Maritime Union, before it had been taken over by right wing types and the CIA so to speak and the government - he was very overtly communistic for several years, from '39 to 41, 42.

Pellec expressed surprise at what Ginsberg had said, and asked if Kerouac had read Marx. Ginsberg replied:

> "Certainly, sure. Kerouac was very learned, you know, he was always very learned. I don't think he read it with any formal scholarship but I 'm sure he read in and out of *Das Kapital* and read through *The Communist Manifesto* and maybe a few other things and he read the *Daily Worker*. It was not a phase that lasted very long. It was only two or three years."

Ginsberg's suggestion that Kerouac may have been a Party member may not have had any basis in fact, but it was the kind of opinion that could be expressed because of the general circumstances it referred to. As we'll see, Kerouac did have an interest in communism in the period that Ginsberg mentioned. And he could well have considered joining the Party. In a 1952 book, *Report on the American Communist* by Morris Ernst and David Loth, it's said that the age when most people were likely to join was between 18 and 23, and that a majority of them had left by the time they reached 23. This would, of course, tie in nicely with Kerouac 's age (he was born in 1922) and the three or four year period when he was supposedly "overtly communistic." But thousands of people went in and out of the American Communist Party in its heyday, not all of them used their real names when joining, and it's unlikely that accurate membership lists survived the eventual collapse of communism in America during the McCarthy years. In other words, it's unlikely that documentary evidence could be produced to back up Ginsberg's claim.

There is, however, evidence to show that Kerouac was on the fringes of the communist movement at one point in his life. In

*Vanity of Duluoz* he even mocked his own early leanings when he reminisced about watching his friend, Sabby (Sebastian Sampas), making "big Leninist speeches" on Boston Common: "There's Sabby in his blazing white shirtsleeves and with wild black curly hair haranguing everybody about the Brotherhood of Man. It was great. In those days we were all pro-Lenin, or pro-whatever, Communists, it was before we found out that Henry Fonda in *Blockade* was not such a great anti-Fascist idealist at all, just the reverse of the coin of Fascism."

Kerouac's reference to being a pro-Lenin, or pro-whatever, Communist shouldn't be taken as an admission of Party membership. He was just indicating that, like many other people at the time, he was inclined to look sympathetically on left-wing ideas. With the effects of the Depression in evidence, and the rise of Fascism in Europe threatening the stability of the world, it was understandable that young people, in particular, would turn towards political movements that appeared to offer overall strategies for combating the social and economic problems that the existing system seemed unable to solve. Kerouac's retrospective idea that communism and fascism were simply two sides of the same totalitarian coin was a conclusion that others also came to, but in the 1930s it wasn't quite as obvious, unless you were an astute political thinker and knew what was really going on in Russia and Spain. The reference to *Blockade*, a 1938 film about the Spanish Civil War scripted by John Howard Lawson, a well-known Hollywood communist, was not just Kerouac being idiosyncratic and makes a point about communist intentions towards the Spanish Republic.

Sebastian Sampas seems to have been much more politically aware than Kerouac, whose politics could often be more emotional than intellectual. According to Dennis McNally, the two formed a "radical study group" and read *Das Kapital* and *New Masses*, the American Communist Party literary magazine which published many left-wing poets and short-story writers. Kerouac's early story, "Birth of a Socialist" (only published many years later in *Atop an Underwood)* could well have been influenced by the kind of writing that appeared in *New Masses* and other magazines of the period. Sampas and Kerouac continued to share their literary and political interests when they corresponded after Kerouac left Lowell. In a brief note dating from February, 1941, Kerouac

says: "Am reading Jan Valtin's *Out of the Night.* Arise Masses!"
Valtin's book was an autobiographical account by a German merchant-seaman who had acted as a communist agent in various
countries and had been arrested and tortured by the Gestapo. By
the time *Out of the Night* was published in the United States in
1941Valtin (or Richard Krebs, to give him his real name) had
broken with the Communist Party and his book was viciously
attacked in both the *Daily Worker* and *New Masses.* Kerouac
would presumably have been aware that *Out of the Night* didn't
toe the Party line, but he seems to have been impressed by the
writing, which certainly maintained a gripping and fascinating
tone. He may also have taken note of Vaitin's anti-Stalinist conclusions. In *Vanity of Duluoz* he says that it's "still a good book to
read today."

Valtin's experiences at sea could have had an influence on Kerouac, who in 1942 joined the National Maritime Union and
shipped out on the *SS Dorchester.* Allen Ginsberg's reference to
the National Maritime Union as left-wing was accurate and it had,
in fact, a communist-dominated leadership. The Party had credibility with many ordinary sailors because communists had played
a major role in the often-violent struggles to organise the Union.
And without going overboard for the mythology which sees every
merchant-seaman as some sort of left-wing autodidact, there was
a radical tradition among them and it was not unusual to come
across sailors who had read widely, if not always systematically.

When Kerouac was on the Dorchester he became friendly with a
man named Pat Reel, a communist who had been with the American volunteers in the International Brigades in Spain. I've checked
several books about Americans in the Spanish Civil War and have
not found any references to Reel, but over three thousand were
involved and they are not all mentioned by name. And the question of names among Party members is always tricky. In *Out of
the Night*, for example, Jan Valtin mentions an American Party
organiser called Appelman who operated under the name of Mike
Pell and had written a novel, *S.S. Utah*, about a communist-led
mutiny aboard an American ship. This book was published in the
1930s and with its seafaring theme, and its radical content, it
makes me wonder if Kerouac had ever come across it? But to return to Pat Reel, Kerouac, seems to have been initially impressed

by him, and in a letter to Sebastian Sampas dated November, 1942, he talks about going back to sea and says: "These are stirring, magnificent times. I feel like a fool each time I think of Pat Reel." Did Kerouac feel that way because Reel was an activist, involved with "the pith of the moment," to use Kerouac's phrase? There's perhaps a foretaste here of his later admiration for Neal Cassady and his devotion to action rather than observation. Reel crops up a few times in letters to Sampas, alongside enthusiastic comments about John Reed: "we must lay a wreath on Jack Reed's grave in Moscow." Reed had been a well-known journalist and a founder-member of the American Communist Party, and his book, *Ten Days That Shook the World* was a classic account of the Russian Revolution. He died in Russia in 1920 and was buried in Red Square. There are also statements about "communal brotherhood" and the impossibility of living "in a world of vested wealth, property, privilege and selfish greed." And a suggestion that "after the war, we must go to France and see that the revolution goes well!" It could be that Kerouac was only saying what he thought Sampas wanted to hear, or that his youthful romanticism was getting the better of him, but even so he does appear to be still thinking of himself as occupying a position somewhere on the Left.

A few months later Kerouac was trying to clarify his relationship to the Communist Party. A long letter to Sampas dated 25th March, 1943, said that the two of them were "generous enough spiritually to embrace Socialism or Progress. I am as rabid about it all as you are, don't kid yourself." But Kerouac then added: "But I'm looking at the working class movement askance, not because it's just that, but because it may not be in good hands. Pat Reel proved to be a very intolerant person. The American Communists, moreover, don't seem to rely so much upon their own initiative and. native ideas than on simple Muscovite policy." This was a common accusation, usually denied by communists in America, but there was a great deal of truth in it that was evident at the time and was later clearly demonstrated when the archives were opened after the collapse of communism.

His letter went on to talk about problems relating to power and he quoted from Eugene Lyons, whose book, *The Red Decade*, published in 1941, carefully detailed the way in which, he claimed, communists and communist ideas had infiltrated many areas of American society, from unions to universities and Hollywood to branches of the Government. Kerouac denied that he was "going reactionary" and said that if Sampas thought that then he was "destined to become another blind American Communist, instead of a discriminating one, in the vein of the great Liberal, Debs." The reference was to Eugene V. Debs, a noted Socialist active in the early part of the 20th century. But Kerouac insisted: "I am a Leftist.....I couldn't be otherwise, I may not be a Party-liner.....they haven't done anything good and most of them are a trifle too intolerant.....and unless the Party improves here, I'll never join it."

And there we have it, an admission that, though he's obviously considered it, he had not joined the Party and didn't intend to unless it altered its policies. Interestingly, there was, in 1944, an attempt by the American Communist Party to broaden its appeal and persuade people that it was not a subversive organisation taking orders from Moscow. Under the direction of its leader, Earl Browder, the Party was dissolved and reconstituted as the Communist Political Association, with a programme of co-operation with liberal democracy. Initially, this did attract new members, among them Carl Solomon, but in 1945 Moscow stepped in and Browder was ousted, the American Communist Party reformed, and a pro-Stalinist, William Z. Foster, put in charge. By this time, of course, Kerouac was involved with a new group of friends (Sebastian Sampas had been killed at Anzio in 1944) and their interests, though often unconventional and sometimes radical in their own way, were not usually linked to a specific political philosophy. The American Communist Party was soon to find itself under attack from the Government, there was a purge of communists in the National Maritime Union, left-wing writing went out of fashion, and attitudes generally changed as the Cold War set in. Carl Solomon later recalled: "I broke with my CP friends that I had made at CCNY, and I moved down to the Village and became interested in avant-garde art and existentialism with a circle of people disillusioned with the left, ex-liberals and progressives I should say." It wasn't long before he set up with the Beats. The left-wing bohemia of the 1930s was replaced by a bohemia that revolved around bebop and the kind of art and literature that didn't adhere to conventional notions of social awareness and left-wing political ideology.

It's perfectly understandable that Kerouac had a brief interest in communism when he was young. As I mentioned earlier, the events of the 1930s and early 1940s caused many young people to look for answers in political involvement and activity, though Kerouac doesn't seem to have done much more than read and talk about politics. He saw himself first and foremost as a writer and political activism was alien to his nature. And that he became increasingly conservative as he grew older (an innate conservatism coming out?) doesn't alter the fact that he had what Allen Ginsberg called "a very overtly communistic" period during his formative years.

# LAWRENCE LIPTON AND THE BEAT GENERATION

When the Beats came to the attention of the general public in the late 1950s there were a handful of books that influenced perceptions of the movement. *On The Road* and *Howl* were important, of course, but two others stand out. One of them was *Protest: The Beat Generation and the Angry Young Men,* which placed Kerouac, Ginsberg, and Burroughs alongside writers like Anatole Broyard, George Mandel, and Chandler Brossard, who weren't Beats, denied the label, and were often critical of the Beats in print. But *Protest* had a fairly wide circulation and tended to influence the views of non-specialist readers. The other book was Lawrence Lipton's *The Holy Barbarians,* an attempt to provide a sociological and literary analysis of what the Beats were doing, where they came from, and where they were going. It was largely based on the Beat community in Venice West, Los Angeles, and constructed around Lipton's own need to create a certain kind of social movement as well as investigate a literary one. And it's necessary to know something about Lipton in order to understand how and why he produced his book.

Lawrence Lipton was born in Lodz, Poland, in 1898 and came to the USA in 1903 living in St Louis and Chicago. His father died when Lipton was 14 and he was "compelled to work for a living from then on; forced to fight a running battle against time for my education (time stolen from sleep, from play, from work - and consequently from food very often.)" He worked as a graphic artist and journalist for the *New York Forward,* but was back in Chicago in the 1920s and met the young Kenneth Rexroth and established writers like Carl Sandburg and Sherwood Anderson. Lipton is mentioned in Rexroth's *An Autobiographical Novel*, where it's noted that he and Rexroth and Samuel Putnam started The Escalator Movement which took its inspiration from the activities of the Dadaists in Europe and staged outrageous performances of poetry and music. Lipton also worked as an assistant editor on Frank Harris's *Pearson's Magazine*, and was active in radical politics. He had links to both the IWW (the Wobblies) and the Communist Party and was reputed to have helped hide Big Bill Haywood, the Wobbly leader, when he jumped bail and fled to Russia to escape a long prison sentence.

Despite his involvement with radical politics, Lipton always seemed able to earn good money from journalism and other jobs. In the 1930s and 1940s he edited the *Detroit Forward*, a Jewish newspaper, was director of publicity for the Fox Theatre chain, and wrote numerous stories, screenplays, and potboiler novels which appeared under different names. He married several times, his third wife being a successful crime novelist who published as Craig Rice. There is some evidence to show that the books were often a co-operative affair and that Lipton did a great deal of the work on them due to his wife's alcoholism. But he had ambitions to be known as a serious novelist in his own right and his first book, *Brother, The Laugh is Bitter*, was published in 1942, though only after heavy editing to ensure that it didn't lead to court cases for libel. Lipton had based it in Chicago and wanted to show how anti-Semitism was rife in the city and could lead to a situation similar to Nazi Germany. The problem was that some of the real-life characters behind the fictional ones could easily be identified. The publishers insisted that Lipton alter the text so that the similarities were less obvious. He couldn't win, though, because although the book was pro-Jewish it angered many people because of the way some Jews were portrayed. A second novel, *In Secret Battle*, published in 1944, didn't fare much better, its anti-fascist message being a standard ingredient in numerous films, books, plays, newspaper pieces, and magazine features by that time. Lipton's novel didn't stand out from the rest.

By 1948 Lipton had divorced Craig Rice, though he maintained a business relationship with her so they could both benefit from sales of her novels and stories. He also continued to pour out other work. In one year alone he wrote two screenplays, ghostwrote a popular science book, produced sixty-five radio scripts, and sold a couple of package deals to television, which was then just beginning to attract a mass audience. But by 1952, encouraged by a new wife, he was starting to think of himself as a poet, an activity hardly designed to boost his income. It was around this time that he went to live in Venice West and began sending his poems to various little magazines, including *Merlin*, the Paris-based publication edited by Alexander Trocchi. Lipton re-established contact with Kenneth Rexroth, the leading figure of the San Francisco poetry world, partly to find ways to get his poems published but also to develop his theories of "voluntary poverty," something which was increasingly engaging his attention. Lipton could always make money if he wanted to but he was keen to show that he thought it was possible to lead a full and meaningful life without sacrificing one's individuality or compromising too much to earn enough to get by on. Rexroth seemed to live the way that Lipton aspired to, keeping his expenses to a minimum and writing what he wanted to write rather than churning out fodder for the commercial market, as Lipton had so often done.

What had also shaped Lipton's thinking were his encounters with some of the poets and artists in Venice West. John Arthur Maynard has described the area in those days as somewhere with "tiny corner markets, warehouses, liquor stores, fleabag hotels, strange little factories, and old fashioned Jewish bakeries," and with cheap rents and a curious, mixed population. Among them were writers and painters and musicians who had drifted to Venice West because it was a place where they would be left alone. As Maynard put it: "They lived in cottages, sheds, garages, warehouses, and empty stores, observing a cheerful and offhanded ethic of non-competition, non-acquisition, and disrespect for established values, however or by whomever established.....almost none of them were poor for lack of opportunity, and many had walked away from what most Americans would have called good jobs."

Fascinated by the life-styles and attitudes of these young poets and painters, who included Stuart Perkoff and Wally Berman, Lipton invited them to his house for poetry readings and hours of discussions about art and other matters. And he began to talk to them about the history of what he saw them involved in, which was a bohemian anarchist tradition stretching back to the 19th Century and even before in Lipton's scheme of things where the wandering scholars of the Middle Ages and even the early Christians could be called into service to back up his arguments about the virtues of voluntary poverty. But what primarily impressed his listeners was Lipton's familiarity with American bohemias in Chicago, New York, and elsewhere in the 1920s through to the 1950s. He'd been there and met all the people. He also knew the politics of those years and while his followers were mainly interested in being left alone to write and paint he wanted to promote their activities as a challenge to the existing social order. Art as a social movement was something that had a major place in Lipton's thinking.

He began to write articles which outlined his arguments. It's often assumed that Kenneth Rexroth's famous piece, "Disengagement: The Art of the Beat Generation," published in *New World Writing* in 1957 was the first one to tackle the subject in detail, but Lipton's "Secession:1953: The State of the Arts on the West Coast" (*Intro: A Magazine of the Arts,* 1953), "Youth Will Serve Itself " (*The Nation*, 1956) and "Disaffiliation and the Art of Poverty" (*Chicago Review*, 1956), all covered some of the same ground. Lipton even wrote about "disaffiliation" and American writers for a British audience in "The World Behind the Billboards" (*London Magazine*, 1955). It was almost as if he had a messianic need to spread his ideas and he certainly had the journalistic knack of making them highly readable. Even Rexroth admitted that Lipton was much better at writing this kind of material than he was, and he suggested that, between them, they had "launched a movement." But it was Rexroth who gained most of the attention, perhaps because the San Francisco scene he represented had more talented writers clustered around it than Lipton was able to muster in Venice West. Rexroth's article also neatly capitalised on the term "Beat Generation" and appeared just as the interest in *Howl* and *On The Road* was starting.

Lipton's own poetry was never as good as Rexroth's and his first book, *Rainbow at Midnight,* published in 1955, didn't break any new ground, though he did try to incorporate big ideas into his work. And that may have been a problem, because he often sounded like he was preaching, something which tied in with his ideas about the poet as a kind of shaman and, of course, his aim to deliver a message to the wider world. A later book, *Bruno in Venice West* (published in 1976, a year after Lipton died, but containing poems from the 1950s), was better and some of the poems, especially the funny "I was a Poet for the FBI," indicated that he'd loosened up a little and picked up some lessons from the Beats. But it was hardly major poetry.

He continued to push the idea of Venice West as a centre of artistic activity and a haven for the disaffiliated, but with the contradiction that he wanted to attack the square world and, at the same time, attract its attention. The one-time advertising man and publicist couldn't resist trying to create a stir so that what he was selling would interest a wide audience. And, as we'll see, it would lead to

problems for the Venice West community. In the meantime, however, Lipton continued to advocate the values of the Venice West
poets. He organised jazz-and-poetry events, using some of the stars
of the West Coast jazz movement like Bud Shank and Shorty
Rogers alongside Stuart Perkoff and others. And he encouraged
writers like Bruce Boyd and Charles Foster in an attempt to show
that they were as creative as the San Francisco crowd. It was true
enough that they were no worse than most of the minor writers
around that city but neither Boyd nor Foster went on to produce
anything of great significance, and it may have been that Lipton's
enthusiasm was in advance of his critical judgement.

Lipton was working steadily on the book that would be published
in 1959 as *The Holy Barbarians*. When it did appear it provided
him with at least some of the success he wanted, not necessarily
success of a financial kind, though that was useful enough for a
man who had reached 60, but of the sort that drew attention to his
ideas about the people he described and the work they were creating, along with the lifestyle that was, to him, almost the point of
the work. Art existed to help establish disaffiliation as a viable way
of life. The book certainly did appear at the right time, the period
between 1957 and 1959 being one that saw the Beats increasingly
noticed not only in literary circles but also in the popular press and
on TV. People wanted to know more about these new bohemians
who were supposedly challenging the complacency of 1950s
America and rejecting its commercial values, and Lipton's slick
prose, with its mixture of journalistic generalisations, literary history, advertising hype, and seemingly serious sociological investigation, was a good place to start. He gave a colourful account of
sex, drugs, and jazz, blended in with poetry, dissident politics, and
advocacy of voluntary poverty. And the book was illustrated with
photos which played up the beards, bare feet, and bongos angle, so
that it was calculated to infuriate those who thought that anything
not cleancut and respectable was part of the communist conspiracy
while at the same time intriguing those who saw cleancut and respectable as signs of the capitalist conspiracy. The fact that what
Lipton was essentially talking about was a group of thirty or forty
people clustered in a down-market section of Los Angeles was
usually overlooked. Photographs of Henry Miller, Robert Duncan,
Kenneth Patchen, and Lawrence Ferlinghetti, included in *The Holy
Barbarians*, probably persuaded the impressionable that they lived

in Venice West, as did references to Kerouac, Ginsberg, and even Charles Olson.

Lipton's book had a disastrous effect on the small Venice West community of poets and painters by persuading people with no real commitment to the arts to move to the area in search of adventure. Stuart Perkoff later remarked: "One morning we who lived in Venice woke up and walked out onto the Promenade and we saw hundreds of people who looked just like us." Along with the would-be Beats came the sightseers, driving around in cars and gaping at anyone they thought even mildly unconventional in appearance. And following them were newspaper and TV reporters looking for stories about drugs, rebellion, and sex, which led to increased attention from the city authorities and the police. The influx of new residents and visitors also brought money into Venice West and that, as Lipton must have known, only served to corrupt the people he'd proclaimed as examples of the joys of voluntary poverty. The police began to crack down on poetry readings, real-estate developers began to consider how they could get rid of the cheap accommodation and build expensive properties, and businessmen looked at the potential for new enterprises. It was the old story of how everything is taken over by the system if there is a chance of making money out of it. But it has to be said that many of the Venice West Beat community were their own worst enemies, with drugs, alcohol, and other indulgences sapping their energies when it came to opposing the consumerist forces of the wider society. By the early 1960s the group, particularly as Lipton envisaged it, had broken up.

Lipton himself continued to live in Venice West and he planned a book about poets and poetry but the communities he thought important, in San Francisco, New York, and Venice West itself, had splintered and the individual poets had moved on to other places and other activities as they established reputations or simply had to find steady jobs. It was not something that Lipton had really considered, though his earlier experiences of bohemias should have told him that they rarely stayed the same. But Lipton, ever-optimistic, continued to promote the notion of new communities and life-styles. He wrote a regular column for the *Los Angeles Free Press,* one of the first "underground" newspapers, taught a course on avant-garde literature at the University of California and, when that was closed because of attacks by right-wing activists, he opened up his own Free University of California at a coffee-house in Los Angeles and persuaded Gary Snyder, Anaïs Nin, and other writers to take part in its programme. His book, *The Erotic Revolution: An Affirmative View of the New Morality,* came out in 1965 and tried to sell, in Lipton's usual blend of advertising slogans and seriousness, the idea of more openness about sexuality and similar matters. The problem was that by that time these themes were being discussed in a wide range of publications and Lipton's views didn't seem at all unusual. But, if nothing else, he continued to be prolific and, though nearing 70, he rattled off articles at a fast rate. *Cavalier,* a sort of poor-man's *Playboy,* signed him to write regularly about the hippies, the "underground," and similar subjects, and said that his articles would form the basis of a new book, *It's What's Happening, Man,* though it never actually appeared. But the articles did and in "Westward Look! The Hipster Armageddon," "The Hip Squares New Status Dropout," and "This Time it's for Real!!" (a typically optimistic Lipton title), all published early in 1968, he hammered away at his theories of cultural and social disaffiliation, the role of the West Coast in their development, and the importance of poets like Ginsberg, Snyder, and Ferlinghetti. He tackled a wide range of other subjects, as if to demonstrate that he was, despite his age, keeping up with the latest trends in literature and art, and in 1968 *Cavalier* sent him to cover the Democratic Convention in Chicago. This was the Convention that turned into a major clash between the Chicago police and an army of demonstrators and Lipton got caught up in the turmoil and though clearly an old man was badly beaten by the police. He never really recovered from this experience and his last few years, before he died in 1975, were marked by ill-health and near-poverty.

It's easy to be critical of Lawrence Lipton, especially for the way in which he promoted disaffiliation, the art of poverty, and art itself, as a range of consumer products which could be neatly packaged and then purchased by anyone attracted to them. He perhaps didn't mean it that way but his undoubted skills at marketing, publicity, and writing for the commercial press, were something he couldn't easily abandon and once in full swing he found it difficult to hold back from going all out to sell his ideas. On the other hand it's possible that he did reach a broader readership than if he'd restricted himself to writing for obscure little magazines seen only by a few specialists, and that he may have persuaded some people to consider what he was saying and, perhaps, question the values by which they were organising their lives. *The Holy Barbarians* may have spread some wrong ideas about the Beats but it wasn't all bad and there were useful things to be found in its pages. Lipton genuinely wanted to get across some alternatives to a consumerist society, and he had a real interest in literature and in writers who were often ignored by the commercial publishers. It's always best to read him with a degree of caution but he deserves credit for the good things he did.

NOTE

I owe a debt to John Arthur Maynard's *Venice West: The Beat Generation in Southern California* (Rutgers University Press, New Brunswick, 1991) for information about Lipton and the Venice West scene generally. Maynard's book has an extensive bibliography which should prove useful to anyone wanting to know more about the subject.

# CARL SOLOMON

Accounts of the Beat movement point to the profound effect that Neal Cassady had on Jack Kerouac and his writing and, by extension, the Beats generally. But it's unusual for the same sort of attention to be focused on Carl Solomon, though there's little doubt that he greatly influenced Allen Ginsberg and, perhaps, other Beat writers. One critic said that Solomon was "the secret heart of the Beat movement, far more influential than his own modest output would suggest." That may well be true but I doubt that many contemporary readers of Beat literature will know all that much about him, probably because despite some colourful experiences when he was younger, in later years he seemed quite conventional. When the Beats began to be noticed by the press and general public in the late 1950s Solomon was out of circulation due to mental health problems and he afterwards chose to lead a relatively quiet life that almost guaranteed him anonymity.

Carl Solomon was born on the 30th March 1928 in the Bronx, New York, to a family that came from immigrant stock, though both his parents had been born in America. His father, who died when Solomon was eleven, was very patriotic and taught his son to salute the American flag whenever he saw it and behave like "an officer and a gentleman." He also took Solomon to baseball games, and the sport, along with fishing, remained lifelong interests. In general, he seems to have had a fairly ordinary and uneventful childhood, at least until his father died. After that he recalled that he had a feeling of alienation, even to the point where he reacted against his father's views: "I was deeply distressed, I had idealised my father. When he died I was more or less adrift. He had been very strict.....I drifted into indiscipline and intellectual adventure that eventually became complete confusion." And he added, "My left wing period of the forties, after he died in '39, must have been a sharp and bitter reaction to his teachings."

There was something of a literary tradition in the Solomon family and his great uncle, Samuel Shipman, was a writer whose plays were performed on Broadway. And Solomon himself was always interested in literature and published short pieces in school magazines. He read Poe, Whitman, Guy de Maupassant, and William

Saroyan, and popular novels like Walter D. Edmonds's *Drums Along the Mohawk*. He also did a variety of odd jobs to make some pocket money. Solomon claimed that his academic work suffered after his father died but he graduated from high school when he was fifteen and enrolled at City College New York in 1943. It was around, this time that he got interested in left-wing politics and joined an organisation called American Youth for Democracy which was the youth wing of the Communist Political Association, as the American Communist Party was then called. He contributed bits and pieces to *Common Sense*, a newsletter published by American Youth for Democracy, and expressed admiration for Henry Wallace who was then Vice-President of the USA and very pro-Russian in his views. In 1948 he was the leader of an ill-fated attempt to establish a third party with left-wing ideas to compete against the Democrats and the Republicans.

In 1945 when he was seventeen, Solomon enlisted in the U.S. Maritime Service to train for work in the Merchant Navy. And he soon joined the National Maritime Union, a left-wing organisation that represented sailors. Its leadership was largely dominated by communists and later in the 1940s there would be vicious factional battles as anti-communists fought to gain control of the union, but when Carl Solomon joined the Cold War hadn't started and being a communist wasn't a problem. Years later, when asked about what had attracted people like himself (and Kerouac) to the Merchant Navy, Solomon replied in a typically idiosyncratic way: "Well, there were movies in those days romanticising it - *Action in the North Atlantic* with Humphrey Bogart - so that sort of thing was in the air then." The film referred to was written by John Howard Lawson, a leading light of the "Swimming Pool Soviet," as the Hollywood branch of the American Communist Party was mockingly called, and it was viewed with suspicion when communist activity in the film capital was investigated in the late-1940s.

Solomon continued to attend college, alternating his studies with stints at sea, and always thought of this period as one of the happiest of his life. He made trips to Cuba, Italy, Greece, Poland, and France. In New York he frequented Books 'n' Things, a bookshop owned by Harold Briggs, a poet with roots in the radical 1930s and an interest in a wide range of modern literature. It was in his shop that Solomon discovered the work of Nathanael West, Rimbaud,

Henry Miller, and others.

It was during a voyage to France in 1947 that Solomon left his ship and made his way to Paris where it's said that he joined the French Communist Party. He visited surrealist exhibitions, witnessed a disturbance at the Sorbonne when André Breton and his followers disrupted a talk by Tristan Tzara, and saw a performance of a play by Genet. On another occasion, he came across a crowd of people outside a small art gallery and, pushing his way inside, heard Antonin Artaud declaiming his poetry. It must have been a heady brew, this mixture of art and politics. Solomon could attend a lecture on Kafka by Jean-Paul Sartre, go to a Communist Party rally, see the Mona Lisa, make French friends who got him to read the poetry of Prévert and Michaux, and discover Isidore Isou and the sound poets whose work he related to the bop vocalising of Jackie Cain and Roy Kral when he heard them in the New York jazz clubs. He also bought books by French writers who were little-known in the USA at that time.

Inevitably, his interest and involvement in the kind of politics he had known among his acquaintances at college and in the communist movement began to falter. He had started to question the nature of communism and the Stalinist rule in Russia. And it's more than probable that his curiosity about surrealism, bebop, existentialism, and avant-garde art, would have been looked on with suspicion by orthodox communists, many of who were, to put it mildly, conventional in their tastes and interests. Solomon left City College of New York and enrolled at Brooklyn College, which was more inclined towards literature and the liberal arts. As he put it: "Well, I broke with my CP friends that I had made at CCNY, and I moved down to the Village and became interested in avant-garde art and existentialism with a circle of people disillusioned with the left, ex-liberals and progressives I should say. I began to read *Partisan Review* and a flock of other little magazines like *Horizon*." Among the people that he knew around this time were Anatole Broyard, whose *Kafka was the Rage* is a lively portrait of Village life, and Robert Reisner, who later put together a book of reminiscences of Charlie Parker.

In Ginsberg's *Howl* there is a reference to someone "who threw potato salad at CCNY lecturers on Dadaism," and it relates to an incident involving Solomon, though the actual details differ somewhat from the poet's version. Solomon and a couple of friends had heard that Wallace Markfield, a writer now remembered mostly for his novel *To An Early Grave*, was giving an off-campus talk about "Mallarmé and Alienation." They decided to go along and make a Dadaist gesture by throwing potato salad at Markfield, with Solomon claiming that it was "an illustration of alienation." But it may also have been an indication of increasing mental instability, something that was further demonstrated when he stole a sandwich from the college cafeteria and then taunted a security guard with it, as if inviting a reaction from the authorities. They, not surprisingly, suggested that he needed psychiatric help and he was referred to the New York State Psychiatric Institute where he asked to be lobotomised: "I was in a very negative, nihilistic mood, things seemed sick to me, and I wanted a lobotomy, or to be suicided. I thought I was a madman."

He was given insulin shock treatment and it was during this experience that he first encountered Allen Ginsberg, himself a patient at the Institute. The story of the meeting is now enshrined in Beat legend, with Solomon saying by way of introduction, "I'm Kirilov" (a character in Dostoevsky's *The Possessed*) and Ginsberg claiming to be "Myshkin" (from the same author's *The Idiot*), and a close friendship then ensuing, They met regularly in hospital to talk about books, friends, and experiences. Solomon told Ginsberg about writers like Artaud, Genet, and the surrealists, and Ginsberg responded with stories about Kerouac, Burroughs, Huncke, and Neal Cassady, all of who Solomon would soon know.

His mischievous sense of humour never seems to have deserted him and to stay one step ahead of his doctors he read a standard work on insulin shock therapy and disguised it in a wrapper from a book about surrealism. He also managed to arouse accusations of communism from some members of staff when they found him reading Trotsky's *The Permanent Revolution*. While all this was going on Ginsberg, ever alert to likely material for his poems, was making notes of the things that Solomon said. Many of them turned up in *Howl* but Solomon's own view of this when the poem became famous and drew attention to him was less than favourable. He said that Ginsberg "published all of this data, compounded, partly of truth, but for the most raving self-justification, crypto-bohemian boasting *à la Rimbaud*, effeminate prancing, and esoteric aphorisms plagiarised from Kierkegaard and others - in the form of *Howl.* Thus he enshrined falsehood as truth and raving as common sense for future generations to ponder over and be misled." His own more factual account of his experiences as a patient can be read in his "Report from the Asylum" published in *Neurotica* in 1950 and later in his book, *Mishaps, Perhaps.*

When he was released from the Institute just before Christmas 1949 Solomon rented an apartment and began to associate with the young writers and bohemians who would soon be called the Beat Generation. He also got a roommate, Olive Blake, who he married, though the marriage only lasted for a couple of years. Solomon worked at casual jobs, including market research and sorting mail, but was then hired by his uncle, A.A.Wyn, publisher of Ace Books. It was largely due to Solomon that *Junkie*, the William Burroughs book published as by William Lee appeared as an Ace paperback in 1953. Negotiations were started to publish *On The Road* but when Kerouac submitted the manuscript it was rejected. Solomon did suggest that it might be acceptable if some revisions were made but Kerouac reacted angrily so the matter was dropped. It's intriguing to speculate what might have happened had Ace Books accepted *On The Road.* Would it have had a sensational cover like *Junkie* and just taken its place on the paperback racks with all the other pulp fiction? It's unlikely that it would have created the kind of interest that it did arouse when it finally came out as a hardback in 1957 and was seen as a key Beat work. In the early 1950s hardly anyone outside a few people in New York knew or cared about the Beat Generation.

Solomon's mental health was never very good and in 1956 he suffered a nervous breakdown and was committed to Pilgrim State Hospital on Long Island. He was to stay there until 1964, with occasional home visits at weekends. It's said that when he was collected from the hospital, he often gave his family the slip and dashed off to see his literary associates in their Greenwich Village haunts. According to Solomon, the psychologists dealing with his case tried to persuade him to stay away from his Beat friends, seeing them as a bad influence, and he was urged to lead "a tame life." But he kept in touch with Burroughs, Ginsberg, and others, and A.A.Wyn sent him manuscripts to read and comment on. But Solomon was mostly out of circulation during an important phase of the Beat years. Ginsberg's *Howl* with its dedication to Carl Solomon and its catalogue of many of his supposed escapades, was published in 1956 and *On The Road* in 1957. After that there was a steady stream of books, anthologies, and magazines, that featured Beat material, though Solomon was overlooked by virtually all of them. It's true that he was included in *Protest,* alongside Kerouac, Ginsberg, Burroughs, and others, but he was represented by "Report from the Asylum," an important piece in its own right though not really representative of what he could do with short, provocative memoirs or sly sketches on a variety of topics ranging from politics to fishing to the problem of how to de-frost a fridge when you've never been used to having to deal with such mundane issues. To be fair to the editors of *Protest* little of Solomon's work was available in the period concerned, and in any case "Report from the Asylum" probably suited their purpose, which was to see madness as a form of protest against a hostile society.

After his release from Pilgrim State Hospital in 1964 Solomon lived with his mother and had routine jobs in bookstores and as a messenger on Wall Street. By the mid 1960s, however, some people had started to acknowledge his literary work for its own qualities and not just because he had been around in the early days of the Beat movement. A small selection of his short pieces, *Mishaps, Perhaps,* was published by City Lights Books in 1966, and a follow-up collection, *More Mishaps,* in 1968. These books brought together his earlier work and later short pieces he'd contributed to various magazines. He was sometimes invited to review new books by Beat writers but also seems to have freely jotted down all kinds of reflections and comments on anything that took his fancy. It made for a very idiosyncratic kind of writing which was easily identifiable despite its brevity.

It would seem, too, that this sort of short sketching enabled Solomon to respond quickly to requests for material, as I can testify from a personal experience. In 1976 I was editing a little magazine called *Palantir* and I wrote to Solomon and asked if he had anything I could publish. The piece that arrived, "Work Day Ended - 1976," was a brief summary of what I assumed was a fairly typical day for him as he caught the bus to work in the morning, carried out some routine tasks in a department store, and took the subway home in the evening, this way reading the paper to pass the time. It seemed on the face of it a totally factual tale of dull activities, but Solomon's little asides about the places the bus passed through and the columnists he read in the paper, coupled with a slightly tongue-in-cheek style of writing, gave it life. And there was a great deal packed into a short space. One of the joys of reading Solomon is that he is completely at home with short statements and can make them memorable. Like good short poems they stay in the mind and seem relevant when certain situations arise.

Solomon's life continued in this way through the 1970s and 1980s, though he was given more attention by historians of the Beats and he was interviewed and invited to conferences that celebrated the achievements of the Beat writers. His cryptic humour was always present, even when he was being acclaimed as a Beat pioneer, and a visit to Boulder or a reading with Ginsberg were likely to be written up in a way that suggested Solomon was a bit bemused by all the attention he was receiving but still wasn't going to take his fellow-Beats too seriously. There's a review of a literary anthology about baseball in which he lightly mocks Ginsberg:

> "However, there is baseball and there is this sort of intellectual approach to baseball. Just as there is fishing when you fish with non-literary types and fishing when you go fishing with Allen Ginsberg in a rowboat at City Island. Others will wait patiently for bites while Allen recites haikus about 'little silver fish'. The literary types inevitably revert to their specialities. What generally emerges, though, is a mingling of corn and erudition."

It was a typically dry Solomon observation, making an interesting point in a seemingly casual manner. He isn't just laughing at Ginsberg but also indicating how literary types have to intellectualise non-intellectual activities once they're involved with them.

It was once suggested that Solomon was working on "an extended memoir of the Beat Generation," but if he was he doesn't appear to have ever completed it. And yet his scattered writings about the Beats do add up to a loose history of what were probably the most important Beat years, those between 1945 and 1955. It was during this period that the main personalities in the movement - Kerouac, Ginsberg, Burroughs, John Clellon Holmes, and a few others, including Solomon - came together in New York and began to document their activities and promote each other's work. Solomon was a part of all that and his own experiences show how varied were the elements that went to make up the Beat philosophy. But like all the writers mentioned he really didn't fit to the Beat label as it was applied by later commentators, and it was possible to see much more than a fixed literary style in his work. He was a Jewish New Yorker and he always acknowledged that the issues he encountered in the 1940s – communism, surrealism, existentialism, French literature, madness - were what had shaped him. His published work is full of asides on these subjects and many others, and as he slid in and out of anecdotes about the people he'd known and reflections on their lives he also provided a running commentary on his own activities.

Carl Solomon died of cancer on February 28th 1993 and after the obituaries had appeared in print little was written about him. He is mentioned in books about Ginsberg and the making of *Howl,* and he usually rates a note or two in general histories of the Beats, but few critics and historians bother to discuss his own writing or note the major impact he had on Allen Ginsberg at a formative time in his life. And Ginsberg passed on much of what he'd learned from Solomon to other Beat writers. It would be a mistake to say that Carl Solomon was a major writer, even if he was a very intelligent and entertaining one, but he deserves better than to be remembered only for his links to Ginsberg and *Howl.*

NOTES

Much of Carl Solomon's best work can be found in *Emergency Messages: An Autobiographical Miscellany,* published by Paragon House, New York, 1989. His earlier books were *Mishaps, Perhaps* (City Lights Books, San Francisco, 1966) and *More Mishaps* (City Lights Books, San Francisco, 1968). Both have material not included in *Emergency Messages.*

# COOL KEROUAC

It's easy to imagine Jack Kerouac listening to some "wild tenor-man bawling horn across the way," as he once wrote. It goes with the notion of the Beat Generation, all excitement and movement and music that typified ideas of endless on the road endeavours. But there was a different Kerouac and it could be that a "cooler" style appealed more to his imagination than some frantic jazz or rhythm 'n' blues. Larry Kart, writing about Allen Eager and Brew Moore, referred to "a meditative inward-turning linear impulse that combines compulsive swing with an underlying resignation - as though at the end of each phrase the shape of the line drooped into a melancholy 'Ah, me,' which would border on passivity if it weren't for the need to move on, to keep the line going." And Kart indicated that Kerouac recognised this and related to it.

So who were those "cool" tenormen that Kerouac liked and wrote about so knowledgeably? His admiration for Lester Young, who can be called the father of the "cool" approach, was made clear in *On the Road*, when he referred to him as that "gloomy, saintly goof in whom the history of jazz was wrapped." Young's style had broken away from the previously-dominant approach illustrated by saxophonists like Coleman Hawkins and Ben Webster. They played with full, rich tones, and improvised in a rhapsodic manner, whereas Young's sound was light.

It has been said that Hawkins's method was to "push hard, pressing every drop of harmonic juice out of a theme," but Young's tone "had no edge at all. It didn't cut, it floated." And Young himself was quoted as saying, "I play a swing tenor, that lag-along style where you relax instead of hitting everything on the nose."

Young affected quite a few other tenormen, including Wardell Gray and Dexter Gordon, but it was during the mid and late-1940s that his greatest influence was felt, and it's interesting that it was most evident among white musicians. Dozens of young tenor saxophonists based their playing on Young, sometimes to the point where they lost all sense of their own individuality. Listen to the big-band records of the 1940s and 1950s and you will hear short solos by them. Only keen jazz collectors now remember the names of Buddy Wise, John Murtaugh, Buddy Arnold, Billy Usselton, and Ben Lary. I'm sure Kerouac must have come across some of them, either on records or in the clubs, though he obviously didn't think it important to mention them. But he did consider it worthwhile writing about Allen Eager and Brew Moore.

In *The Subterraneans*, the action of which takes place around Greenwich Village in the early1950s, there's a reference to "Roger Beloit, the great bop tenorman." Beloit is actually Allen Eager, one of the leading lights of the New York modern jazz world, and a musician who Lester Young thought the best of the "gray boys," as he called his white disciples. By 1953, though, Eager's career was faltering. His main period of activity had been in the 1940s when he was featured with the Buddy Rich orchestra, recorded under his own name, and included in Tadd Dameron's group where he played alongside the brilliant, though doomed trumpeter, Fats Navarro. This group which appeared at the Royal Roost in 1948, was one of the finest of the bop years, its music making absolutely no concessions to popular taste. If you didn't like pure bop then that was your problem. As for Eager, the jazz critic Ira Gitler recalled that "whatever he played swung with a happy, light-footed quality and pure-toned beauty..... many a night in the Roost he had us ready to get up and start dancing along the bar."

There was another side to Eager, one very much related to the problems that became associated with bop. Leonard Feather, a noted jazz writer, knew Eager and described him as a Jekyll and Hyde character: "His Dr Jekyll is an amusing, well-read and highly articulate guy, while the Hyde side is a typically gloomy product of the frustrations and neuroses of 52nd Street, with ornithological overtones." In other words, Eager, like so many bop musicians, had a problem with drugs.

When Kerouac referred to him in *The Subterraneans* he described him listening to a Stan Kenton record and, upon hearing a young tenorman named Ricci Commuca (real name Richie Kamuca) supposedly playing the "music of tomorrow," commenting dryly, "This is the music of tomorrow?".

What Beloit (Eager) was saying was that Commuca (Kamuca) was only playing in a way that he had been using since the mid-1940s. To be fair, Richie Kamuca was a fine musician who made many excellent recordings on the West Coast in the 1950s, but it's true that he hadn't progressed much, stylistically, beyond what Eager had done.

Eager slipped into obscurity in the 1950s. He made some excellent recordings with trumpeter Tony Fruscella, who Kerouac wrote about in *Lonesome Traveller*, spent some time in Paris, then became a member of the international jet set. His parents were reasonably wealthy and Eager had always been noted as a sharp dresser with sophisticated tastes, including skiing and motor-racing. But from a jazz point .of view he was virtually inactive. It is said that he did get involved with Frank Zappa and the Mothers of Invention and possibly played on some of their recordings. In the 1980s he did attempt to get back into jazz and I remember seeing him in clubs in London and Manchester. It was admittedly fascinating to see and hear a jazz legend, but his playing was less than exciting. He retired to Florida, played occasionally in local clubs, and died in 2003.

The other tenor player who Kerouac had a liking for was Milton "Brew" Moore (Kerouac called him "Brue," but I'll stick to Brew) who appears in *Desolation Angels*. There's a long description of Moore at work in a San Francisco club, where he's seen

"blowing on tenor saxophone, which he holds mouthpieced in the side of his mouth, his cheek distended in a round ball like Harry James and Dizzy Gillespie, and he plays perfect pretty harmony to any tune they bring up - He pays little attention to anyone, he drinks his beer, he gets loaded and eye-heavy, but he never misses a beat or a note, because music is his heart, and in music he has found that pure message to give to the world - The only trouble is, they don't understand."

Moore had arrived in New York in 1948 and soon got involved with the city's modern-jazz scene, though he wasn't at first sure that his playing tied in easily with that of the boppers. Moore worshipped Lester Young and said that anyone who didn't play like him was wrong, but he soon realised that he could work alongside musicians who were more inclined to look to Charlie Parker for lessons. He appeared on records with Howard McGhee, Machito, Gerry Mulligan, Stan Getz, and others, and he worked in the clubs with Charlie Parker, Miles Davis, and Tony Fruscella. In the 1950s he was a regular performer at the Open Door (Kerouac called it The Red Drum in *The Subterraneans*), the New York club that was a hangout for musicians and the hipsters described by Kerouac in his novel. Moore's playing was always warm and swinging and he never deviated from a style that was totally rooted in the music of Lester Young. Even when he was playing above the churning rhythms of Machito's Afro-Cuban orchestra, or working in a small group that was being kicked along by the driving bop drummer, Roy Haynes, he produced smooth, easy-flowing lines and could be exciting without resorting to the honking sounds that rhythm 'n' blues saxophonists used.

If Moore, like Eager, had an active period for a few years, little was heard of him by the mid-1950s and he moved to San Francisco. The story is that he was sitting on a bench in Washington Square, thinking that nothing was happening in New York, when Billy Faier who was delivering a car to the West Coast, asked if anyone wanted to go there.

Moore decided to go with Faier and two others, Woody Guthrie and Ramblin' Jack Elliot, though he and Guthrie didn't exactly get along due to the folk-singer's dislike of modern jazz. They did share a taste for alcohol, though, so seem to have come to some sort of agreement about buying booze as the trip progressed.

San Francisco was where Kerouac came across Moore, though he'd probably also heard him in the New York clubs. Moore stayed on the West Coast for a few years before moving to Europe. He was in Paris for a time and then settled in Copenhagen, with occasional trips back to the United States. He recorded in Denmark and worked in clubs in Germany and elsewhere, but without ever becoming prominent on the jazz scene again. Always a heavy drinker, he fell down some steps while drunk and died in 1973.

If, as Jack Kerouac claimed, he wanted to be a jazz poet in the sense of his writing paralleling the sound of the music then it's probable that he achieved it by focusing on how jazzmen like Allen Eager and Brew Moore played rather than the way that Charlie Parker and Dizzy Gillespie approached their performances. It's the line from Lester Young through his white followers like Eager, Moore, Stan Getz, Warne Marsh, and all the others now forgotten, that shaped him, even if he admired what Parker and Gillespie were doing. Larry Kart reckoned that there was something essentially "boyish" about the music of Eager, Moore, and the rest of the white "cool" musicians, and that, similarly, there was a "boyishness" about Kerouac's vision. He could be right.

I've quoted from Larry Kart's article, "Jazz and Jack Kerouac," and it can be found in his *Jazz in Search of Itself* (Yale University Press, 2004). It's well worth reading in full for the insights it gives on Kerouac's relationship to jazz.

There are two excellent CDs which fully illustrate the music of Allen Eager and Brew Moore. These are, *Allen Eager; An Ace Face* (Giant Steps GSCR 023) and Brew Moore: *The Kerouac Connection* (Giant Steps : GSCR 025) .

# JACK MICHELINE : POET OF PROTEST

Writing about Jack Kerouac in *Beat Scene 41*, I discussed his youthful interest in left-wing ideas and the suggestion that he may even have considered joining the Communist Party, though no evidence exists that he actually did. Kerouac's inclinations were not at all unusual, bearing in mind the social and political situation in the 1940s, and it's worth noting that several other writers associated with the Beat movement had, at one time or another, some form of involvement with groups on the Left. Carl Solomon had actually belonged to the Communist Political Association, which was the American Communist Party under another name in 1944, and Allen Ginsberg had a close awareness of left-wing theories picked up from his socialist father and communist mother. Gary Snyder was more inclined towards anarchism and knew the traditions of the Industrial Workers of the World (the famed Wobblies) while John Clellon Holmes described himself as "a committed and studious Marxist" who read *The Daily Worker* and similar publications. Bob Kaufman was an activist in the seamen's union and possibly a member of the Communist Party and the story is that he was blacklisted because of his associations. Stuart Z. Perkoff also seems to have been a Party member, if only for a brief period. And Jack Micheline was, in his own words, "in the radical movement for a short time" though which group he belonged to isn't known. He also claimed to have been a union organiser. What is interesting about Micheline is that, more than the others I've mentioned, his work can be seen as having close links to what was in the 1930s often referred to as proletarian writing. It was Seymour Krim who described one of Micheline's poems as having "a fullness and juiciness reminiscent of the Depression 30s," and I think it's possible to identify those characteristics as evident throughout his writing.

Micheline was born in the Bronx in 1929 his real name being Harvey Martin Silver and his ancestry Russian-Rumanian Jewish. He grew up in a working-class neighbourhood (largely Irish-American, from his own account) and from an early age was much influenced by his surroundings. The poverty, injustice, and money-grubbing he observed soon began to shape his attitudes towards society in general.

Attracted to reading, he discovered James T. Farrell's *Studs Lonigan*, a classic of 1930s radical literature and a book that was to have a great effect on him. Farrell's massive account of the hard lives of his characters (the three novels that make up the book amount to around 900 pages) "brought to American fiction a new voice, for the previously inarticulate and a sustained criticism of urban life," to quote one critic. It was about an Irish-American community in Chicago but the problems it dealt with would have been recognised by Micheline as similar to those he was experiencing.

Leaving school early, Micheline joined the army when he was seventeen, serving in the Medical Corps, and on his release went to live on a kibbutz in Israel. On his return to the United States he drifted west and worked at a variety of routine, blue-collar jobs. He was still using his real name and doesn't seem to have shown any interest in writing poetry until 1953 or so, when he began to consider the possibilities it offered to express his thoughts and feelings about both personal and social matters. By 1955 he was living in Greenwich Village and identifying with a tradition of American bohemianism and especially the lives and literature of street poets like Vachel Lindsay and Maxwell Bodenheim. Lindsay had wandered around America, "travelling as a combination missionary and minstrel" who preached "the gospel, of beauty." As he wandered he distributed a small pamphlet entitled, *Rhymes to be Traded for Bread*, hoping that way to make enough to live on. One commentator described him as "singing to convert the heathen, to stimulate and encourage the half-hearted dreams that hide and are smothered in sordid villages and townships." And he developed a chant-like method of delivering long poems such as "'The Congo" and "General William Booth enters into Heaven." It's unlikely that they're known to many people today and political correctness would probably rule out public performances of "The Congo" which has the attitudes and language of the period (the early 1900s) when it was written. Some of Lindsay's short poems ("To a Golden Haired Girl in a Louisiana Town," for example) still have charm and in their openness can resemble some of Jack Micheline's quieter poems.

As for Maxwell Bodenheim, he had been a prolific novelist and poet in the 1920s and early 1930s, and had appeared in most of the major magazines of those years, but he slid into alcoholism and destitution later in life and became a Greenwich Village character, roaming from bar to bar and selling poems for his drinking money. He was murdered in 1954 so was just a legend when Micheline arrived the following year. It was probably the legend that attracted him because most of Bodenheim's poetry was fairly orthodox from a technique point of view, though it sometimes expressed radical sentiments and was published in left-wing magazines. He had some loose links to the Communist Party in the 1930s and was included in an influential anthology, *Proletarian Literature in the United States*, which appeared in 1935. It's possible that Micheline may have come across this book some years later. I wonder, too, if he ever read Bodenheim's *Bringing Jazz*, published in 1930 and with various sections called "Greenwich Village Jazz," "Bronx Jazz," and so on. Bodenheim intended these poems to be read aloud, preferably with jazz accompaniment, and he incorporated slang into his street-wise commentaries on city life. The slang has dated., of course, and the poems are now only readable for their curiosity value but some of the energy behind them still comes through.

Micheline's heroes often cropped up in his poetry, as in "Chasing Kerouac's Shadow," where he imagines:

> Bodenheim hustling another poem for wine
> Franz Kline singing a sad song at the Cedar
> Kerouac talking to the moon again
> James T. Farrell chasing a waitress at Yankee Stadium

Like so many others by him this poem almost becomes a catalogue of the people he admired, most of them outsiders in relation to American society, a procession of jazz musicians, writers, painters, bohemians, Spanish Civil War veterans, and others, and a footnote to the poem says that it was written during a bus journey between San Francisco and Santa Rosa. It stressed that, whether in life or literature, Micheline did not believe in a detached and tidy approach to things. His stance set him apart from bourgeois conventions of taste, order, aspirations, and comfort.

Micheline's identification with the Bohemian tradition and his presence in Greenwich Village meant that he met Jack Kerouac, Allen Ginsberg, Gregory Corso, and other Beats. And when a publisher expressed interest in bringing out a small collection of

Micheline's poems provided a well-known writer could be persuaded to contribute an enthusiastic introduction, the poet contacted Kerouac. But his desire to be recommended by Kerouac wasn't just opportunism. He'd also recognised that Kerouac was a kindred spirit, someone he admired as "...a saint. An experimental writer. A genius with total memory. A loving and open human being. A ball player, a player of words". And it was the mixture of optimism and pessimism, the "upbeat" and the "downbeat" that critics have noted in Beat writing generally, that also appealed to Micheline, whose own work could veer wildly between harsh descriptions of cities he saw as falling apart and expressions of belief in the possibility of redemption through joy and freedom. Kerouac's celebrations of the ordinary had their parallels in Micheline's poetry and prose, with their elegies for failures, down-and-outs, and the common people. Additionally present, and this perhaps as a lingering element of his earlier political activism, are the occasional laments for the decline of working-class radicalism. *River of Red Wine,* his first book, has a poem which says:

> In youth we
> possessed
> so much hope and
> passion.
> Money boys have given
> you a time card
> and a gold plated watch
> after thirty five years.
> The politicians have
> fed you with promises
> and left you with doubts.

The style, functional at best, aims for the simple structures which make for easy reading. It seems that the poems were originally written with longer lines and were then changed to their printed form at the request of the publisher so that they would appear "more unconventional." It's evident that a feeling of protest is central to Micheline's work, though he never offers glib political solutions to the problems he describes and usually suggests that the only hope lies with individuals and worthwhile personal encounters and relationships. Talking about *River of Red Wine,* almost thirty years after its original publication Micheline claimed that Kerouac had found "affirmation of life" in his poetry and that he himself considered it an essential part of his approach to writing. Whatever else may be said about the poems they do often assert that things could be better, given a major shift of emphasis in people's attitudes about what they think is important in life.

It was about this time that Micheline stopped using his real name and began to publish regularly as Jack Micheline. He added an "e" to his mother's maiden name of Michelin and took the Jack from Jack London, the radical novelist and journalist of the early part of the 20th Century. London was another of the American rebels who Micheline had read and admired for his freedom of spirit and the energy and intensity evident in his writing.

His friendship with Kerouac and other Beats, his presence in Greenwich Village during the heyday of the movement, and his inclusion, in anthologies like *The Beats and The Beat Scene,* not to mention such magazines as *Yugen, The Outsider,* and *Beatitude,* ensured that Micheline was categorised as a Beat by those documenting events. But he was wary of the label. He never disassociated himself from it, but he preferred to see the overall situation in America in the 1950s, when painting, jazz, and poetry flourished, as linked to a longer bohemian tradition. Interviewed in 1985 and asked about what had happened thirty years before, he came up with a typically idiosyncratic answer that nonetheless provides a good picture of the period:

> "Artists exist in this country no matter what. You can't put a lock on the spirit of a man's soul. That's why the arts flourish. It was that way in the 50s. There was something new going on. Freaks spent the winter in New York cafes and automats discussing life over a cup of coffee. Brothers wandered the country looking for girls in fast cars."

If Kerouac's influence was important to Micheline he also, in 1959, encountered another man who was to play a significant role in shaping his poetic consciousness. Ed Balchowky was a pianist who had volunteered for the International Brigades and had lost his right arm fighting in Spain in the 1930s. He later began to paint and write but got into trouble with the authorities when he was convicted of possessing heroin. This mixture of the outsider roles of political radical, and struggling artist, must have appealed to Micheline immensely. He stated that Balchowsky opened his eyes to the world around him, making him see how society worked against the interests of the individual. In return, Micheline placed Balchowsky high on his list of bohemian heroes and frequently mentioned him in poems:

> They walked among the people
> With their open eyes
> They never knew each other
> But these men were brothers
> A guy named Ed Balchowsky
> And a guy named Franz Kline

Balchowsky clearly had radical ideas rooted in the 1930s and one of the characteristics of Micheline's poetry is its similarity to the proletarian verse of that period. It has often been the fashion to dismiss much 1930s writing but to read it is to discover a vitality, concern, and directness very much like Micheline's. Forgotten American poets such as Joseph Kalar, Michael Gold, Norman MacLeod and Herman Spector, spoke out against a system that had damaged or destroyed many of their contemporaries, and Micheline's work can easily be seen as following in their footsteps when he writes in a condemnatory manner:

> He worked for a hundred a week
> A worker on steel
> they cut off his limbs
> crushed in a rock called construction
> he sits in a wheelchair in Bellevue Ward 9
> some guy out of Memphis
> who had a good heart and read papers
> crippled for life on a merry-go-round

The straightforward statements, the down-to-earth language, and the bitterness which spits out of every line, are typical of both Micheline and the earlier poets, as is the poem's angry conclusion:

> and the poor they still suffer
> and the rich they keep weeping
> and escape is a six letter word
> this American dream out of rock
> and the grave of my father on a stock market page
> and the dead they are buried before they're sixteen
> and the power still crushes and stamps out the cripples
> this killing called profit
> this American dream out of rock

It is the mixture of bohemianism and social protest that places Micheline directly in a line leading to the left-wing poets of the 1930s and beyond them to the poets who published in radical magazines like *The Masses* and *The Liberator* earlier in the 20th Century. It's perhaps true to say that, unlike those writers, Micheline couldn't identify with a particular political ideology, so he tends towards a wide-ranging emotional commitment to the poor, the downtrodden, the misfits, and the outsiders of various persuasions. But there is a consistent stand made against bourgeois society and its values. In the poems and the short stories he wrote over the years Micheline constantly harangued his fellow-Americans, condemning the system under which they chose to live and at the same time always suggesting that they have the capacity within themselves to be different:

> "America is a seduced land where money is God and goods have spoiled the people, crushed their spirits, proclaimed false gods, raped the minds of its workers, taken the life from its very own land. Yet Americans are beautiful people. They are people that love, hope, pray, practice kindness and love. But the tide of power that corrupts and destroys human life - in masses, in hordes, in groups - has taken a hold, has twisted and squeezed and milked dry the very life that brings the spirit of more life."

In many ways Micheline's work never developed. His style remained the same, always a piling up of images in staccato lines, and his basic concerns hardly changed at all. To read a selection of his poems, ranging from the 1950s to the 1990s, is to be struck by the degree to which the same angry voice can be heard. This is not necessarily a bad thing, though the reader may well start to wonder how the poet can sustain such a fierce, emotional attack on an unchanging, even worsening society without it having an effect on his mind and spirit. Certainly, some of the earlier radical poets got disillusioned, though that was sometimes because they'd put too much faith in the revolutionary potential of the working-class or had believed that a particular party had the answer in its manifesto. Micheline seems to have avoided both of these traps, though he did once say that he hoped that someday he hoped his work would be "read out loud by the masses," which is a rather starry-eyed view of what is likely to happen. It may be significant that his output slowed down in the 1980s, though he continued to be active as a performer at readings and as an artist. There is a poem from 1987 called "The Last Bench," which celebrates the lives and misadventures of a selection of ill-fated writers, painters, and musicians, and it's tempting to wonder if it was also speaking for Micheline:

> you had no more to give
> and you gave everything you had
> and that was all
> everything and nothing
> and you gave it all

I've concentrated on aspects of Micheline's poetry but it's worth adding some comments about the short stories published in *In The Bronx and Other Stories* (1965) and *Skinny Dynamite* (1980). Like the poems they have radical antecedents in that they can be seen as related to the tough-guy prose of the 1930s that could be read in some left-wing magazines and in the pulp publications printing crime stories which occasionally touched on harsh commentary on the social system. I doubt that many people have heard of Benjamin Appel but in the 1930s he wrote for a radical magazine like *The Anvil* and also produced crime novels, including *Brain Guy*. It strikes me that Micheline's stories wouldn't be out-of-place alongside Appel and similar writers. And they would surely have found a place in 1930s magazines, their directness and concern for the disadvantaged placing them in a category that the proletarian authors belonged to.

There are few niceties in a Micheline story and the general theme is of the struggle to survive a brutal and uncaring society. But there are suggestions of possible ways out of the problem. In one of his stories Micheline says of two men, "They were not looking for revolution - they were the revolution," indicating that their lifestyle is to be preferred to that of the wider society, or at least the respectable elements of it. And the story goes on to say, "In the despair and futility of a modern age, there is a world still to win" and the echoes of 1930s radicalism can be heard in that. *A World to Win* was, in fact, the title of a novel by the proletarian writer, Jack Conroy, whose first book, *The Disinherited,* described what it was like to be on the road and hunting for work. Conroy had also been involved with a bohemian community in St Louis which brought together radical workers, writers, artists, and a variety of oddball characters. Micheline would surely have been at home there. A

119

critic, writing about *A World to Win*, referred to its "grotesque realism of unsavoury behaviour, irreverent parody, and grim description as Conroy's figures bump up against the concreteness of an everyday world," and it's equally a good description of many of Micheline's stories. Their realism is often extended to the point where it touches on the grotesque.

I've looked at Jack Micheline's work largely in terms of how it relates to a bohemian radical tradition because it seems to me that its strength lies in that relationship. Other Beat writers expressed various forms of dissent, but he was the one who, consciously or not, most closely identified with the 1930s radical poets and a tradition of bohemian protest that stretches back to the Greenwich Village of the first two decades of the Twentieth Century. It would be wrong to claim that he was a major poet but Jack Micheline had an individual voice that developed out of his own experiences and he never stopped using that voice to speak out against what he thought was wrong. He was a genuine poet of protest.

# JOHN CLELLON HOLMES

John Clellon Holmes was the quiet man of the Beat Generation. He was always overshadowed by Kerouac, Burroughs, Ginsberg, and others, when he was alive, and even though he's now included in anthologies of Beat writing and mentioned in histories of the Beat movement, he tends to be taken for granted. He's noted as someone who was there in the early days in New York and who wrote a novel which portrayed the world of the Beats in fairly accurate detail, but beyond that he rarely rates much attention. And much of his work, including novels, short stories, essays, and poetry, is sadly overlooked, and perhaps even forgotten.

Holmes was born in 1926 in Holyoke, Massachusetts, but because his father was a salesman the family moved around and lived, at various times, in New Jersey, New York, New Hampshire, and Connecticut. He seems to have left school early and in 1943 was working in the *Reader's Digest* subscription department and taking evening classes at Columbia University. In June, 1944 he was drafted into the United States Navy Hospital Corps, and though he wasn't sent overseas he did work in a hospital for wounded servicemen. It was an experience that had a profound effect on him and in an interview many years later he said: "Anti-fascist though I had been since 12, the experience ended war for me. Fifty boys my own age died while I watched, helpless to help. A hundred more were crippled forever, and no June night would promise them anything but bitterness. I feel a solidarity with them still."

Along with hospital work Holmes read a great deal, delving into Shakespeare, Tolstoy, Dostoevsky, Spengler, Darwin, Blake, and many others. He was discharged from the Navy in 1945 and settled in New York with his wife, Marian, who he had married during his Navy service. Holmes continued to read widely and took an interest in painting. He recalled visiting galleries to see the work of the artists who would become famous as the Abstract Expressionists, including Jackson Pollock and Franz Kline, and he worked on his own paintings. At this stage of his life Holmes was also, as he described himself, "a committed and studious Marxist," and he was working on something for the communist magazine, *New Masses*, which was never published because the magazine closed down.

The onset of the Cold War and the communist takeover of Czecho-slovakia in 1948 caused him to reconsider his views and break his links with Marxism.

It was in 1948 that Holmes was drawn into the world of the Beats. He had started to publish poetry and reviews in magazines like *Partisan Review* and *Poetry*, and he also contributed a short story, "Tea for Two," described as "an experiment with the language of jazz," to Jay Landesman's *Neurotica*, which was also publishing early work by Anatole Broyard, Carl Solomon, Chandler Brossard, and Allen Ginsberg. Holmes's story, written before he had listened to Charlie Parker, Dizzy Gillespie and modern jazz in general, was "a fanciful take on Max Kaminsky and the Condon crowd at Nick's-in-the-Village," a club which featured Dixieland jazz. And he was getting to know various young writers in New York. Alan Harrington, later author of *The Secret Swinger,* a novel which looked back on 1940s New York and featured Holmes in fictional form, had told him about the manuscript of Kerouac's then-unpublished *The Town and the City*, as well as Kerouac's journals, and Holmes had been impressed by the way they were described as "bursting with life." Eventually, on the weekend of July 4th, 1948, Holmes went to a party in Spanish Harlem where he met Kerouac and Ginsberg. It isn't true to say that the encounter was momen-tous, and Holmes's own accounts of it do not suggest that the three struck up any great associations of interest at the time. Holmes did say that the others impressed and intrigued him, and that "there was a vividness about them, in their different ways, that spoke to me." But he added: "But certainly I had no suspicion that some-thing had begun that night that is not over yet."

The friendship between Holmes and Kerouac did develop, how-ever, and with Holmes increasingly involved with the new jazz sounds of the 1940s they shared interests that went beyond writing. Holmes had floundered intellectually after abandoning his Marxist sympathies and the curious world that opened up to him as he got to know the Beats and their followers, and explored the sounds of bebop and the habits of the hipsters, gave him new possibilities for writing. He was always more intellectually orthodox than Kerouac in the way that he wanted to work out what made things happen and people behave the way they did. And he looked for cause and effect in the events that took place around him. Looking back on the 1940s, he remarked: "*The Hunt* (Wardell Gray and Dexter Gordon): listen there for the anthem in which we jettisoned the intellectual Dixieland of atheism, rationalism, liberalism - and found our own group's rebel streak at last." It was not unexpected that some of Holmes's best writing would later turn out to be in the essay form, where he was provided with an opportunity to combine an intellectual appreciation of a subject with a talent for evocativeness and a flair for striking phrases. When he wrote about Kerouac in a wonderful essay called "The Great Rememberer," he described him in detail and, in one passage, referred to his mood swings:

> "He was moody. There were always weathers in his soul. You would see the cloud pass over his sun; you would see the light go out of his face; he would become as dismal as November, and sit there with an odd heaviness about him, saying only the perfunctory least, ungiving, dour beyond help of a joke, as gloomy as an old New England house on a rainy afternoon."

Holmes was a traditional writer, in the sense that he didn't experiment with language or form, but he could describe and explain and he knew how to make each word count.

Spurred on by his new friends and enthusiasms, Holmes began to work on a novel describing New York life, or at least that part of it he was involved with. Looking back on the period between August, 1949 and September, 1951 when he wrote the book, Holmes said:

> "These gloomy lofts and tenements, these thronging streets and bars, these continual parties and confrontations - can it really have been like that? Did we resemble these feverish young men, these centreless young women, awkwardly reaching out for love, for hope, for comprehension of their lives and times? Can this picture of the New York of twenty-five years ago be accurate? I can attest that it is. These were the places we lived in, the events that occurred, the way we talked, and the things we talked about. In this sense, the book is almost literal truth, sometimes a truth too literal to be poetically true, which is the only truth that matters in literature."

And it would seem that from the point of view of historical accuracy, *Go*, which is what Holmes called his novel, probably gives a clearer picture of the early Beat days than anything else written by

a participant. As Kenneth Rexroth put it, "if you want to understand what Allen Ginsberg called 'the best minds of my generation,' *Go* is the book." All the well-known Beats, such as Ginsberg,
Kerouac, Neal Cassady, Herbert Huncke, are there under fictional
names, along with numerous others who never became famous and
died or disappeared. And I'd guess that Holmes's views of them
were less-romanticised than in other versions. Neal Cassady, for
example, appears as Hart Kennedy, and though Paul Hobbes
(Holmes) is fascinated by his energy and speech patterns he does-
n't go overboard for him in the way that Kerouac did. Taking
Holmes at his word when he said that the book was "almost literal
truth," what comes through is the fact that, while Kennedy (Cassady) affects Hobbes (Holmes), the latter is too conventional to let
himself be fully overwhelmed by his amorality and enthusiasms.
There was, I suspect, always a conservative side to Holmes's character which didn't allow him to throw off all the constraints of
middle-class behaviour, though like many of his kind he had a
sneaking admiration for people who could. Holmes recalled: "I
was reasonably close to Neal, and always liked him," but he added,
"he wasn't a mythic character - he was simply a fascinating human
being." This is a sober view of Cassady but it is more positive than
the one expressed by Holmes's friend, Alan Harrington, who
thought that "according to any medical model ever devised, Cassady qualified as a complete psychopath."

Holmes's need to analyse what he was experiencing is evident
throughout *Go*, as in the passage dealing with a visit to a jazz club
called *The Go Hole*. After briefly describing the physical appearance of the club and the audience, Holmes turns to the social reasons for its existence

> "The Go Hole was where all the high schools, the swing bands,
> and the roadhouses of their lives had led these young people; and
> above all it was the result of their vision of a wartime America
> as a monstrous danceland, extending from coast to coast, roofed
> by a starless night, with hot bands propelling thousands of lonely
> couples with an accelerating, Saturday-night intensity. In this
> modern jazz, they heard something rebel and nameless that
> spoke for them, and their lives knew a gospel for the first time. It
> was more than a music; it became an attitude toward life, a way
> of walking, a language and a costume; and these introverted kids
> (emotional outcasts of a war they had been too young to join in,

or in which they had lost their innocence), who had never belonged anywhere before, now felt somewhere at last."

It's hard to imagine Kerouac writing something like that, and
though Holmes may have abandoned Marxism as a belief it's clear
that some of its analytical processes still shaped his attitudes. But I
don't want to overstate the idea that *Go* is simply a thinly-
fictionalised sociological survey of the Beat experience of the late-
1940s. Holmes wrote as a novelist and whatever he himself said
about his book being almost "literal truth" it is best read as a novel
that also provides a fairly accurate picture of people and places. It
is its evocation of how a young writer encounters a group of adventurous and sometimes talented people, and how they affect his
life and ideas, that gives it strength and enables it to describe what
it was like to be alive at a certain time and in a certain place.

While Holmes was writing *Go* he had continued to publish poetry
in *Epoch, The Chicago Review,* and similar magazines, and had
ghost-written speeches, produced advertising copy, and worked on
public-opinion surveys. Like any young writer he had to find a
variety of ways to earn money. He also attended the New School
for Social Research, studying comparative religions, medieval literature, French Impressionist painting, and sitting in on a course
on Melville's *Moby Dick* given by the noted critic, Alfred Kazin.

*Go* was published in the autumn of 1952 and sold around 2,500 in
hardback and was bought for paperback publication, though that
edition never appeared due to worries about censorship problems.
It attracted enough attention for Holmes to be asked to write an
article about the Beat Generation (a term used in *Go* and correctly
attributed to the character based on Kerouac) for *The New York
Times Magazine.* This also created some interest, though not
enough to sustain it beyond the initial impact. Kerouac's *The
Town and the City* had appeared in 1950 and had what might be
called a Beat section, and Chandler Brossard's *Who Walk in Darkness* came out in 1952 and focused on Greenwich Village types,
while George Mandel's *Flee the Angry Strangers*, also from 1952,
touched on the Village and drugs. But at the time very few people
saw these books, and *Go*, as having some sort of common identity.
They weren't the only publications dealing with groups and individuals - junkies, bohemians, hipsters, to name some of them -
operating outside the conventional frameworks of society. Nelson

Algren's *The Man .With the Golden Arm* (1949) and a curious short story, "The Heroin Addicts" (1950) by Larry Rivers, published in *Neurotica*, can also be mentioned, along with stories by R.V. Cassill, Herbert Gold, and Anatole Broyard, and articles by Broyard and Milton Klonsky. Something was stirring, but it would be several years later, when the Beats were in the headlines in the late 1950s, before these early manifestations of new or different sensibilities could be seen as significant.

Holmes's marriage had broken up under the pressures of the bohemian life of New York, but he re-married and, in 1953 moved to Old Saybrook in Connecticut, where he started to work on a jazz novel, a portion of which was published in *Discovery* that same year. But he soon had to put the novel on one side while he struggled to earn enough money to live on. A few stories and articles were published in magazines like *Holiday* and *Nugget* between 1954 and 1957 but the period generally doesn't appear to have been a very productive one. He said he was "desperately broke in those years," and he spent a lot of time renovating the old house he'd bought in Old Saybrook. Things began to look better in 1958 when the upsurge of interest in the Beats after the publication of *Howl* and *On the Road* focused some attention on Holmes. He had finally completed the manuscript of his jazz novel, *The Horn*, and the book was published in 1958 so managed to be drawn into the debate surrounding the literary talents of the Beats and their supposed social ideas. *The Horn* was not the first jazz novel, by any means, but it was the first to try to deal with the world of modern jazz. It wasn't a complete success as a novel and at times reads like a slightly hysterical version of the jazz life, with romanticised notions of its central characters (clearly based on prominent jazz people like Lester Young, Billie Holiday, and Dizzy Gillespie) being tormented artists struggling to create in the face of a hostile society. In a letter to Kerouac, Holmes had said that he saw jazzmen as the people who "most perfectly epitomise the sorry, and often, fabulous condition of the artist in America." But while Holmes was telling an often colourful story which seemingly aimed to draw a parallel between beboppers and Beats he tended to overlook the fact that the jazz musicians in real life "thought of themselves, above all else, as professionals," to quote the critic, Jon Parrish. It's always difficult to describe music in words and jazz, in particular, has seen some outlandish examples of overdone prose, but Holmes tried to create the atmosphere of live music being made. And he created a few notable scenes, as when a sardonic Edgar Pool, a tenor saxophonist not unlike Lester Young, watches a big-band rehearsing and remarks, "Man, what a lot of paper," as the musicians sort through the arrangements. *The Horn* lacks the authenticity of Ross Russell's *The Sound*, which was flawed as a novel but had some convincing descriptions of jazzmen at work, but it has a sincerity which enables it to finally overcome its limitations. Holmes said that it was "well-reviewed almost everywhere, sold modestly well, and disappeared."

As I said at the start of this piece, Holmes never got the publicity that Kerouac and Ginsberg attracted, even if he did appear in a couple of popular Beat anthologies like *Protest* and *The Beats.* But, to be fair, there is little evidence to show that he cultivated a Beat image. He wrote articles for *Esquire, Nugget, Playboy* and *Harper's Magazine* in the early 1960s, often about non-Beat topics, and he worked on a third novel, *Get Home Free,* which was published in 1964. He once commented that it "got luke-warm-to-bad reviews and didn't sell. Even people who know my work somewhat have never read it," but I've always thought it the best of his novels from a purely literary point of view, with wonderful descriptive passages and one or two memorable characters. Seen by Holmes as a record of the "emotional aftermath of the experiences" described in *Go* and the "changing milieu of the Fifties," the completed work perhaps didn't match up to what Holmes had envisioned. He admitted that he'd written the two longest sections of the book as "stand-alone novellas" and then decided to tie them together, which may explain why it doesn't totally convince as a novel. It's still worth reading, though, and its ambitions, if flawed, are real. There are, also, the passages I referred to earlier. In the "Old Man Molineaux" section the central male character in the novel leaves New York and goes back to the small town in Connecticut where he was born. He takes up with Old Man Molineaux, the town drunk, and the two embark on a series of drunken escapades which are brilliantly created and matched by some vivid descriptions of the area where they ramble and drink and talk.

Obviously, none of Holmes's novels ever brought in enough for him and his wife to survive on for very long, and he had to turn his hand to other literary work, especially essays. And it may be that the essays will turn out to be his most lasting contribution to the Beat story in particular and American writing in general. They were eventually collected into three volumes published by the University of Arkansas Press in the 1980s, though an earlier collection, *Nothing More to Declare*, published in 1967, contained many of Holmes's Beat-related pieces. Writing about Kerouac, Jay Landesman, Gershon Legman, Ginsberg, the Beat movement, and adding a couple of fast-moving accounts of the 1940s and 1950s, Holmes built up a powerful picture of the people he'd known and the events he'd observed. His essay on Kerouac, "The Great Rememberer," is one of the warmest ever written about him and captures the spirit of the man. Holmes, reminiscing about what he'd seen in a small town in Iowa, says: "Instantly, I thought of Kerouac, for the place was quintessentially his America, the America he knows down to its last stained mattress ticking and its final broken bottle in the railroad weeds; the America he taught me how to see, full of the anxious faces in which his eye had spied an older, more rooted America (of spittoons, and guffawing, and winter suppers) now vanishing bewilderedly behind the billboards and TV antennas."

*Nothing More to Declare* didn't sell well and the fact that his writing alone wasn't likely to bring in enough money pushed Holmes into taking teaching jobs. For a time these were, as he described them, "gypsy-teaching," with short-term stints at the Iowa Writers' Workshop, Brown University, and Bowling Green State University, but by the mid-1970s he'd settled at the University of Arkansas, where he eventually became a Professor of English. In an interview he said of his decision to take a permanent post: "After two decades of staying alive by my wits, writing for magazines, occasionally teaching a semester here or there, I was faced with having to acknowledge that I would never be able to live by writing, that I was fifty years old, and wearied beyond belief with having to think about money day in and day out." His idea was that, despite its demands, "the Job in Arkansas left me free to write what I wanted (money or no)," and he began to produce poetry again, though in a much freer technical style than his earlier poetry had used. It was around this time that I wrote to Holmes to ask him to contribute to *Palantir*, a little magazine I was then editing, and several poems by him did appear in its pages in 1976 and 1977. From our brief correspondence he came across as open and friendly, and when I explained to him that the usual financial fragility of a small magazine wouldn't allow me to pay anything for use of the poems, he simply said, "Never mind, we're all in the same boat, baling together." It was a relaxed and generous gesture and seemed typical of the man I'd got to know from his novels and essays.

Holmes continued to work on novels, including one called *The Quincy Girls*, which covered the lives of four sisters over a sixty years timespan. He also had a completed novel, *Perfect Fools,* which was a sequel to *Go*. Neither of these books were ever published, but several new short stories did appear in print and his poems were used by a variety of magazines. He additionally turned to making films and to painting again. He described himself as living "quietly, rather simply," and added that he'd no wish to be famous and "the work is all. The rest is only ego-massage." Several small collections of his poems were published in the late-1970s and early 1980s, along with a couple of memoirs of Kerouac, and the University of Arkansas began work on the three collections of his essays which appeared in 1987 and 1988. As I said earlier, it may be that these will be his lasting legacy. In them he covered cultural, biographical, and travel topics, and always with deep respect for what he was writing about and a highly personal, though never prejudiced, approach to the subject in question. They weren't just essays written to order, or to earn some quick money, and the fact that Holmes brought an individual emphasis to the writing will enable them to survive.

John Clellon Holmes died of cancer in 1988. It would be wrong to claim that he was a major novelist. *Go* is an important text if seen in the context of the Beat experience, and *The Horn* and *Get Home Free* are interesting but minor works. The best of his poetry has warmth and sincerity but doesn't break any new ground. His essays are, as I've indicated, often first-rate and worth preserving. And, whatever criticisms might be levelled against it, there is in virtually all his writing, whether poetry or prose, always something that gives it life and makes it of value. The reader has the feeling that Holmes was never content with the obvious and was searching for something beyond it. As he said of his aims: "To tell the truth, neither to explain nor apologise, is a decent and demanding enough endeavour to occupy a serious and honest man."

# WILLIAM BURROUGHS: HIP NOT BEAT

"I have some close personal friends among the Beat movement: Jack Kerouac and Allen Ginsberg and Gregory Corso
are all close personal friends of many years standing, but
we're not doing at all the same thing, either in writing or in
outlook.....I don't associate myself with them; it's simply a
matter of juxtaposition rather than any actual association of
literary styles or overall objectives."

So said William Burroughs when asked about his relationship to
the Beat movement. And it may be that what sets him apart is that
he was, if I can use handy labels, Hip rather than Beat. There has
been a tendency to use Hip and Beat as if they were merely two
sides of the same coin, a tendency which isn't surprising given the
way in which the terms have been corrupted by use. We all know
how Beat was used by the media, and Hip is now virtually mean-
ingless, fashionable magazines and advertising agencies having
turned it into something to do with a slick and sophisticated image.
It wasn't that way in the 1940s, which is when Burroughs came to
it through his drug addiction, and it is in that era that true definitions of Hip and Beat need to be located.

It was during the 1940s that the notion of the hipster as a definable
type began to take shape. Robert Creeley once said: "This was the
time of the whole cult of the hipster, which is a forties designation,
the crew is defined then, the whole thing of being hip or with it."
There are various suggestions about where the term "hip" came
from, but it's more than likely that it originated in West Africa in
the language of the Wolof tribe. They have a word "Hipi" which
means "to open one's eyes," and it is from West Africa that most
American Negro slaves came, so it clearly carried over. A hip-cat
(from the Wolof, "hipi-kat") or hipster was someone who had
wised-up and opened his eyes to the ways of the world. By the
1940s, hip was very much linked to a detached approach which
was adopted by jazz musicians, especially those playing bebop.
Many of them were junkies, of course. You didn't have to be a musician to be a junkie, and Burroughs himself never displayed a
great deal of interest in bebop, but the style and the language

(some of it from carnival slang, as well as the jazz world) inter-mingled. The point is that it's difficult to understand what hip meant unless you see narcotics as central to the experience.

To be hip was to be addicted, and it shaped one's attitudes. The hip world was a small one, small enough for many of its inhabitants to know each other and to share experiences. It's a world evoked in *Junky* and *Naked Lunch*, with its paranoia, conspiracies, crime, corrupt cops, and the continual search for the next fix or the money to buy it. All other activities focus on this. Burroughs, by choosing to immerse himself in that world, had taken on its characteristics, and they shaped his fiction, especially his early work. And the hip world was not a pleasant one, no matter how glamorous it may have seemed when represented by a brilliant jazz musician. It did-n't encourage much loyalty. If the hipster seemed a conman, or locked into his own thoughts and likely to raise an eyebrow at the functions of the square world, then that was totally understandable. Experience had taught him to be wary and see everyone else, even fellow-hipsters, as a possible threat. Junk, as Burroughs said, was "a way of life." Anatole Broyard, who wrote an early analysis of the hipster, thought that being hip meant that the external world could be simplified and that a "manageable mythology" could be constructed in this way. Broyard also said that the hipster "still wanted terribly to take part in the cause and effect that determined the real world," but that he was frustrated and "not allowed to con-ceive of himself functionally or socially." He therefore, "conceived of himself dramatically, and, taken in by his own art, he often en-acted it as actual defiance, self-assertion, impulse, or crime." Burroughs' biographer, Ted Morgan, wrote: "In his search for a viable identity, Burroughs deliberately sought out a criminal life....Using junk made him part of the group, it was a sort of rite of passage."

The hipster, though some might see him as a rebel, had no desire to change the world. It was enough to survive it. *Junky* and *Naked Lunch* incorporate no programmes or any alternatives to faults per-ceived. The world is evil because it deprives the junkie of his fix. There is a difference between Hip and Beat, and I'd suggest that politics, even if of a decayed kind, is at its centre. Most of the members of the early Beat clique had a link to liberal/left-wing ideas, even Kerouac who, Allen Ginsberg suggested, went through

131

a communistic phase around 1940. Kerouac's political thoughts were always hazy at best, and any involvement would have been the product of enthusiasm rather than reflection, but other Beats - Ginsberg, Carl Solomon, John Clellon Holmes, Gary Snyder, Lawrence Ferlinghetti, Jack Micheline, Bob Kaufman, Stuart Perkoff - had more substantial connections, ranging from membership of the Communist Party to writing poetry full of social comment. Beat bohemianism can be placed in a tradition of American protest writing, but Burroughs doesn't belong there. He was too hip to think that change could come through established forms of opposition. When asked if he shared Ginsberg's aim to "transform the world by love and non-violence," he replied, "Most emphatically no." He was a man who had opened his eyes to the realities of the world, and he knew that those in power were hardly likely to step down voluntarily, nor take much notice of "love and non-violence."

In any case, Burroughs' social ideas, insofar as they existed, certainly didn't incline towards left-wing oppositional activity. In 1949 he scoffed at Ginsberg's dream of becoming a labour leader, and said that his opinion of labour leaders and unions was close to that of Westbrook Pegler, a right-wing columnist with pronounced anti-communist views. Burroughs also referred to Britain as a "socialistic police state," and added that socialism and communism were synonymous and both unmitigated evil. There is, too, a story about Burroughs, later in life, walking out of a party because he thought that the Scottish writer Tom McGrath was the American radical poet, Thomas McGrath.

It's true that, once the Beat movement hit the headlines, Burroughs was often published alongside Ginsberg, Kerouac, and the others, and that critical studies, literary histories, and anthologies, emphasise the connection. But I'd still insist on his separation from the main impulses of Beat thinking, whether they be jazz, social protest, Eastern religions, ecological concerns, or bohemianism. The Beats, it seems to me were, in many ways, part of a final fling of an old-style literary bohemia, with its politics and social commentary, and its overt cultivation of a life-style that challenged the bourgeois world through a rebuttal of its values. But after the Beats things changed. The Old Left could understand what the Beats were about, even if they didn't always like their work, and Kerouac spoke to an audience reared on a social tradition of literature. But

Burroughs appealed to a largely different audience, one more in touch with drugs and new methods of communication, and sharing with Burroughs a mistrust of the whole state apparatus. Interzone was a concept understood by that audience. It knew what Burroughs meant by "total control," and it related to the individualistic and ironic point of view of Hip rather than to the group-minded and enthusiastic mood of Beat. The critic Jennie Skerl wrote of Burroughs' humour:

"But in spite of all the parallels with traditional satire, *Naked Lunch* is ultimately a parodic rather than a satiric work. It attacks without implying any positive standards as traditional satire does. The individual, anarchic freedom that lies behind the destructive satire exists in a vacuum, with no moral or social structure to support it or to give satire any function but destruction. The only values upheld by Burroughs' parodic style are the energy, delight, and laughter that come from the freedom from controlling structures and the joy in spontaneous response to inner impulses and external context. These are the hipster's values, and *Naked Lunch* is a Beat masterpiece, embodying the hipster mentality, which Burroughs had explored in life and in *Junky.*"

Jennie Skerl makes the common mistake of associating Hip with Beat, but I doubt that the work of Ginsberg, Ferlinghetti, Corso, Kerouac, and all the minor Beats, could be described in the way that she refers to Burroughs. As Ginsberg once said: "I sit because after Lunacharsky got fired and Stalin gave Zhdanov a special tennis court I became a rootless cosmopolitan." The satire in that does not exist in a vacuum, and its political background is clear. There is nothing like it in Burroughs, who was far too hip to think that any state might have offered hope at any time.

One other point I want to make with regard to Burroughs and his role as a kind of spokesman for Hip rather than Beat relates to his status as an American writer. Obviously, he is, being American born and educated, and using mostly American backgrounds in his early books. There is, also, his use of the American storytelling tradition, or at least a parody of it, with its tall tales and cracker-barrel philosophies. But he is, I'd suggest, far less American than Ginsberg, Kerouac, Snyder, Corso, and the rest. The Beats were all-American boys, and that includes Ginsberg, despite his claims of rootless cosmopolitanism. They could not have been anything else, and that was true whether they were in San Francisco, Paris, Tangier, Mexico, India, or wherever. Like the expatriates of the 1920s they constantly examined their relationship with their homeland. There is, in Kerouac, often a sad lament for an older, imagined America which was better, or so he supposed, than the one he sees around him. And Ginsberg's poetry is often a critique of American society, and so is the work of lesser poets like Jack Micheline and Diane di Prima. But this is not necessarily true of Burroughs, and he was probably the most genuinely international of the group. He spoke out strongly in favour of abolishing "the whole concept of the nation." His vision of the world cut across what Lawrence Ferlinghetti referred to as "the obscene boundaries."

I've only provided a brief analysis of Hip, but even so I think it shows how it differed from Beat, and why Burroughs stands to one side of the movement. The personal links are there, and without the interest and encouragement of Ginsberg, Kerouac, and others, Burroughs may never have become a writer and certainly wouldn't have had his work promoted to the same extent. But this does not make him a Beat. He was Hip and although he went beyond the limitations of that term, as anyone familiar with his whole body of work will know, he always retained some aspects of Hip in his response to the world and its ways. He had opened his eyes and, as the title *Naked Lunch* implies, had seen what was truly on the end of every fork.

# BEATITUDE

There are books on my shelves that I bought almost half-a-century ago and which I've probably not looked at in recent years. But every now and then, searching for something else, I come across one of them, blow off the dust, and settle down to see what attracted my attention when I was younger and a little more optimistic than I tend to be now. I try to fight off nostalgia and instead look at things objectively so I can evaluate the merits, or otherwise, of what I'm reading. It doesn't always work and sometimes the past does creep up and it makes me tolerant of poor writing simply because when I first read it I felt that it represented something new or different. And that's what I wanted at the time. There's a parallel with music and the way in which a popular song can overcome its limitations and still have meaning many years later. It doesn't have to be wonderful just so long as it triggers the relevant memories.

I can't recall exactly where I bought *Beatitude Anthology* in 1960, and even then I knew that, compared to other collections of new American writing published in the same year, it hardly typified the best of Beat and related work. For real quality you had to turn to Donald Allen's *New American Poetry* (Grove Press), and a lively survey could be found in Seymour Krim's *The Beats* (Gold Medal Books) though Krim did stretch the definition of "Beat" to include writers with only a limited relationship to the movement. Stanley Fisher's *Beat Coast East* (Excelsior Press) mostly outclassed what was printed in *Beatitude Anthology* (City Lights Books) and Elias Wilentz's *The Beat Scene* (Corinth Books) had much of interest, though like Krim he used a fairly loose interpretation of what "Beat" meant.

But, despite its drawbacks, *Beatitude Anthology* represented something beyond the literary claims and aims of the other anthologies. The writers they featured were mostly people who, whether they eventually succeeded or not, wanted to be seen as writers. And more than a few of them went on to publish books and establish literary reputations of varying kinds. It's true that the same could be said of some of the poets in *Beatitude Anthology* (Ginsberg, Corso, Whalen, McClure, and others were there) but, in a way, the

135

whole ethos of the anthology almost worked against literary prestige. It mixed good and bad poetry without apology, and what
came across was that a community was on display and that literary
quality was not a first priority in such circumstances.

What needs to be noted is that the anthology was drawn from the
first sixteen issues of *Beatitude* magazine, a mimeo publication
started in 1959. According to the introduction to the anthology, the
idea for *Beatitude* "was conceived by Allen Ginsberg, Bob Kaufman and John Kelly or someone at Cassandra's Coffee House in
May, 1959." It was intended to be a cheaply produced "weekly
miscellany of poetry and other jazz designed to extol beauty and
promote beatific life among the various mendicants, neo-
existentialists, christs, poets, painters, musicians, and other inhabitants and observers of North Beach, San Francisco." Like many
good intentions the weekly publication schedule soon slipped and
only fifteen issues appeared in the first year. Distribution seems to
have been a problem, as it is with all small literary magazines, and
there are varying accounts of the number of copies sold. Warren
French, in his detailed critical study, *The San Francisco Poetry
Renaissance, 1955-1960* (Twayne Publishers, 1991), describes
*Beatitude* as a "slapdash publication," and says that because of its
poor production standards, sporadic appearances, and low sales,
few complete sets of the early issues survived, so the anthology is
the best easily-accessible source for finding out what was in the
magazine.

A different opinion about how popular *Beatitude* was can be found
in *The Real Bohemia* by Francis J. Rigney and L. Douglas Smith,
which was published by Basic Books in 1961. According to them
the magazine did have support and "its thousand copies usually
were sold within two weeks." It should be noted that Rigney and
Smith did actually spend a lot of time in San Francisco and would
have been there when Beatitude was appearing. They quote from
an editorial in the second issue which mentions the "overwhelming
response to our magazine," though that could have been something
of an exaggeration. A further reference to "the flood of poems
coming into our office" rings truer, as any editor of a poetry publication will tell you. Magazines always receive more poems than
subscriptions. And the editorial continued, "there are very likely
more poets per square foot here in North Beach than anywhere else

in the world."

John Kelly appears to have been responsible for producing the first seven issues of *Beatitude* from an office in Bannam Alley, and it then moved to The Bread and Wine Mission, an establishment run by Pierre Henri Delattre, who described himself as "a kind of non-denominational street priest." His book, *Episodes* (Gray Wolf Press, 1993) has a lively reminiscence of what it was like in San Francisco before the Beat idea was publicised and exploited by journalists and commercial interests: "Poets joined with jazz musicians; folk singers with street poets. Lefty labourers were meeting with artists and intellectuals in the coffee shops, bars, galleries, jazz cellars, and bookstores to celebrate a break from institutional life." As for *Beatitude,* wherever it was published from it was described as being "edited co-operatively by various types from Grant Avenue, Mill Valley, and other scenes," though Rigney and Smith say that William Margolis and Bob Kaufman did most of the editorial work. Other people may have been involved, and not everything ran smoothly. Warren French quotes from a letter he received in 1960 from Jory Sherman, a poet then active in San Francisco, which refers to one of the editors of *Beatitude* who had "absconded with 500 bucks of the money, and worse, the entire subscription list."

*Beatitude Anthology* was, as I noted earlier, compiled from the first sixteen issues of the magazine, and I don't want to give a detailed account of what happened later. There were some further issues and it continued, in an occasional way, for some years. But for the purpose of this article it's only really necessary to say that by the seventeenth issue, dated October/November, 1960, *Beatitude* was being published from City Lights Bookshop. That issue, incidentally, focused more on the better-known names in the Beat world and there were contributions from Kerouac, Ferlinghetti, Ginsberg, Whalen, McClure, Kaufman, Meltzer, and Corso.

It's possible to get an idea of what those early issues of *Beatitude* were like by combining *Beatitude Anthology* and *The Real Bohemia* because the latter included a thirty-two page selection of poems from the magazine and quoted liberally from others elsewhere in its text. What interested me in 1960/61, when I first read these books, were the poems by the lesser-known names. Work by Ginsberg, Corso, and others, was already available, but what about B.

Uronovitz, Anabel Kirby, Raymond Samuel Meyerbach, and the poets who simply signed "Marc" and "Jo" to their poems? Marc's "Mexico 5, '59" was the kind of poem that, at one time, would have been thought of as typically Beat, with its references to hitch-hiking, drugs, a truck driver "driving like crazy at a thousand miles an hour," and an encounter with a man named Harry from San Francisco, and all of it written without capitals and strung down the page like a catalogue. As for "Jo," she wrote lines like, "take me and I take Thee/your lips touch my body/I shivering/with each kiss," which sounded wonderfully old-fashioned and close to a parody of popular romantic literature.

What these poems, and others like them, demonstrated was the gap that existed between the leading Beat writers whose work appeared in *Beatitude* and the mass of would-be poets who must have been around San Francisco in the late-1950s. In the introduction to *Beatitude Anthology*, Lawrence Ferlinghetti says that by the time the sixteenth issue was published "most of the early contributors had made off to faraway scenes and could not be found even to receive their share of the bread produced by the sale of this anthology," which perhaps indicates how they comprised a floating population which drifted from one bohemian community to another, or just spent a short time in San Francisco and then settled down to a routine life and got a steady job and gave up writing poetry. I'd guess that quite a few of the now-forgotten names were those of people for whom writing poetry was just a phase they went through. All bohemias have had, besides the dedicated writers, a larger group who come and go and don't produce anything of significance. Henry Murger, chronicler of Parisian bohemia in the 19th Century, noted this, and dryly remarked how the temporary bohemians would later in life, when they were respectable and comfortable, reminisce nostalgically about their youthful experiences. Are "Marc" and "Jo" now somewhere in America, elderly and half-remembering their poems in *Beatitude*?

I'm possibly being unfair if I give the impression that all the minor poets in *Beatitude* were mediocre writers. William J. Margolis had been around the North Beach and Venice West bohemian scenes for most of the 1950s and, in fact, edited a magazine called *The Miscellaneous Man* which ran for fifteen issues between 1954 and 1959. His own work, if the samples in *Beatitude Anthology, The*

*Real Bohemia,* and *The Outsider,* where he also published, are anything to go by, was tidily written and varied between poems that were neat and carefully composed and others that took a looser approach. A long work, *The Hegira Cycle,* seemed to show a Ginsberg-influence and had a series of statements ("I nearly died in New Jersey on oilslick trucktoppled roads and drove all night in the moon with the rain...." and so on) that added up to an autobiographical chronicle. Was it ever published in full? It has been said of Margolis that his "life was forever stamped by an impulsive romantic act." In 1960, quarrelling with a lover, he jumped out of a second-story window and injured himself so badly that he spent the rest of his life in a wheelchair. He continued to write, though not with any great success in terms of his work reaching a wide audience, and died in 1998.

It's perhaps not too important to try to track down all the obscure poets who were in *Beatitude,* and it probably wouldn't be easy to do it. Lew Gardner, John Chance, and Anne Frost soon disappeared from view. And how about Richard Gumbiner who was working on *The Canticle of the Wanderer,* which he said was a long poem "to be continued over life." Fragments appeared in *Beatitude* and *Gemini,* a British magazine, but did Gumbiner ever complete it? It is possible to find a few facts about some poets. Jory Sherman had a large family to support and soon realised that he couldn't do it writing poetry for magazines like *Beatitude,* so he turned to more-commercial forms of literature and produced popular books on a number of subjects. Warren French says that Sherman wrote "western romances - often under pseudonyms - for a German audience that still enjoys them." But the trail soon runs cold for most of the others. Alan Dienstag, like Richard Gumbiner, was in *Beatitude* and *Gemini* and was said to be an editor of *Underhound,* though copies of this publication, if it ever got off the ground, are impossible to find. Dienstag does seem to have had a sense of humour, if his poem-sequence, "Three Women," was anything to go by, but the longer "The Meeting" in *Gemini* was a predictable attack on some typical Beat targets, such as the police, government, the military machine, etc. I'm not suggesting that they shouldn't have been attacked, but simply indicating that the sort of declamatory poem that Dienstag wrote added little to what had already been said in a more-effective way by Ginsberg and older poets such as Kenneth Rexroth and Kenneth Patchen. A lot of Beat poetry was "protest poetry" of one kind or another, but too many of the poets made the mistake of thinking that making the protest was enough and that the literary quality of what they were doing wasn't of real importance. I once saw Alan Dienstag described as "a poet and novelist," but I don't know of any books that he had published other than a slim volume of poetry about ten years after his links to *Beatitude*.

Despite all my doubts about the uneven literary qualities of many of the poems in *Beatitude Anthology* it still has a certain appeal and not only because of the nostalgia it evokes. It may be that it still speaks for a time when a sense of community existed, even if only briefly, and there was a belief, however hazy, that something good might come of trying to get poets, painters, musicians, and others, working together. And the way *Beatitude* magazine was produced perhaps pointed to a do-it-yourself spirit that wanted to operate outside a commercial framework. This may sound very idealistic, and there's no point in denying that the better-known writers would be keen to have their work accepted by established publishers. But they were also willing to be part of a bohemian community that, in many ways, was their first and most attentive audience. Looking back, it's easy to see that the venture was doomed from the start and that the combined forces of ambition, publicity, establishment hostility, and too much self-indulgence, especially in relation to drugs, would force the community to break up. Pierre Delattre charts it all in a bleak short chapter in *Episodes* and puts it this way: "The so-called beats would soon be driven out of North Beach by beatniks and merchants trying to exploit them commercially. Overwhelmed by all the attention, they would mostly burn themselves out." Is that what happened to many of those obscure contributors to *Beatitude*? They probably all didn't "burn themselves out," and some may have just decided it was time to move on when the original intentions of the Beat community were degraded by newcomers attracted to North Beach by publicity about the Beat Generation in the popular press.

With the exception of Warren French's informative book very little has been written about the minor writers in San Francisco in the 1950s. Rigney and Smith's *The Real Bohemia* is worth mentioning, too, though their intentions were essentially sociological and psychological and the poems they used were often meant to back up their arguments about such matters. Neither of them were all that impressed by the literary achievements of the Beats. But their book is at least a source for some otherwise forgotten writing. As for myself I'm prepared to concede that a lot of Beat poetry, especially of the minor variety, wasn't very good, and some of it was down-right bad. That's probably true of most poetry, anyway. Only a lit-tle of the poetry written at any time deserves to survive. Still, whenever I look at something like *Beatitude Anthology*, with all its faults, I can't help wondering what happened to "Marc" and "Jo" and Alan Dienstag and all the others. I almost said "all the other failed writers," but I'm not sure that they did completely fail if they were, even for only a brief period, part of something worthwhile .

# WHAT BECAME OF CLINT NICHOLS?

I recently came across an old copy of *Gaslight Poetry Review*. It isn't dated but I'd guess it was published around 1958 and inside it says, "Poetry of the Beat Generation as read at the Gaslight, 116 McDougall Street, New York." It includes some of the usual names - Ginsberg, Bremser, Micheline, Ted Joans - but also several others whose appearances on the New York Beat scene seem to have been short-lived. They crop up in a few magazines and anthologies of the period and then disappear, and I began to wonder what happened to them. Histories of the Beat movement rarely, if ever, mention such people but they deserve some sort of recognition, if only because they provided the general context in which the better-known writers could function. Books written years after the events they describe often give the impression that only a handful of famous writers were active but a study of magazines and other material published at the time will easily show that this was not the case.

There's a photograph by Fred McDarrah on the cover of *Gaslight Poetry Review* and his famous book, *The Beat Scene* (Corinth Books, 1960), does contain a number of photographs taken at the Gaslight readings. Work by some of the poets is also included, though Clint Nichols only managed to have his picture in the book. He's sitting with his back against a wall and appears to be scowling. He has something of the look of Ray Bremser and a poem by Nichols that appeared in *Beat Coast East; An Anthology of Rebellion* (Excelsior Press, 1960) suggests that, like Bremser, he had spent time in prison. In *Gaslight Poetry Review* his "The Little Prophet" refers to "songs, laughter and poems of saintly madness", and follows the Beat pattern of piling up a series of images and ideas in a catalogue style that probably works better read aloud than when seen on the page. A couple of poems by Nichols were published in *Between Worlds*, a curious magazine based at the Inter-American University in Puerto Rico, and a note mentioned that he was then (1960) touring the Virgin Islands. One of the poems mentions Charlie Parker, another sign of Nichols falling in line with Beat concerns. What happened to Clint Nichols after these fragmentary appearances? If he carried on writing he must not have had any great success in getting his work published.

*Between Worlds* is worth hunting for, incidentally, as an example of how some people recognised the links between the Beats and older literary groups. Gilbert Neiman, the editor, used work by Ginsberg, Snyder, Corso, Whalen, and Ferlinghetti, as well as minor figures like Nichols, alongside such older radicals and bohemians as Henry Miller, Marcel Duchamp, Malcolm Cowley, and Harry Roskolenko. It was a demonstration of the fact that the best Beat work was in a recognisable tradition and not something simply fashionable. And the magazine contained much more, including such fascinating asides as the note on Tram Combs, described as "the first poet to settle on San Francisco's North Beach" after World War Two.

The importance of Charlie Parker as a Beat icon was also apparent in Stephen Tropp's "Elegy for a Broken Bird" in *Gaslight Poetry Review*, and Tropp, a tidy-looking figure in a dark jacket, is shown reading his work at the Gaslight in *The Beat Scene*. He was born in Vienna in 1930 and spent some years playing drums with jazz and rhythm-and-blues groups. By the late 1950s he was active around New York as a poet and had work published in *Beat Coast East*, *Yugen,* and the short-lived *Exodus,* which also featured Seymour Krim and Ray Bremser. In 1964 Tropp was one of *Six American Poets* (Harvard Book Company of New York, 1964), a collection edited by Jack Micheline. A small book by Tropp, *Mozart in Hell*, was published by Tuli Kupferberg's Birth Press in 1959. I can't say that Tropp was a major Beat poet, nor even a major poet of any kind. His work was conventionally avant-garde with its broken lines and juxtaposed images, but it had little individuality and was no better, nor worse, than much of what was in the little magazines of the time. Tropp died some years ago and would probably be totally forgotten now but for his brief appearance on the Beat stage.

Fred McDarrah in *The Beat Scene* proved that if many of the minor Beats were not exactly great writers they did photograph well. William Morris is seen in two shots, one taken in Washington Square Park where he's giving a reading and it's mentioned that he'd once been arrested for a similar performance, and the second where he's barefoot and perched on a high chair, presumably in the middle of another reading. Morris travelled around a bit and in *The Expatriates* by Mack Reynolds (Regency Books, 1963) he turns up in San Francisco, Torremolinos, and Paris. Getting arrested came easy to him and he spent six weeks in a French prison after he and some friends had, according to Reynolds, tried to trick Air France into paying compensation for a painting by Morris that had supposedly been lost in transit. In *Gaslight Poetry Review* an excerpt from a long poem called "Return to New York" celebrates his desire to meet and make love to someone called Britt ("rose of my flame/you are the reason for my return"), and in *The Jazz Word* (Ballantine Books, 1960) he came up with a short prose piece which testified to his liking for jazz and its influence on his writing. According to Fred McDarrah's *Beat Generation: Glory Days in Geenwich Village* (Schirmer Books, 1996), Morris was born in Glasgow, moved to England in the 1960s after his brief involvement with the Beats, and died in London in 1996. Does anyone know what he did during those years?

The bearded John Fles crops up in *The Beat Scene* and *Glory Days in Greenwich Village* and was clearly very much part of the scene when McDarrah's photos were taken. He had been connected with *The Chicago Review* when its editor, Irving Rosenthal, was slipping the Beats into its pages. Rosenthal fell foul of the university authorities and started *Big Table* so he could use the material banned from *The Chicago Review* and Fles stepped in to help him. Fles also had links to *Kulchur*, one the finest magazines to appear in the 1960s, and his own work was published there and in *The Beat Scene*, though none of it, prose or poetry, added up to a great deal. Perhaps the one piece of his that still has some value, mainly for its documentary interest, is "The Great Chicago Poetry Reading," a long account of a benefit event for *Big Table* which involved Ginsberg, Corso, and Orlovsky. It was published in the March, 1961 issue of *Swank*, a men's magazine that, thanks to Seymour Krim, published four special sections of Beat-related writing. Fles had accompanied the three poets on their car journey to Chicago and his article captures their enthusiasm and the responses of the people who came to hear them read. His other main contribution to the Beat story was editing and publishing a one-shot review, *The Trembling Lamb*, which had prose by Leroi Jones and Carl Solomon alongside work by the French writer, Antonin Artaud. A rare document, which also included a letter from Gregory Corso, it was a useful reminder of how the best Beat writing could operate in an international context.

Another writer who published in *Swank* was Dan Propper and he also appeared in another men's-magazine, *Nugget,* when Seymour Krim had an editorial job on it. But Propper was also in *The Beat Scene, Evergreen Review, Provincetown Review, San Francisco Review*, and *The Beats* (Gold Medal Books, 1960), edited by the highly active Seymour Krim. And he continued writing well into the 1970s with a book, *The Tale of the Amazing Tramp*, published by Cherry Valley Editions in 1977. A second small book, *For Kerouac in Heaven* (Energy Press, 1980), was part of a manuscript he'd been trying to place with publishers for some time. Propper at one point lived in California but seems to have moved to Woodstock in more recent years. His work was always very readable and he had a wider range of references, and I'd guess a broader political sensibility, to draw on when compared to other minor Beats. But without a sympathetic environment and its network of magazines and anthologies to function in, he seems to have slipped into near-obscurity.

Earlier in this piece I referred to *Six American Poets*, the anthology edited by Jack Micheline, and among those included was Roberts Blossom, a poet, playwright, and actor who was a bit older than most of those I've mentioned so far. He was born in 1924 and had appeared on stage in New York as well as at various poetry readings. His photograph in *The Beat Scene* shows a somewhat shy-looking man clutching his manuscripts to his chest and perhaps bowing his head slightly because the sun was in his eyes. He had poems in *Beat Coast East* and the same issue of *Swank* that John Fles was in, and his book, *Excusology of the Ocean* was published by Interim Press in 1964. Blossom's poems tended to be fairly introverted, sometimes looking at his childhood and sometimes taking a cryptic view of events and ideas, and from that point of view they don't correspond with the open and social approach that was in use among many minor Beat poets. His acting career occupied much of his time and he eventually moved to Hollywood and had small parts in films like *Home Alone, The Great Gatsby*, and *Close Encounters*. I don't think Blossom really belonged with the Beats other than that he took part in their poetry readings and appeared in a few of their publications, but he benefited from the publicity which surrounded the Beat movement and was often extended to just about any writer who spent time in and around Greenwich Village. It's often forgotten that *The Beat Scene* was, to quote from

145

its back cover, "the world of the young Bohemian writers of New York's Greenwich Village," and that the word Bohemian described many of them better than a Beat label did. And they weren't all young, either, and some of them - Paul Goodman, Thomas McGrath, May Swenson, Kenneth Patchen, and Edward Dahlberg, to name a few - would have scorned the Beat tag. Or how about David Galler, who has his photo and a poem in *The Beat Scene,* but whose book, *Walls and Distances* (MacMillan, 1959) shows him to have been a conventional poet in terms of his technique. He was, perhaps, a Bohemian but never a Beat.

Returning to *Gaslight Poetry Review,* it throws up a few more names, none of them of any real consequence. Ambrose Hollingworth can be seen in one of the more amusing photos in *Glory Days in Greenwich Village,* his appearance, and that of his girl-friend, almost designed to match the general public's idea of what a Beat should look like. He wears a leather-fringed jacket and a shirt fastened with just one safety pin. His trousers are a couple of inches too short and his shoes seem to have some sort of tassels on them. The girlfriend wears tight jeans, a dark shirt, and bells around her neck and is carrying a long walking stick. You can imagine how they'd attract attention and welcome it. The only Hollingworth poem that I've ever come across is "Mental Toilet" in *Gaslight Poetry Review* and it hardly adds up to much. The same could probably be said of the poems by Joan Block, John Brent, Kitty Donovan, Bob Freidman, Claus Stamm, and Connie Rothschild, and none of them, as far as I can tell, went on to make any kind of mark on the literary scene. They presumably sank without trace once they'd had their moment of fame at the Gaslight readings. We do know what happened to a couple of others who were in *Gaslight Poetry Review.* Bob Lubin, who photographed well enough to get into *The Beat Scene,* abandoned poetry and concentrated on carpentry and architectural design. And Hugh Romney later went around calling himself Wavy Gravy and turned up at the Woodstock Festival.

I've concentrated on the New York scene and most, though not all, the poets I've mentioned had a link to *Gaslight Poetry Review.* I'm aware there were others who made fleeting appearances in print during that late-1950s and early 1960s period when the Beats were in the news but my main concern has been to show that the range of writers included under the Beat banner was far wider than later surveys suggest. Literary movements do not begin and end in ways that can easily be fixed in terms of dates and personalities. People drift in and out of them and it's only in retrospect that we think we can tidy everything so that it looks as if it happened according to some neat plan. It was never that way, of course, and we just need to look at something like *Gaslight Poetry Review* to see how varied and flexible the guidelines were.

# ANATOLE BROYARD

Recently, I read a small book by the late Anatole Broyard. Called *Intoxicated By My Illness*, it is an account of how he came to terms with being told that he had prostate cancer and that it was probably incurable. With reflections on the nature of the illness, his relations with the doctors, the reactions of his friends, a couple of surveys of the literature of illness, and a fictionalised account of the death of his father from cancer, this slim book (just 135 pages) impressed me more than most of the massive biographies, overlong novels, and extended academic exercises, I come across. Broyard was an elegant writer, and his prose, always poised and precise, is a pleasure to read, even if he is dealing with a grim subject.

But who was Anatole Broyard? I'd guess that few readers in this country will have heard of him, and if they have it may be because of some misleading links to the writers of the Beat Generation. But he was far more interesting than that, and although his output was small he nonetheless produced a body of work which is worth looking at.

Broyard was born in New Orleans in 1920, but his family moved to New York when he was young. He was educated at Brooklyn College and The New School for Social Research, spent time in the army during the Second World War, and when he returned to civilian life he opened a bookshop in Greenwich Village. His wife later recalled that "lacking the patience to sit and talk to his customers, he turned to writing essays and stories that were published in literary magazines and anthologies." He soon became part of what was, in Seymour Krim's words, "a highly intellectual but not necessarily artistic group of brilliant minds which roved with barely believable and almost illegal freedom over the entire domain of the thinkable and utterable. Some of these minds - like Isaac Rosenfeld, Dave Bazelon, Manny Farber, Weldon Kees, Willie Poster, Chandler Brossard, Anatole Broyard (plus the occasional appearances of Saul Bellow, Delmore Schwartz, Alfred Kazin, James Agee) and the inimitable Milton Klonsky - were in literature partially or completely; some like Will Barrett, Herb Poster, Clem Greenberg were more interested in 'ideas' than expression. All of us were broadly part of the *Partisan Review* and

*Commentary* worlds where ex-Trotskyites, ex-anarchists, ex-Stalinists (everybody seemed to be an ex something) mingled with fancy Ph.Ds and metaphysical poets to produce that modem eclectic monster who is as much at home with surrealist poetry as British radical politics, with baseball and boxing (the big sport for intellectuals then) as with the foolproof technique for banging a girl."

Krim's description of this milieu is colourful but accurate, though a darker version perhaps comes through in Chandler Brossard's 1952 novel, *Who Walk In Darkness*, in which a fictional character named Henry Porter is clearly based on Broyard. It is easy to recognise him in this brief passage:

> "When his money ran out Porter got a job writing promotion copy for a publishing company. On the side he pursued his literary career by writing fiction and book reviews. His fiction was not bad. It did not knock me out, but it was not bad. Three or four of his stories were accepted by small literary magazines. This gave him some literary status. His reputation with women gave him more status though. I had to hand it to him. He could pick up almost any woman he saw."

Broyard did, in fact, work in advertising in the 1940s and he did have stories published in *Modern Writing, Discovery,* and *New World Writing*, three leading pocket-book format little magazines. He also contributed articles and essays to *Partisan Review, Neurotica, New Directions*, and a glance at the lists of other contributors to these publications will show that he was appearing alongside some of the brightest young writers of the period. It's interesting to see what he chose to write about when not writing fiction, and in a 1950 issue of *Neurotica* he turned his attention to the mambo, the Afro-Cuban dance then sweeping America. It's significant that Brossard's novel includes a major scene in which Porter and others visit a dance-hall which features authentic mambo music. Porter (Broyard) is portrayed as something of an authority on it. In his article, Broyard placed a sociological emphasis on his description of mambo, looking at the dance element and describing what he saw as its sexual connotations. He took a similar view in a second *Neurotica* piece, *"American Sexual Imperialism"* which told how, as the craze for mambo spread, the American dancers began to change its tone as they introduced a different emphasis, in particular a less submissive role for the woman.

There is a highly-relevant angle to Broyard's writing in these and other pieces from the period. Unlike an older generation of intellectuals in New York he didn't appear to be involved with formal politics, or even all that much interested in the subject. In this he was fairly typical of his generation and it perhaps indicated a "shift of intellectuals away from Marxian and radical political criticism toward non-political cultural criticism." In a short article in *New Directions* in 1950, Broyard discussed this change of direction. Referring to a piece by Mary McCarthy about Greenwich Village cafes, he mocked her comment about her contemporaries being used to "the battle of ideas and standards," and went on to say: "Marx is passé, the bourgeois already épaté; the students here are from the New School, where they've just been asked "What is the meaning of meaning?" Someone - he's not here - shouted something about the machinery of production, rattled the workers' ghostly chains, but the others know that the machinery of production is for beer and bombs, and they'll take beer. Art? - the art of self-defence! God -Moloch, the jukebox." It was racy writing, and its sardonic view of the situation suited the mood of the late-1940s and early-1950s when, as Seymour Krim said, everyone seemed to be an "ex-something" or other and no-one had much faith in anything.

Another Broyard piece, *"Ha! Ha!,"* looked at the role of laughter in society, and it said things that still apply today. Commenting on the way in which the accusation of not having a sense of humour is often likely to upset someone, he wrote:

> "No sense of humour! This dread deficiency must surely find its place in the medical lexicons. Already some initial research has been done on its nosology. Another psychologist, writing on laughter, observed that it is the most psychopathic and the healthiest persons who laugh easiest. Assuming that this is true, I think it would be useful to determine who's who. It would certainly seem that most of us should fall between the two classifications, that, accordingly, laughter should come grudgingly to the majority. The evidence, however, is to the contrary, and this leaves an uneasy choice of interpretations."

It was lively and provocative, and Broyard, summing up, indicated that Freud meant more than Marx to his contemporaries:

> "The twentieth century will be remembered as a century of great

concussions. Not the least of these will be laughter. If the nineteenth century was the age of rationalism the twentieth is the age of rationalisation. From one to the other is but a simple slip. In many ways, the nineteenth century was an adolescent period; having outgrown some of his childish illusions, man was beguiled by his comparatively aggressive insights into the truth. By the twentieth century, he has realised that these insights are merely the beginnings of an understanding of his ultimate limitations. As Freud put it, the child grows up only to discover that he will always be but a child to mother Nature. Realising this, he laughs to recover his child's innocuous immunity."

Broyard's best-known essay, one which was reprinted several times in later years and extensively quoted from, was *"A Portrait of the Hipster,"* published in *Partisan Review* in 1948. In it, Broyard attempted an analysis and a definition of a new type then appearing around Greenwich Village who had, in his view, been welcomed by intellectuals who "ransacking everything for meaning, admiring insurgence... attributed every heroism to the hipster." But Broyard was less enthusiastic about these supposed new rebels, and saw the attempts to escape from the restraints of society through narcotics, jazz, and general disaffiliation, as merely ways to a new conformity. People who were once shadowy presences in the jazz underground began to take themselves seriously and to crave the adulation others gave them. In Broyard's words: "The hipster promptly became in his own eyes, a poet, a seer, a hero." And he added that the hipster lifestyle "grew more rigid than the Institutions it had set out to defy. It became a boring routine. The hipster - once an unregenerate Individualist, an underground poet, a guerrilla - had become a pretentious poet laureate."

Of course, what Broyard was doing, as well as attacking the hipsters, was criticising his fellow-intellectuals for failing to accept that the hipster rebellion was a sham. It was the intellectuals, in their desperate search for types who seemed to stand against the society intellectuals despised, who had idealised the hipster, something which had deep implications for their own state of mind and lack of broad political vision. Broyard's essay was written fifty years ago, and yet it has relevance to current practices where intellectuals try to find cultural heroes amongst pop musicians and the like.

The magazines which carried Broyard's essays usually mentioned that he was working on a novel, and that portions of it had appeared in various journals. A 1954 issue of *Modern Writing* printed *"Sunday Dinner in Brooklyn"* a story which was about a Greenwich Village intellectual visiting his parents in Brooklyn and trying to come to terms with the fact of the growing distance between them. It was a sharply observed piece, and I recall that when I first read it in the 1958 anthology, *Protest: The Beat Generation and the Angry Young Men,* it seemed to speak for and to me in terms of how I felt about my own background, and the way in which I was moving away from it. There were astute little scenes in Broyard's story, as when, on arrival at his parents' house, they rush to find him the book supplement from the Sunday paper, as if to show that they understand his needs.

Another Broyard story, again clearly part of his novel, was called *"For He's a Jolly Good Fellow"* and describes the way the narrator encounters an old friend and realises how little they now have in common. The friend is locked into a pattern of work, home, marriage, and all the other involvements that creep up on people. And he's shocked when told that the narrator is "going to school" and doesn't appear to have any ambition to settle into a career or marriage. The narrator, for his part, wonders what has happened to change the man he once knew into the one he sees before him:

> "I ran my eyes over his pearl-gray suit with its broad lapels and tried to picture him seven or eight years before: the fine, tough, tight laugh he had, the restless originality which showed in his clowning ...He was the handsomest guy in our bunch, wiry, with a laughing ferocity in his face that wrinkled his lean cheeks. We used to wear each other's clothes, but now he outweighed me by twenty pounds, he didn't have that hungry, starving-for-life look any more."

The novel was never finished, or at least was never published, though some other excerpts from it did get into print. "What the Cytoscope Said" appeared in *Discovery* in 1954, and is the story later used in *Intoxicated By My Illness.* It is about the death of Broyard's father, and the way in which the event makes the son re-examine their relationship. Another story, *"The Choice,"* which was in the 1960 anthology, *The Beats,* has a son visiting his father in hospital and trying to make a decision to ease the older man's suffering by leaving an overdose of pills within his reach. Both stories are tightly written and raise serious questions about how we deal with death. As Broyard says: "Expecting the worst - that's another phrase for you. We never expect the worst."

The inclusion of fiction by Broyard in two anthologies which were widely linked to the Beats probably caused some people to think that he was part of the movement. But, as mentioned earlier, he was a member of a broader group of Greenwich Village intellectuals, and his tastes and activities were not those of the Beats. What little he seemed to have in common with them related to the feeling of alienation that comes through in his writing, and which was a not uncommon factor in much fiction of the late-1940s and early-1950s. But Broyard's alienation, if it was that, was an intellectual position, one which enabled him to cast a critical look at the world. He had no liking for Beat excesses in both life and literature, and could be highly critical of both Kerouac and Ginsberg. In a review of *Visions of Cody* he said: "The irritating thing about both Ginsberg and Kerouac is their habitual assumption that only they and a few of their friends have known reality, and the rest of us will have to find it in their books." He also added some comments about the Beat taste for spontaneity:

"Kerouac can describe people and places, but what he cannot do is find anything meaningful for them to do in those places. Usually, they get drunk or high, have maudlin conversations and leave for another place where exactly the same thing happens. Regarding these conversations, I would like to propose, once and for all, a pox on spontaneity in fiction: spontaneity is a psychological, not a literary, quality. Though it may sometimes be pleasant to experience spontaneity it is almost never interesting to read, and while I'm at it, I'd like to point out that there are all kinds of spontaneity, good and bad, and the notion that what comes naturally is naturally welcome is one of the great idiocies of our age."

Broyard's life after the 1950s largely revolved around teaching - at The New School, New York University, and Columbia University - and book reviewing. He was a reviewer for *The New York Times* for many years, and for long periods wrote a daily review for the paper. A collection of some of these reviews, published under the title, *Aroused By Books*, included just over one hundred from the three hundred he wrote between 1971 and 1973. A rate of production like that, as anyone who has written regular book reviews will know, uses up a lot of time and energy. It can lead to other work being neglected, and Broyard was said to be still working on a novel when *Aroused By Books* was published in 1974. But he does seem to have genuinely loved books and writing, and his reviews are not simply summaries of plots and subject-matter but do instead try to say something of value about the work. His style was brisk and to the point, as befits reviews published in a daily newspaper, but he still managed to be insightful in a few sentences. A review of Bernard Malamud's novel, *The Tenants* began:

"In his new novel, *The Tenants*, Bernard Malamud has rushed in where angelic liberals fear to tread. In exploring the relation between blacks and Jews - and carrying it to its implicit conclusion - he has seized contemporary history by the horns. And because he is one of our better writers, his book is more radical than those who call themselves radicals. Like Saul Bellow in *Mr Sammler's Planet,* like Ralph Ellison in *Invisible Man*, Malamud goes beyond the rhetoric of the revolutionaries to the very root of the matter, to man's inhumanity not only to others, but to himself."

Writing about Anaïs Nin, Broyard remarked that, "turning her into a vogue may be the best solution to the ungallant task of evaluating her critically," and looking at a book about Dada and Surrealism, he said:

"Dada was not so much a school of art as a parodying of all schools. But, since brevity is the soul of wit, the Dadaists soon exhausted their material, and in the early twenties Surrealism was born. Surrealism set itself the task of cleaning out the attic and the closets of the modern imagination."

It was crisp, perceptive reviewing, not designed for a specialist audience, and with some inevitable limitations resulting from the need to keep to a few hundred words. But Broyard always made good points, as when he said:

"Breton was himself the most surrealist feature of the entire movement; totally humourless and pedantic, he had a compulsion for issuing manifestos. He was constantly defining and redefining their position - while the Surrealists as constantly ignored or transcended these definitions."

These words came back to me during a recent visit to a Surrealist exhibition in Paris where the poems and paintings often went their own way despite what the manifestos said.

Broyard published another book in 1980, *Men, Women and Other Anticlimaxes,* which centred on the life he lived when he moved to Connecticut, and he worked for *The New York Times,* and carried on writing. His wife noted that, even when he was terminally ill, he managed to juggle the "pain and medication in a way that allowed him to keep writing his weekly column for *The New York Times Book Review.*" He died in October, 1990.

Obviously, it would be foolish to claim any kind of major literary status for Anatole Broyard. He was a literary journalist, and most of his work - a few excerpts from an unpublished novel, scattered essays, short book reviews - was hardly likely to be remembered, at least by the majority of those who read it. Ironically, the work most likely to have a lasting impact only appeared after his death. I've already mentioned *Intoxicated By my Illness,* and Broyard's name also appeared on another book, *Kafka Was The Rage: A Greenwich Village Memoir,* which was published in 1993. He had worked on it for sometime, and Alfred Kazin remembered that "he was strangely slow and too deliberate in completing it," although Kazin had been impressed by the sections Broyard had shown him. Writing in *The New York Times Book Review* a month or so after Broyard's death, Kazin said: "What caught me was not the racy old days in the Village, much as I envied some of his experiences, but the tone, poised without being falsely detached, very comic at times without cheapening some crucial memories. The memoir was all representation, all picture. Anatole was certainly bringing all this back from a most unexpected point of view. And one quite at variance with the growling, all too seasoned and debonair New York literary reviewer I had known and read without being unduly impressed. In the memoir Anatole somehow created a new Anatole for me to regard, and this on the basis of Greenwich village memories that elsewhere had become as conventional as life in the suburbs."

It was Kazin who also recalled that Broyard's

> "growling intensity.. had to do with a love of books, the primary books, against which, as a measure and representation of human existence, the life around him often seemed hollow and mean to the point of being disgraceful. I am a writer who has had to earn his living as a professor, and Anatole's burning, grasping insistence upon recalling the immortal life in certain favourite books

was in such contrast to most of the professors of literature I knew that I almost felt guilty for not caring.. .as sharply and even accusingly as he did."

We need people like Anatole Broyard who care about books and writing, and we need to preserve their work and not let it disappear simply because it was not widely praised nor published in large selling editions. I've kept the magazines in which his early stories and articles appeared, and I've got his later books on my shelves, but there are dozens of other novelists, poets, and critics, whose books, once I've read and reviewed them, have been given away or taken to the second-hand bookshops. Anatole Broyard means much more to me than that.

NOTES:

The 1950s pocket-book format magazines in which Broyard's early stories and articles were published are difficult to find, but for the record, "Ha! Ha!" was in *Discovery 2* (1953), "What the Cytoscope Said" in *Discovery 4* (1954), "Sunday Dinner in Brooklyn" in *Modern Writing 2* (1954), and "For He's a Jolly Good Fellow" in *New World Writing 10* (1956). "Sunday Dinner in Brooklyn" was reprinted in *Protest: The Beat Generation and the Angry Young Men* (Souvenir Press,1959).

"Mambo" was in *Neurotica 6* (1950) and "American Sexual Imperialism" in *Neurotica 7* (1950). "Village Cafe" was in *New Directions 12* (1950). "The Choice" was published in *The Beats* (Gold Medal Books, 1960), edited by Seymour Krim. "A Portrait of the Hipster" was originally published in the June 1948 issue of *Partisan Review,* and was reprinted in *Jam Session* (Peter Davies, 1958), edited by Ralph Gleason, and *The Scene Before You* (Rhinehart & Co., 1955), edited by Chandler Brossard. A memoir of an encounter with Dylan and Caitlin Thomas appeared as "A Fling With Dylan" in the September 1964 issue of *Cavalier.*

*Aroused By Books* was published by Random House in 1974, and *Men, Women and Other Anticlimaxes* by Methuen in 1980. *Intoxicated by My Illness* was published by Ballantine Books in 1993, and *Kafka Was The Rage: A Greenwich Village Memoir* by Vintage Books in 1997.

# BEHIND THE SCENES

Chandler Brossard's *Who Walk in Darkness* is sometimes said to be the first Beat novel, though Brossard himself tended to have an ambivalent attitude towards being identified with the Beats. In the late-1950s he wrote an article, "The Dead Beat Generation," for *Dude*, a slick magazine of the time, but on the other hand he once said that his generation of the late-1940s and early-1950s in Greenwich Village "were the first beats," and that he "was there among them and part of them before, during, and after the writing of my first novel, *Who Walk in Darkness.*"

This article is not going to debate whether or not Brossard was a Beat writer. What I want to do is to look at the background to *Who Walk in Darkness*, with particular emphasis on the real-life models for two of the main characters in the book. Brossard said that his novel was not directly autobiographical, but I think he was being disingenuous because other people familiar with the Greenwich Village scene of the 1940s recognised that several of the supposed fictional characters were easily identified as being based on some of Brossard's acquaintances. The poet and critic, Delmore Schwartz, got to read the book prior to its publication and told the people concerned, and at least two of them threatened to sue for libel unless changes were made. One or two others didn't seem bothered about being in *Who Walk in Darkness.* William Gaddis, whose massive novel, *The Recognitions*, was published in 1955, thought that the heavy-drinking Harry Lees was based on him. And Stanley Gould could have objected to the way he was portrayed as the junkie Cap Fields, but neither he nor Gaddis took any action.

Anatole Broyard objected to the fact that he could be linked to the Henry Porter of the novel. Porter was said to be a "passed" Negro, meaning someone from a black family who could pass for white because of his light skin colour. Broyard was exactly that but he didn't want to have it widely acknowledged. In the race-conscious environment of America in the late-1940s it would have limited his activities, literary and otherwise. The opening of the book was changed to "People said that Henry Porter was illegitimate," which was seen as acceptable but tended to reduce the impact of the

157

story. A Negro trying to pass for white in a society hostile to his race is at once more dramatic than someone having to deal with being illegitimate, even if some narrow-minded people attached a stigma to that. The story of Broyard's struggle to conceal his true identity has been dealt with in detail by Henry Louis Gates in his long essay, "White Like Me: Anatole Broyard," (it's reprinted in *Beat Down To Your Soul*, edited by Ann Charters) so I won't repeat it here. I'm more interested in the literary and cultural environment that *Who Walk in Darkness* relates to.

Seymour Krim, in his wonderful autobiographical essay, "What's This Cat's Story?," wrote about being in Greenwich Village in the 1940s as "part of a highly intellectual but not necessarily artistic group of brilliant minds which roved with barely believable and almost illegal freedom over the entire domain of the thinkable and utterable. Some of these minds - like Isaac Rosenfeld, Dave Bazelon, Manny Farber, Weldon Kees, Willie Poster, Chandler Brossard, Anatole Broyard (plus the occasional appearances of Saul Bellow, Delmore Schwartz, Alfred Kazin, James Agee) and the inimitable Milton Klonsky - were in literature partially or completely; some - like Will Barrett, Herb Poster, Clem Greenberg - were more interested in 'ideas' than expression. All of us were broadly part of the *Partisan Review* and *Commentary* worlds where ex-Trotskyites, ex-anarchists, ex-Stalinists (everybody seemed to be an 'ex' something) mingled with fancy Ph.Ds and metaphysical poets."

Krim mentions the "inimitable Milton Klonsky" and he also crops up several times in Anatole Broyard's unfinished Greenwich Village memoir, *Kafka Was the Rage*, which covers the period just after the Second World War. I'll talk about Klonsky later, because he's in *Who Walk in Darkness* and objected to the way he was portrayed, but for the moment I'm focusing on Broyard. In the novel the narrator says:

"When his money ran out Porter got a job writing promotion copy for a publishing company. On the side he pursued his literary career by writing fiction and book reviews. His fiction was not bad. It did not knock me out, but it was not bad. Three or four of his stories were accepted by small literary magazines. This gave him some literary status. His reputation with women gave him more status though. I had to hand it to him. He could pick up almost any woman he saw."

Broyard did have stories and articles published in magazines like *Modern Writing, Discovery, New World Writing, Neurotica, Partisan Review*, and *New Directions* in the late 1940s and early 1950s, and for a time he was seen as having great potential and perhaps likely to produce a definitive Greenwich Village novel. But for a variety of reasons he never did complete a novel, despite still claiming to be working on one well into the 1970s. He turned to teaching (the New School, New York University, Columbia University), advertising, and book reviewing in order to earn a living. In the late 1950s he was briefly linked to the Beats due to a couple of his stories being included in *Protest:The Beat Generation* and the *Angry Young Men* and *The Beats* (Seymour Krim described Broyard as "a white-collar Beat" in the introduction to his story) but the truth is that Broyard had little sympathy with the Beat approach to writing. He wrote: "The irritating thing about both Ginsberg and Kerouac is their habitual assumption that only they and a few of their friends have known reality, and the rest of us will have to find it in their books." Elsewhere in the same review of *Visions of Cody* he made some disparaging comments about Kerouac's style.

Broyard's own writing skills were directed mostly into book reviewing for many years, with occasional other short prose pieces also written for *The New York Times*. It may give an idea of the time-consuming aspect of book reviewing if I mention that, in a period between 1971 and 1973, he wrote three hundred reviews, often on a daily basis. As someone who has written book reviews for magazines and newspapers on a regular basis for around forty years, I can testify to how the work can eat into the time and energy needed for more creative activity. And I doubt that I ever had to produce reviews as often as Broyard seems to have done. Seymour Krim, in "What's This Cat's Story?," offers a poignant account of how in his case writing reviews stopped him completing a novel. But it may also have been true that Broyard, like Krim and other people, never had the talent and dedication to write a novel and that their inclination towards book reviewing, articles, and short stories, might have been what they were best suited to do. William Gaddis thought that Broyard's womanising also distracted him: "that's where his career went, his creative energies."

The portrait of Henry Porter in *Who Walk in Darkness* gives the impression that he is capable of hurting people with his comments, and it has been suggested that Anatole Broyard could be malicious when reviewing books by people he'd taken a dislike to or who he envied. His own failure to complete a novel and get it published may have pushed him into negative reviews of some of his contemporaries. In *A Tragic Honesty: The Life and Work of Richard Yates*, Blake Bailey says that Broyard would even ask to be given certain books to review so that he could write disparagingly about them. He and Richard Yates had been friends, but as Yates's career flourished (he published seven novels and many short stories) Broyard became increasingly dismissive of his writing. R.V. Cassill, who knew both men, wrote to Yates and said: "Back in the time I knew Anatole he was among the white hopes, deservedly so for the merit of the few things he published in the fifties. After that.... well, only the competent malice of what he has written as a reviewer."

There were people who did speak highly of Broyard's skills as a reviewer, though, and reading *Aroused By Books,* a collection of one hundred reviews, it strikes me that he could be witty and astute, and that he was not always negative about the books he dealt with. Perhaps his nastiness only came out when he was faced with something written by a contemporary who he saw as some sort of competitor in the literary stakes? He didn't only review novels and he does seem to have had a genuine love of literature. He could write well, and another book, *Men, Women and Other Anticlimaxes*, has some engaging sketches of life in the country, old Greenwich Village characters, his relationship with his children, and other topics. Like his reviews the pieces were written for newspaper publication and were consequently short. And when Broyard knew he was dying of cancer he wrote several articles which were later collected in *Intoxicated by My Illness*, along with one of his old short stories, "What the Cystoscope Said," about the death of his father. There are many things that can be said about Broyard, but it's unfair to deny him his due as a writer within a certain kind of framework.

Seymour Krim said that of all the writers he met, and he listed Mailer, Kerouac, Ginsberg, Brossard, Broyard, and others, the one with the "greatest potential" was Milton Klonsky, who was the prototype for Max Glazer in *Who Walk in Darkness*. Krim's long, admiring essay about Klonsky in *Views of a Nearsighted Cannoneer* refers to his wide range of interests, the breadth of his reading, and his general intellectual capabilities. He wasn't the only one to look at Klonsky in this way and Anatole Broyard admired him, as did the older poet-critic, Allen Tate. Brossard's portrait, assuming we accept that Glazer is Klonsky, doesn't bring out the intensely intellectual side of his character, and instead sees him as a pot-smoking "underground man" who is not averse to sponging off other people to get by. He is also described as "a spiritual desperado" whose ideal is "to look like a street-corner hoodlum and be the finest lyric poet in America at the same time."

Klonsky was, in many ways, an archetypal Greenwich Villager who, from the moment he arrived there in 1945, took to the life of an intellectual bohemian. As someone said of him: "he never left the Village, and never gave up on the spirit of the Village as he encountered it in his youth.....He was first and foremost a Village intellectual, meaning that not only did he remain in the Village all his life, but that he was quintessentially of it as well." Klonsky began publishing in the 1940s but never had a book out in his lifetime. He wrote some poetry, edited various books including a couple on William Blake and a very good anthology of modern poetry which was wide-ranging enough to take in Kerouac, Bukowski, and Corso, as well as Philip Larkin and Kingsley Amis, and produced quite a few essays.

The argument over *Who Walk in Darkness* didn't stop Chandler Brossard including Klonsky's "Greenwich Village: Decline and Fall" in the 1955 anthology, *The Scene Before You*, along with Anatole Broyard's "A Portrait of the Hipster" and work by Seymour Krim and other Greenwich Village writers. Klonsky's piece had originally been published in *Commentary* in 1948, but his bitter version of what the Village had become as opposed to what he thought it should be must have still had resonance in 1955. It's curious that Klonsky still lived in Greenwich Village despite his misgivings about it. Did he think that there might be a return to "the spirit of the Village" he'd encountered in 1945?

What happened to the potential that Seymour Krim saw in Milton Klonsky? And why did he never complete a book or even what could be called a consistent and reasonably large body of work? It seems that he hit a writer's block and for almost twenty years, between 1949 and 1968, he published only eight or nine essays and three poems. What puzzled his friends was how he managed to survive. He never had a steady job, though he worked for a time for a vanity publishing house, did a little private tutoring, and had some short teaching stints at various colleges. He got a grant and occasional summer fellowships at artist colonies like Yaddo and MacDowell. And as Mark Schechner said, "there was, its seems, always a woman around to help with the rent, among them Beverly Kenny, a jazz singer who sang with some major jazz sidemen in the 1950s." She recorded a number of albums with musicians like Johnny Smith, Nick Travis, and a small group from the Count Basie band. Klonsky did begin to be active again in the 1970s, editing the anthologies referred to earlier, and writing long pieces for *New American Review*, including "A Discourse on Hip," which pointed to his continued fascination with Greenwich Village and its characters. This essay became the title piece of a collection of Klonsky's writings published by Wayne State University Press in 1991, exactly ten years after he had died from cancer in 1981. It was well in keeping with the way Klonsky had lived that he died in a public ward because he was penniless. And I'd guess that his one book, the posthumously published *A Discourse on Hip*, attracted little attention, despite the quality of the writing and its intellectual rigour.

Anatole Broyard and Milton Klonsky were talented but flawed men whose early promise was never fulfilled, and Chandler Brossard may have spotted their flaws early on and developed them to create the fictional characters he wrote about in *Who Walk in Darkness*. And it's more than likely that they may be remembered only for being the real-life personalities behind Brossard's inventions. But they deserve better than that and their best writing ought to be acknowledged for its own merits.

# HOW BRAVE WE LIVE

Greenwich Village plays a central role in any account of American bohemianism, and the atmosphere of the area in the late - 1940s has been evoked in various memoirs by Anatole Broyard, Seymour Krim, and others, and in novels like Chandler Brossard's *Who Walk in Darkness* and George Mandel's *Flee the Angry Strangers*. Histories of the Beat movement mention the bars and cafes where the bohemians congregated, though the word "Beat" wasn't in general use before the 1950s. But the types were easily identifiable, that's for sure. Writers, artists (and all the would-be writers and artists) various hangers-on, misfits, drunks and junkies. Fertile ground for a novelist.

I came across *How Brave We Live* by Paul Monash gathering dust in a junk shop some years ago and got it for next-to-nothing. I think the owner of the shop was glad to get rid of it. I was attracted to it by the blurb about the characters it dealt with: a novelist, an artist who sometimes resorts to mugging drunks to get the money for his paints and canvases, an alcoholic female, and other assorted oddballs. It seemed like it might be lively, if not exactly great literature, but it turned out to be more interesting than I thought.

It was published in 1950 and the action appears to take place around 1948 or 1949, so it has some links to those novels and memoirs I mentioned earlier. The central character, Breedon Rawley, has had some success with a novel about Greenwich Village, though not all the people who think they can see themselves in the fictional individuals in the book are happy with how they're portrayed. It's a situation similar to the one that Chandler Brossard faced in real life when he wrote *Who Walk in Darkness*. And because the book has been successful there's an element of envy in the reactions of the mostly unsuccessful bohemians who frequent a bar called the Marino. It's the descriptions of these people and the bar that give *How Brave We Live* a great deal of interest in the context of post-1945 bohemia:

> "Even at one in the morning on a Wednesday night the Marino was tumultuous. It was filled with people and conversation; words seemed to choke the air like great massed clouds, lightning phrases playing along their edges and pontifical pronun-

ciations rumbling inside them. The usual gaunt faces leaned towards each other in all the booths, the jaws all chopping out simultaneous sentences. Beard almost touching beard in wagged argument. There was too a restless harried movement, people moving along the bar from booth to booth, talking, talking. These were the young intellectuals of the Village, drained into the Marino through all the subterranean channels of American life, now clogging the Marino through a process of damp yet sympathetic groupings. A couple of years before, Breedon knew, they had gathered up the street at a place called the Biretta; in a couple of more years it would be another bar. These were the young intellectuals, talking of sex and of drinking, of marijuana and perversion and poetry, talking about each other and the people they despised, talking as always with a desperate resolution to crystallise all the indecencies of their unhappy, threatened young lives into words."

I think it's fairly obvious that the Marino is based on the San Remo, which is referred to in many accounts of the period. And the Biretta is clearly the Minetta. Fred McDarrah in his book, *Greenwich Village* (Corinth Books, 1963), said that the San Remo "became famous after World War 2 as a rendezvous of Village Existentialists," and Steven Watson in his *Birth of the Beat Generation* (Pantheon Books, 1995) described it as "a hipster hangout." He also mentioned that Allen Ginsberg thought of its clientele as "subterraneans" and that Jack Kerouac "appropriated the term as the title of his novel about the San Remo crowd." It's perhaps significant that Paul Monash also uses the word "subterranean" in his description of the Marino/San Remo.

There's a female singer in Monash's book who reflects on how she's been portrayed in Breedon Rawley's novel:

"She had recognised instantly the character which he had based on her, physically at least. But he had missed her, missed her completely. Damnit, he had even maligned her. She was not trying to pass as anything. She had never denied that she was a Negro, even though she had never been convinced of it."

I don't want to draw too many parallels with *Who Walk In Darkness*, which was certainly about at least some of the San Remo crowd, but one of the problems that Chandler Brossard faced was because he'd based one of his fictional characters on Anatole Broyard, who was trying to pass as white. Monash's character is female and she says she's not trying to pass as anything, but it raises the question, of whether or not he knew about Broyard and Brossard's book. *Who Walk in Darkness* was only published in 1952, two years after Monash's novel, but it had been written earlier and the manuscript was seen by various people before it finally appeared in print. Monash would have been familiar with many people who frequented the San Remo and possibly was aware of Brossard's novel. It's not my intention to outline the whole plot of *How Brave We Live*. It takes its characters into various situations in Greenwich Village and elsewhere, and Breedon Rawley eventually heads for Hollywood and a job writing screenplays. But Paul Monash does have more to say about the people in the Marino:

> "I may be wrong, but I do not think these people have ever been so lost and so hurt as they are in our time. The sense of hope was blown up by the atomic bomb; it disappeared in the fumes of the debates of the United Nations, Strictly Ltd. They are the younger generation of creative people, and they are sick, much much sicker than most of the young men and women who went to the Continent after the First World War. They have cut loose from the professed principles of a society which doesn't bother to live up to its principles, but they have been able to formulate no positive standards of their own. They are almost afraid to be happy, because they can understand better why they should be unhappy. For them at this time there is no quietness, no peace, no certainty."

That doesn't seem to me much different from the sort of commentary that John Clellon Holmes wrote about the mood of the late 1940s. Or far from Kerouac's "a weariness with all the forms, all the conventions of the world." It would be foolish to claim that *How Brave We Live* was an early Beat novel on the lines of books by Holmes, Brossard, and George Mandel. But it does have some fascinating things to say about Greenwich Village in the late 1940s and the kind of people also dealt with in *Go, Who Walk in Darkness*, and *Flee the Angry Strangers.*

I don't think Paul Monash ever wrote anything else like *How Brave We Live* but that book is worth considering when post-war bohemianism and the origins of the Beat Generation are discussed.

Published by Scribner's, New York in 1950.

# THE AMERICAN CONNECTION
## *A Lost History*

"I have finished *The Journal of Albion Moonlight*. I feel like becoming a missionary and preaching the Old Testament of Miller and the Gospel according to Patchen.

These books have come to me now that I am ready for them."

So wrote Wrey Gardiner in his book, *The Dark Thorn,* published in 1946 and providing a vivid picture of bohemian literary life in Britain during the war years. I've referred to it because of Gardiner's taste for Henry Miller and Kenneth Patchen, two American writers who were not even widely known or appreciated in their own country but whose work had crossed the Atlantic and reached at least some British writers and readers. But Miller and Patchen weren't the only Americans whose writing was in circulation in this country, and a brief glance at the little magazines of the 1940s will reveal that Kenneth Rexroth, William Carlos Williams, Philip Lamantia, and others like them, were known to British readers.

And there is evidence to show that, in some cases, they were in touch with each other, despite the difficulties of the war years and the immediate post war period. Amongst the key factors influencing British writers, certainly with regard to an awareness of Patchen and Rexroth, were the anarchist or libertarian ideas they shared. George Woodcock, who was later the author of a classic text on anarchism and in the 1940s was closely linked to *Freedom*, the anarchist publication, edited a magazine called *Now* which was influential in printing British and American writers alongside each other. In his autobiography, *Letter To The Past*, Woodcock recalled that he used work by George Orwell, W.S. Graham, Philip O' Connor, Alex Comfort, and George Barker, and then added:

"I also published work by such varied American writers as Henry Miller, who hailed *Now* as one of the best magazines of its time and me as 'a Pharos in the English night,' Paul Goodman. e.e. Cummings, Harry Roskolenko, Philip Lamantia and Richard Eberhart. Some of my contacts with American writers in fact led me much farther than the pages of *Now*. Dwight McDonald, when he founded *Politics* in 1944, invited me to write regularly on English books and English life, and this I did as long as the journal lasted. My favourite among the articles I wrote for Dwight was the essay on Orwell which appeared in 1946. Holley Cantine invited me to write a regular London letter for the anarchist magazine *Retort* which he edited from Woodstock, then in the hinterland of New York State: I continued it from 1945 to 1948. The poet William Everson wrote to me from a conscientious objector's camp in Oregon where he and other poets were keeping their art alive by publishing a magazine, *Compass* and eventually, in 1947, Untide Press published in Pasadena my third book of poetry, *Imagine the South*. Finally, I owe to *Now* my long friendship with that fine poet, Kenneth Rexroth, who had started a literary anarchist group in San Francisco."

I think that gives the flavour of what was happening at a time when it seemed important to make contact with kindred spirits in America as a kind of defence against the darkness that had engulfed Europe. It's worth noting that Linda Hamalian, in her biography of Kenneth Rexroth, (*A Life of Kenneth Rexroth* published by Norton) refers to *Compass* and similar magazines and says that they "were widely distributed throughout the United States and England."

It's obvious that well known American writers were also read in Britain and books by Hemingway, Steinbeck, Faulkner, Dos Passos, James T. Farrell, and Erskine Caldwell, to mention just a few, were available from established publishers. But I'm mostly looking at writers who were largely outside the establishment framework and more identified with what might be termed alternative approaches to literature. I'd guess that, between 1945 and 1950, a lot of information about such writers was picked up from books published by New Directions in the United States. These circulated in Britain, and George Woodcock recalled that James Laughlin often sent him copies of New Directions publications, and that they were avidly read by his friend, Denise Levertov, who was then still living in England. The New Directions annuals could be bought in Britain in the post war years, as could *Spearhead*, a large anthology compiled from the first nine issues of the annuals and described as "Ten Years Experimental Writing In America." Peter

Baker's Falcon Press distributed these books in Britain. Rexroth, Patchen, Anaïs Nin, Henry Miller, Charles Henri Ford, Paul Goodman, and William Carlos Williams, were in the *Spearhead* collection. And Seymour Krim, Robert Duncan, Paul Bowles, Paul Blakburn, Anatole Broyard, Charles Olson, and others, were in New Directions annuals published between 1948 and 1950. The notion that most of these writers only became known to British readers later in the 1950s is clearly wrong, though it would be a mistake to claim that they were widely known here.

Let me return to Wrey Gardiner, whose own books like *The Dark Thorn* and *The Flowering Moment* are unfairly forgotten. He edited a little magazine, *Poetry Quarterly,* which somehow managed to survive from 1939 to 1953, despite Gardiner's poverty and such problems as the paper shortages of the 1940s. Copies still surface in second hand bookshops and, looking through a few I've picked up over the years, I find Paul Potts reviewing a book by William Everson in a 1944 issue. Everson (or Brother Antoninus, as he was known for a time) was very much part of the San Francisco Renaissance in the 1940s and went on to be published by New Directions and, later, Black Sparrow Press. Potts himself was a colourful figure on the British scene, writing highly emotional poems and selling them on the streets of London. He's only remembered now for his prose work, *Dante Called You Beatrice,* which stands outside the usual style of careful British writing and isn't afraid to wear its heart on its sleeve. George Barker, a British poet who spent time in America in the 1940s and knew Rexroth, said of Paul Potts: "A critic in New York once called my poems the poems of a hoodlum angel and I would call Paul Potts' poems the poems of an angelic hoodlum." This remark was made in a 1945 issue of *Poetry Quarterly* which included work by Kenneth Patchen. And there was an advertisement for a book by Patchen, with an introduction by the British poet David Gascoyne, which Wrey Gardiner's Grey Walls Press was due to publish. The issue of *Poetry Quarterly* for Winter 1946/1947 had work by Rexroth and William Carlos Williams, an appreciation of William Saroyan by Paul Potts, and an advertisement for Editions Poetry London (which didn't only publish poetry) listing books by Henry Miller and Paul Goodman.

Wrey Gardiner clearly needs to be seen as important in extending the awareness of American poetry, and he said, in 1945, that "Hart Crane, Robert Frost, John Crowe Ransom, Allen Tate, Wallace

Stevens are avowed influences on and mean much more to the young English poet than the older generation of poets over here." Gardiner is a neglected figure, though the critic A.J. Tolley, in his informative *The Poetry of The Forties* did try to do him justice by saying,

> "he was out in front in recognising how influential American writing was to be. Like George Woodcock, he published work by American writers who were still far from achieving recognition in their own country - among them Kenneth Patchen, a selection of whose poems, *Outlaw Of The Lowest Planet* (1945) he published from The Grey Walls Press. The Press was also to bring out work of F.Scott Fitzgerald and Nathanael West, both little known in England at the time. Unhappily, it combined with Peter Baker's Falcon Press, and when Baker was convicted for a financial offence in 1948, it brought bankruptcy on the Grey Walls Press."

The Editions Poetry London advertisement I mentioned earlier also listed *The Pl Yearbook of Jazz*, compiled by Albert McCarthy, who later edited *Jazz Monthly* and other magazines, and who wrote several books on the subject, and got to know many leading American jazz musicians. McCarthy, like George Woodcock, had anarchist connections, and he met Rexroth when the American poet visited Britain in 1949. He knew Kenneth Patchen's work too, and that of other American writers. If I can throw in a personal note, I knew Albert McCarthy in the 1960s when I was contributing articles and reviews to *Jazz Monthly* and occasionally spent time with him in Soho drinking clubs. I asked him about the 1940s and his replies made it evident that he didn't think it was all that surprising or unusual to have been in touch with the Americans at that time. In this respect, it's relevant to quote from Linda Hamalian's book again. She says that Rexroth's reputation was prospering in San Francisco in the late 1940s, and adds:

> "He was also becoming known to a small but important coterie in England. A London edition of *The Phoenix and The Tortoise* was published by Falcon Press in 1947, the same year as the *Selected Poems Of D.H. Lawrence* with Rexroth's introduction. For a time, Rexroth's attention shifted to England, especially after he had signed a contract with New Directions for the anthology of modern British

169

poets. He had also established an overseas correspondence with fellow anarchists and writers like George Woodcock, Alex Comfort, and Derek Savage."

And with Wrey Gardiner, it's worth adding. To return to the jazz angle, another British writer with an interest in the music was Nicholas Moore, a poet and essayist who often wrote about jazz. He also edited *The Pl Book of Modern American Short Stories*, which was published in 1945 and had work by William Carlos Williams. Henry Miller, William Saroyan, and Paul Goodman, as well as Hemingway and Faulkner. Moore, like Gardiner, is almost unknown these days though Iain Sinclair, in his idiosyncratic novel, *Downriver*, devoted several pages to him. Sinclair inserts his interview with the poet and bookseller, Peter Riley, into his book, and it includes the following comment by Riley on how a post-war decline in readership affected many of the British poets mentioned in this article: "It affected a lot of people. Wrey Gardiner, David Gascoyne , and W.S. Graham (who ended up living in Cornwall, in penury). Perhaps George Barker too. Many of them left the country."

Another magazine of the 1940s, *Modern Reading,* edited by Reginald Moore, published Patchen, Miller, Saroyan, Nelson Algren, and an essay by Bern Porter on new art trends in America. Porter was a significant figure in California and an acquaintance of Robert Duncan, Rexroth, Lamantia, and Patchen. He had been a nuclear physicist but quit after Hiroshima and took up printing and publishing. He co-edited the little magazine, *Circle*, and brought out books by Lamantia, Rexroth, Patchen, and others, in the late 1940s and early 1950s. There weren't as many Americans in *Penguin New Writing*, which survived for fifty issues, but Paul Bowles and Nelson Algren appeared in its pages, and in 1948 it printed Lionel Trilling's story, *Of This Time, Of That Place*, with its portrayal of a rebellious student who, it has been suggested, may have been based on Allen Ginsberg. Of course, in 1948, few in America and probably no one in Britain would have been aware of that. Trilling was very much part of a well established New York intellectual scene, and he also appeared in print in Britain in Cyril Connolly's *Horizon*, which was likewise intellectually respectable. But Connolly wasn't averse to picking up other work from America, and he'd published Henry Miller in 1940. In 1947 he produced a major issue which was completely devoted to American literature, art, and music, and which included *A Letter From San Fran-*

*cisco* by Philip Lamantia. A 1948 issue had a review of the *Spearhead* anthology by Philip Toynbee and though he wasn't enthusiastic about Patchen and Rexroth he did say that "America is in the process of producing an iconoclastic literature of real importance." Rexroth's friend, Thomas Parkinson, later editor of the excellent anthology, *A Casebook on The Beat*, was represented by a long poem in a 1949 issue of *Horizon*. It's of interest to note that Cyril Connolly visited San Francisco in 1946 and met Rexroth, Everson, and Lamantia.

I've referred to some of the links between British and American writers in the 1940s, with particular emphasis on those who were generally identified with alternative or radical or non-establishment structures, though these terms were not necessarily used at the time. The American writers I've mentioned weren't the only ones published in Britain, and I've referred to books by Hemingway, Faulkner, and others, being easily available. And copies of *Modern Reading* and similar publications have stories by all kinds of American authors, as for example Albert Maltz, a communist who worked in Hollywood and was one of the Hollywood Ten, the group jailed for refusing to name names when questioned by the House Un-American Activities Committee. By 1950 or so many of the magazines mentioned in this article had closed down. And publishers like Grey Walls Press, Falcon Press, and Poetry London Editions no longer existed. The reading boom of the war years had declined as the austerities of the post-war period sapped people's energies. They were too busy trying to re-establish their family lives and return to a kind of normality to spend time reading. And some of the hopes of the war years faded under the pressures of the daily struggle to survive shortages, rationing, long hours of work, and little money. Editors like Wrey Gardiner and Reginald Moore finally admitted defeat and faded into obscurity. George Woodcock left England and went to live in Canada. Many of the poets, like Nicholas Moore, Paul Potts, Ruthven Todd, David Gascoyne, Kathleen Raine, stopped writing for long periods. Some resurfaced in later years, but Paul Potts sank into a long decline which led to alcoholism and destitution.

The 1950s saw the rise of a new generation of poets and writers, most of them university educated (few of the 1940s writers had attended university) and with their sights set on successful careers, often as academics. Their writing reflected this conservatism and was more carefully shaped and less ambitious than that of the 1940s poets. G.S. Fraser, considering a 1956 anthology, *New Lines*, which featured the "Movement" poets, as the newcomers were called, said that it represented "the ousting of the bohemians by the academics." The kind of literary bohemianism that Wrey Gardiner described in his books was either forgotten or frowned on. So was the anarchism that some of the 1940s group had believed in. The early 1950s tended to the orthodox, Philip Larkin made no secret of his dislike of modernism in literature, art, and music, and he rejected modern influences. And Kingsley Amis's *Lucky Jim* was dismally provincial and anti-intellectual in tone. Many of the new writers seemed content to operate in a British (if not just English) setting and were not as keen to make contact with America. Even if they did, they rarely extended their interest to the non-establishment American writers, like the Black Mountain School, the New York poets, the writers of the San Francisco Renaissance, and the Beats. It was only in the late 1950s that another generation of British writers began to make close contact with their counterparts in the United States.

The "lost history" ought to be rediscovered, partly to counter the impression that Patchen, Rexroth, and others like them, were unknown in Britain before the late 1950s, but also to revive interest in many 1940s British writers (have a look at Rexroth's *New British Poets,* if you can locate a copy) who are ignored or dismissed in standard histories of literature in this country.

# MAXWELL BODENHEIM

Milton Klonsky once recalled being in a bar in Greenwich Village in the early 1950s and suddenly hearing the owner and many of the drinkers shouting and jeering at someone. When Klonsky turned to see what was happening he noticed "a tall, glum, scraggly, hawk-nosed, long-haired, itchy-looking, no doubt pickled, fuming and oozing, Bowery-type specimen" standing near the door. People were calling to him to read a poem or even make up one on the spot. The man turned and glared at them and wrapped his "old dung-coloured horse blanket of a patched overcoat" around him in a way that reminded Klonsky of Marc Antony drawing his toga to him as he faced the Roman mob. And then he said "Pimps! Patri-ots! Racetrack touts!" in a contemptuous voice, and swept out of the bar. It was, as Klonsky said, the kind of exit that stays in the mind, and it gave the victim of the sneers of the crowd a kind of nobility.

The man was Maxwell Bodenheim, near the end of his life and reduced to living on the streets and peddling his poems around bars but still able to rally himself sufficiently and turn on his tor-mentors when he knew that he was being ridiculed to his face. He figures in histories of bohemianism in America, usually because of his years as an alcoholic drifter, but little attention is given to the work he produced before his fall from grace. Between 1918 and 1934 he wrote thirteen novels, eight books of poetry, and appeared in many of the leading magazines, from *The New Yorker* to the *New Masses*. That he was a forgotten figure, in literary terms, by 1950 says a lot about the transience of literary reputations. And I always think of Bodenheim whenever I see some new writer being acclaimed, and wonder what will happen to him or her in a few years. Of course, we live in different times and today's failed or forgotten writers might still pick up some work teaching creative writing. And perhaps even qualify for a grant if they go around pubs, selling their poems. Maxwell Bodenheim was made of sterner stuff.

Bodenheim was born in 1892 in a small town in Mississippi and moved with his family to Chicago in 1900. He was dismissed from high school when he was sixteen and left home to join the army.

Various accounts indicate that he was not an ideal soldier, with one suggesting that he deserted and another that he hit an officer who mocked him because he was a Jew. What does seem certain is that Bodenheim spent a year in a military prison. When he was released he wandered around and mixed with migrant workers, labour organisers, petty criminals, and other footloose types. In 1912 he arrived back in Chicago, did various odd jobs, and began to establish himself as a poet. His work was published in *Poetry* and *The Little Review*, he knew writers like Ben Hecht and Sherwood Anderson, and he was an active participant in the upsurge of artistic activity which was known as the Chicago Renaissance. But Bodenheim was never one for fitting in with groups and he soon fell out with various people in Chicago. He already had a reputation as a hard drinker with a penchant for outrageous behaviour with some of his escapades offending the influential. When Ben Hecht asked him why he didn't temper his opinions so that he wouldn't always upset people, Bodenheim replied, "I was born without your talent for bootlicking," and carried on as before. Hecht later wrote: "Despite the continuing, unvarying defeats of his life, it is this strut I remember as Bogie's signature. Ignored, slapped around, reduced to beggary, Bodenheim's mocking grin remained flying in his private war like a tattered flag. God knows what he was mocking. Possibly, mankind."

When Bodenheim got bored with Chicago he moved to New York, arriving on the poet and editor Alfred Kreymborg's doorstep with one arm in a sling and the other holding a small bag that contained all his possessions. Kreymborg soon noticed that Bodenheim had a talent for self-destructive behaviour, almost as if he felt that things would probably go wrong anyway so why not help them along. In Kreymborg's words, Bodenheim "betrayed the impression that he was about as happy as he could allow himself to be without neglecting to keep an eye on the disillusion certain to follow." Kreymborg's colourful autobiography, *Troubador,* speaks warmly of Bodenheim but admits that he wasn't the easiest person in the world to get along with.

Bodenheim's first book, *Minna and Myself,* had been published in 1918 to a certain amount of critical praise. He wasn't a major poet, nor an innovator in any way, but his early poems, written in free verse, were tidy and direct and not without charm:

An old silver church in a forest
Is my love for you.
The trees around it
Are words that I have stolen from your heart.
An old silver bell, the last smile you gave,
Hangs at the top of my church.
It rings only when you come through the forest
And stand beside it.
And then it has no need for ringing,
For your voice takes its place.

Other collections appeared in 1920 and 1922, and in 1923 Bodenheim's name was on two new books of poems. His first novel was
also published in 1923, to be followed by twelve more, and further
volumes of poetry came out in 1927, 1928, and 1930. And he contributed articles and reviews to leading magazines. Whatever else
can be said of Bodenhelm, he wasn't lazy and seems to have had
an amazing amount of energy despite a life-style that was often
chaotic. He drank and travelled (to Europe in 1920 and 1931 and
to Hollywood, where he tried to interest the studios in buying his
novels for screen adaptation) and he had numerous liaisons with
women, some of which brought him a notoriety he could never live
down.

In 1925 his novel, *Replenishing Jessica*, was the subject of an ob-
scenity trial. Reading the book now it is difficult to understand
why the melodramatic story of a sexually active woman caused so
much fuss. The writing certainly isn't pornographic, but perhaps
the subject-matter itself attracted the attention of the censors?
Women, after all, were not supposed to be hunters in the sexual
game. Whatever the reason for the prosecution, the jury came up
with a 'Not Guilty' verdict, sales of the book rose, and Bodenheim
got his name in the papers. Young women flocked around him and,
in 1928, one of them attempted to commit suicide because she
thought the poet had spurned her. The newspapers highlighted the
story, and soon another woman contacted Bodenheim, had an affair with him, and also decided that suicide was the answer when
he lost interest in her. Sadly she succeeded and her body was
fished out of the East River. In the meantime, the first woman was
pursuing Bodenheim again and was, in turn, pursued by her family
and a gang of reporters. These events not only made headlines in
New York, but spread across America and were even reported in

British and French papers. Things got worse when a third woman killed herself in a Greenwich Village room and was found with Bodenheim's portrait in her hand. All this had the makings of a black comedy and probably reinforced his conviction that you could always count on life to add to your troubles. And it did, again. Bodenheim had been involved with a woman who he seems to have genuinely liked and he wrote some passionate love letters to her. She was killed in a major subway disaster in New York, and the letters, which she always carried with her, were found scattered across the tracks by some of the news-hungry journalists who were there.

Bodenheim carried on writing, and his novel, *Georgie May*, published in 1928, was a stark portrayal of an ill-fated prostitute. It was, like all his novels, variable in its literary qualities, with vivid passages which effectively captured the atmosphere of the streets alongside others which turgidly philosophized about the lives of the lower-depths types the book describes. At his best, Bodenheim could use a stream-of-consciousness technique to create a mood:

> "Turned out of her room, just no place to go, because she had depended on Dopey Watkins to pay her the twenty dollars which she had loaned him a month back - oh what did a coke-sniffer know about being decent, what did anyone know about being decent, and doggone if they weren't making flies bigger this year, and wouldn't it be heaven if life was just one, never-stopping night with Sunnybrook and Three Feathers whisky free of charge, and plenty of daddy-loving ragtime music and turkey-trots and bunny-hugs - Bill McCoy was a musical boy on the steamer Alabama steaming down to Yokohama. ..Oh-h-h everybody's doing it, doing what? the Turkey-trot!... Oh, you beautiful doll, you great big, beautiful do-oll, I am simply wild about you, I could never live without you... .Ah, just to cake-walk along like the niggers did, kicking her legs high up in the air, and straining her shoulders back, and lifting her chin... Pickled and soused and telling everything to go to hell....just mad and happy . ...never cain't stop till I die. ...God how hot it was."

Elsewhere in *Georgie May,* there are comments on political matters, as when one of the toughs tells how he makes some money "Around election time he strung with the Democrats because they paid the most money - beating up negroes to keep them away from the polls was a lucrative and enjoyable job." And information about prison conditions, and the way in which the warders and some favoured prisoners exploit the rest of the inmates.

Another Bodenheim novel, *Ninth Avenue*, touches on Greenwich Village types and deals with the relationship between a white woman and a black man. It opens with an effective description of an urban landscape - "When the light of morning touches the buildings and pavements of a city, it always seems to borrow their hardness and to lose in some degree its quality of flowing detachment" - and it has been called an almost classic example of the American city novel. Bodenheim often thought up eye-catching titles, and *Naked on Roller Skates* went to Harlem for its story of Jazz Age thrill-seekers on a downward spiral. By the early 1930s, though, he was, like many American writers, taking note of the economic situation as the Great Depression caused mass unemployment and hardship. Bodenheim's 1932 novel, *Run, Sheep, Run,* covered both and also had scenes of a demonstration that is brutally broken up by the police. In the end it is suggested that communism might offer a worthwhile alternative to the failings of the capitalist system. The same message eventually comes through in Bodenheim's last novel, *Slow Vision,* published in 1934, and offering a bleak picture of the period and the way in which people are slow to move beyond established systems. The hero, Ray, sits on a park bench, hungry, unemployed, and wondering how he will survive. A young, black man offers him a copy of *The Daily Worker* but Ray rejects it, saying that he knows there are problems but "I believe in my country and I believe in democracy just the same. We're improving slowly, all the time, and we'll keep on improving, too, if we get more sense in our heads and elect better men to office." He's all for reform, but "no dirty Bolshevism for us: If the Russians want it, O.K., but it's got no place over here."

Ray's views slowly change as circumstances force him to look more closely at what is happening, and he realizes that people like him have to "stick together and fight with our own kind. We'll never get anything otherwise, you can bet on that." And he adds, "There's no use blinking it in the face - about the only damn time they ever pay any real attention to a worker is when they're holding an election, or when they're asking him to pick up a gun and get killed in a war. I don't know whether Communism's the solution or not, but believe me, I'm going to read up on it and find out what it's all about, before I'm through."

Bodenheim's poems also displayed his enthusiasm for leftwing politics, one of the most significant being *Revolutionary Girl*, which appeared in the Communist magazine, *New Masses*, and was reprinted in the influential anthology, *Proletarian Literature in the United States,* published in 1935. In this poem, written in short-lined free verse and having a declamatory effect, the poet acknowledges that the girl would like to be self-indulgent and that she longs "for crumpled 'kerchiefs, notes/Of nonsense understood/Only by a lover," but he calls on her to apply her energies to the struggle "against the ruling swine." Interestingly, Bodenheim also used traditional forms when writing political poetry. A late collection, *Lights in the Valley*, published in 1942, had poems with titles like *Home Relief Bureau, Answering a Trade Union Man,* and *Southern Labour Organiser,* all of them using formal rhyming patterns. An idea of the politics and of the style and tone of the poems in this book is given by the following, simply called *Sonnet:*

> The element of beauty does not thrive
> Within the acts of those who mouth it most.
> Beauty is unobtrusively alive,
> Self-hidden, fresh and not a tired boast.
> It cleaves the lower planes of life - the top,
> In probing music, form, has only dreamed
> The brief, heroic time when burdens drop
> And words are irresistibly redeemed.
>
> Coal miner, Anthony Rubetti broke
> His back to check a sheriff's rifle, save
> A son from death, and he will not invoke
> Quick-flowered poems, lines above his grave,
> But in remembered force, beyond mere pen,
> He will remain alive in other men.

It was around the mid-1930s that Bodenheim seems to have really started to go to pieces, though Jerry Mangione recalled that when the poet was employed on the Federal Writers' Project (a job creation scheme which was part of Roosevelt's New Deal programme) he carried out his work conscientiously and efficiently and was, in fact, given a supervisory post. Mangione thought that the regular work and the responsibility helped Bodenheim cut down on his drinking. Other accounts, however, say that he was already selling his poems in the street. As for his political commitment, it's likely that he was a member of the American Communist Party for a short time, though as Ben Hecht saw it, "Bogie was the sort of Communist who would have been booted out of Moscow, over-night." Hecht pictured Bodenheim as a defiant street orator who was regularly beaten up by the police, but said, "He not only angered the police but disturbed, equally, the Communist Party leaders of New York." His communist links were enough to get him fired from the Federal Writers' Project in 1940.

Bodenheim's publishing record almost stopped after 1934. The small collection of poems, *Lights in the Valley,* appeared in 1942, he was in an anthology of anti-fascist poetry published in 1944, and his *Selected Poems* came out in 1948. But it was In the late-1940s that a new generation of Greenwich Village bohemians came to know him as a drink-sodden wreck wandering the streets and calling in the bars to sell poems and sometimes copies of his old books. Dan Wakefield, drinking in the San Remo, was con-fronted by "a wild man who looked like a bum, waving sheets of paper at us with poems he had written. He wanted to sell them, for either a dime or a quarter a piece (the price was negotiable). We got rid of him as quickly as possible and laughed as he left. A long-haired woman on her way back from the bar saw us laughing and said reproachfully, "That's Bodenheim." The name meant nothing to Wakefield, nor could he understand why the woman had reproached him. It was only later that he found out who Max-well Bodenheim was, and he then felt ashamed that he'd mocked him.

When Bodenheim's second wife died in 1950 he lost what little connection he had to any kind of settled existence. Friends in Greenwich Village tried to help him with money and meals, but he often wandered into the Bowery, where he mixed with the hope-less drunks and misfits of the area. Usually homeless, he was ar-rested for sleeping in the subway. And it was reported that he sometimes hung a sign around his neck and pretended to be blind so that he could beg on the streets.

In 1951 he met a woman named Ruth Fagan, a onetime teacher with a history of mental problems. She was around thirty years younger than the alcoholic old poet, but they established a relationship and soon married. Bodenheim was hired to write his memoirs by Samuel Roth, a curious character who hovered in that grey area where serious and salacious literature mix. A book called my *Life and Loves in Greenwich Village* did appear under Bodenheim's name after his death, but it's doubtful if it was his work and it's more than probable that it was written by someone else from rough notes that the poet had made.

Bodenheim and his wife roamed around New York, sometimes staying in cheap hotels, sometimes sleeping rough. They made a trip to Chicago in 1952 for a reunion of writers involved in the Chicago Renaissance, but Bodenheim got drunk and disgraced himself. He was still writing poems, and when Dorothy Day, a long-time Greenwich Villager and stalwart of the Catholic Worker movement, arranged for the couple to stay at a retreat outside New York he even managed to sell one or two for publication in newspapers. But the period in the retreat came to an end and so did Bodenheim's period of calm. Back in New York he sold his poems on the streets, and it was in 1953 that the poet Aaron Kramer, who had been printed alongside Bodenheim in the 1944 anti-fascist anthology, came across him. There had been an event in Washington Square Park, with poets reciting and selling their work. But everyone had gone by the time Kramer arrived, and the cool Spring day was beginning to close down. Kramer noticed someone in a side street, and found Bodenheim

> "motionless and alone.. ..a face fleshless and red with wind, eyes dead, as if he had no awareness that the sun had long since given way to icy shadows around his chair. I did not introduce myself, but told him that I had loved his work since boyhood and shook his limp, frozen hand. Four or five of his autographed poems were displayed on the wall, flapping against the weather. Afraid he might think me patronising, I bought only one poem - the longest and most expensive - for a dollar. At the corner I turned around for a last look. He sat exactly as before, in the deepening shadow."

Drinking and drifting, Bodenheim and his wife were joined by a man named Harold Weinberg, who had a police record and had been discharged from the army as mentally unfit. Weinberg was sexually attracted to Ruth and she may have encouraged his attentions, and there was a degree of animosity between Weinberg and

Bodenheim. On a cold February night in 1954, when the Boden-heims had nowhere to sleep, they accepted an invitation to go to Weinberg's room. What happened after that is debatable. Weinberg may have tried to rape Ruth and Bodenheim may have intervened. Or Weinberg and Ruth may have agreed to have sex and Boden-heim, who had been asleep, may have woken up and objected. Ei-ther way, the result was that Weinberg shot and killed Bodenheim and then stabbed Ruth to death. It was reported that when the bod-ies were found Bodenheim had a copy of Rachel Carson's *The Sea Around Us* in his possession and that poems he had been working on were on the table. When Weinberg was tried, he said, "I ought to get a medal. I killed two communists," which may have been the ravings of a madman but also points to the power of the McCarthy-ite hysteria then in full flow and the way in which even bohemian-ism was seen as un-American.

I doubt that many, if any, people read Maxwell Bodenheim's work these days, other than for academic reasons, and it's true that it would be hard to make a case for him as a major writer in either poetry or prose. He was a competent, though uneven, novelist, and a skilful, if largely unoriginal, poet. But those descriptions could easily be applied to any number of writers, past and present, and there are things worth preserving in Bodenheim's work. A few po-ems, some passages from his better novels, perhaps even a couple of the novels themselves. *Georgia May* still has power, and *Slow Vision* is worth reading for its sombre portrayal of the effects of the Depression. He certainly deserves to be remembered for more than his days as an inebriated hawker of hastily written verses.

There is little point in giving publication dates, etc., of all Boden-heim's books, but the details can be found in Jack B. Moore's *Max-well Bodenheim,* Twayne Publishers, New York, 1970. This is a good, short survey of Bodenheim's books and Moore deals with the subject seriously, whilst acknowledging Bodenheim's personal waywardness. As far as I know, there is currently nothing of Bodenheim's in print, apart from a short, one-act play, *The Gentle Furniture Shop* written for the Provincetown Players in 1917, and reprinted in *The Provincetown Players,* edited by Barbara Ozieblo, published by Sheffield Academic Press, Sheffield, 1994. Milton Klonsky's *Maxwell Bodenheim as Culture Hero* is in his *A Dis-course on Hip:Selected Writings of Milton Klonsky,* Wayne State

University Press, Detroit, 1991.

Allen Churchill's *The Improper Bohemians,* Cassell, London, 1961, tells the bohemian side of the Bodenheim story, as do other histories of American bohemianism. Most recount the same anecdotes and escapades.

# CLIFFORD ODETS: SWEET SMELL OF SUCCESS

Clifford Odets did not have a distinguished career in Hollywood and most of the films he worked on have been forgotten, though there are moments in *Deadline at Dawn* and *None But the Lonely Heart* when the writing is reminiscent of the Odets of the plays that made his name in New York in the 1930s. The usual assumption is, of course, that he sold out to Hollywood and that it corrupted him and destroyed his talent. The critics point to the poor quality of most of the films he was involved with and make reference to his final years when he wrote a script for a weak Elvis Presley western and did some routine work for television. Add to that his less-than-heroic stance when called to testify to the House Un-American Activities Committee in the earty-1950s and it's not hard to understand why his reputation suffered.

I've never been convinced that such an easy dismissal of Odets is justified. His later plays, like *The Big Knife* and *The Country Girl*, have much to recommend them. And as for working in Hollywood, Odets went there to earn money writing and I doubt that he had many illusions about what he would be able to do. Screenwriting at any time, and especially in the days of the Hollywood studio system has never been a job for the over-sensitive, and writers have to accept that their scripts will be tampered with, not only by other writers but also by directors, producers, and actors, just as they have to be prepared to meddle with other writers' work or produce scripts based on ideas they think are ridiculous. In the old days, Hollywood was like a factory turning out mass-production goods, and the fact that some writers managed to do decent work in that atmosphere says a lot about their resilience and urge to create. It's unlikely that many of the writers who worked in films would want to claim that most of what they wrote was great art (or even minor art) and I suspect it satisfied the majority to think of themselves as craftsmen who did the best they could in the circumstances. As Woody Haut says in a recent study of the effects on writers of working in Hollywood, they "have often had to reject the world of literature and embrace the role of literary worker."

I don't intend to make this piece an apology for writers who went to Hollywood. There is now sufficient material available for anyone interested in the subject to look in detail at why writers worked in films, the problems they encountered, and what they thought they'd achieved, besides making money. What I want to do is examine a film with which Clifford Odets was involved and which, despite an indifferent and even sometime hostile reception when it first appeared in 1957, is now regarded as something of a classic. *Sweet Smell of Success* has been described as "the smartest, most cynical American film of the 1950s," and the story of how it came to be made is a fascinating exercise in creativity triumphing over the odds.

*Sweet Smell of Success* first started life as a novella published in the magazine *Cosmopolitan*. It was written by Ernest Lehman, who had worked in New York as a press agent, a job which required him to hang around the notorious columnists of the day hoping to get his clients favourably mentioned in the newspapers they wrote for or the radio programmes they presented. Lehman had ambitions to be a novelist and tried to construct a book about the seedy world of columnists, press agents, public relations people, hack journalists, hustlers, and others who frequented the clubs and bars of the city. Lehman never did finish the novel but he salvaged enough from it to produce two short stories and a novella revolving around Sidney Falco, an ambitious agent ready to do almost anything to succeed, and J.J. Hunsecker, a famous gossip columnist who ruthlessly uses everyone to keep his own name in lights. It was no secret that Hunsecker was based on a real columnist, Walter Winchell, who could make or break reputations and had the ear of famous politicians, businessmen, film stars, FBI officers, and others in a position to feed him information and receive it from him. That similarities could be seen between Hunsecker and Winchell caused problems for Lehman when he tried to get his novella published, and even after it appeared it was shunned by Hollywood for fear of offending Winchell if it was turned into a film. But Hollywood did ask Lehman to work as a screenwriter and he moved there in the early-1950s.

By the mid-1950s the old Hollywood studio system was breaking down and independent producers were becoming more active. One of these organisations, Hecht, Hill and Lancaster (the latter was Burt, the film star) asked Lehman to let them film his story, with him writing the script and directing, but he refused, partly because he didn't want to revive the controversy about the way he'd portrayed the seamier side of the relationship between press agents and gossip columnists. He'd been almost ostracised in New York after his novella was published and he didn't want the same to happen in Hollywood. But Hecht, Hill and Lancaster continued to press him, and after they'd made an impressive film version of Paddy Chayefsky's TV play, *Marty*, Lehman relented. It was a decision he came to regret, at least in the short term.

The film business has never been noted for high ethical standards and Lehman soon discovered that, despite the promises made, he was not going to be allowed to direct the film. Hecht, Hill and Lancaster may have looked impressive on paper, but the three names represented three competing egos who were not against using underhand methods to get their own way. A story about Harold Hecht perhaps gives an idea of the prevailing ethos. He'd been summoned to appear before the House Un-American Activities Committee and he asked Roland Kibbee, a writer who worked for him, to help him prepare a statement he could read out at the hearing. Kibbee wrote the statement and listened to Hecht read it to the Committee and then immediately name Kibbee as a communist. Lehman had seen the sleazy side of New York at close hand but he thought of what he was experiencing in Hollywood as "a whole new level of corruption." Hecht, Hill and Lancaster did not impress him as people but, as he later said, they were the only ones prepared to buck the system and film his story.

The producers brought in Alexander Mackendrick to direct *Sweet Smell of Success* in what was seen as an unlikely choice for a film dealing with American big-city themes. Mackendrick had made his reputation in Britain, directing Ealing comedies like *The Ladykillers* and *The Man in The White Suit,* but he proved adaptable. Unfortunately, Lehman, under pressure to produce a script and having to cope with Mackendrick's way of working (Lehman said: "You had the feeling he wasn't even listening to you because his mind was going so fast."), not to mention interference by Burt Lancaster, fell ill with stress and was advised by his doctor to withdraw from any involvement with the film.

It was Mackendrick's idea to bring in Clifford Odets to rewrite the script that Lehman had prepared. He'd always admired Odets for his work in the theatre and he knew him to be conscientious about completing writing tasks he was given. And Odets badly needed the work. He was living in reduced circumstances, divorced, looking after his two children, and selling off some of the paintings he'd bought in better days so he could pay his bills. The great days of the 1930s were long past and he'd hardly carved out a successful career as a screenwriter. He had written plays in the early 1950s which were praised but they didn't revive his fortunes. Harold Clurman tried to persuade him to return to New York, but Odets wasn't foolish enough to believe that the world of the 1930s, with the Group Theatre and the whole left-wing artistic and social scene, still existed, or would ever re-appear. No-one would want to watch *Waiting for Lefty* in the relatively affluent 1950s, especially when Senator McCarthy and his associates were on the rampage. But Odets did think that *Sweet Smell of Success* might at least bring in some money and perhaps help him re-establish a reputation in Hollywood. He was worried about one thing, and that was the fact that some of the filming would take place in New York and he had to be in attendance. He worried about running into old friends from his left-wing past and how they would treat him.

The biggest problem that Odets faced was that filming was due to start the week after he was hired and he literally had to write as the film was being made. There was also a battle going on between Lancaster and Mackendrick about how the film should develop, so the writer's situation wasn't at all perfect. Tony Curtis, playing the part of Sidney Falco to Lancaster's J.J. Hunsecker, struck up a friendship with Odets, and recalled him sitting in his overcoat in one of the prop trucks in Times Square in New York, in the early hours of a bitterly cold morning, hammering away at his typewriter because the scenes were needed for that day's filming. Alexander Mackendrick remembered: "One of the most frightening experiences in my life was to start shooting in the middle of Times Square with an incomplete script." And he added: "There never was a final shooting script for the movie....it was all still being revised, even on the last day of principal photography. It was a shambles of a document."

Despite all these drawbacks the film was an artistic, if not a commercial, success and much of the credit for that lies with the script. In terms of the basic story it doesn't stray far from Lehman's novella. Hunsecker has a sister, Susan, who he has an unhealthy interest in, to the extent of resenting any men who pay attention to her. She is having an affair with a young jazz musician. In the novella he's a singer but jazz was going through a brief popular phase in the 1950s so the music could be neatly incorporated into the film. Hunsecker wants the relationship broken and Falco, ever anxious to curry favour with the columnist, connives to do just that. He arranges for some other columnists to smear the musician as a drug user and a possible member of the Communist Party, thus playing on two fears of 1950s America which would place someone outside polite society. Odets had his own reasons for wanting to show how smears spread by columnists easily damaged reputations, but the idea originated in Lehman's story so he was clearly aware of what went on. It's a fairly simple storyline but intertwined with it are a series of other sketches as Falco hustles for business with possible clients, pimps for another columnist he wants a favour from, and explains his philosophy of life in a number of asides and responses to people he encounters. Talking to his long-suffering secretary who raises a mild objection to his behaviour and asks, "where do you want to get?" Falco replies:

> "Way up high, Sam, where it's always balmy! Where no-one snaps his fingers and says, 'Hey, Shrimp, rack up those balls! Or, 'Hey, mouse, run out and get me a pack of butts: I don't want tips from the kitty -I sit in the big game and play with the big players. My experience I can tell you in a nutshell, and I didn't dream it in a dream: dog eat dog."

This is pure Odets and it isn't in Lehman's novella in that form. Lehman was a decent enough writer and kept his dialogue moving, but he didn't have Odets' talent for creating a streetwise language that sounded authentic even if, coolly analysed, it can seem somewhat overdone. Mackendrick, in fact, did raise objections along those lines, worrying that the dialogue sounded "stagy," but Odets countered his comments by saying, "You're probably worried that the dialogue is exaggerated and may sound implausible. Don't be. Play it real fast - and play the scenes not for the words but for the situations. Play them on the run and they'll work just fine." Odets also explained to Tony Curtis how to play the role of Falco: "Don't be still with Sidney. Don't ever let Sidney sit down comfortably. I want Sidney constantly moving, like an animal, never quite sure who's behind him or where he is." The fast-talking lines Odets created for Sidney match the moving man on the screen. A telephone rings in Falco's office and he snarls at his secretary, "If that's for me, tear it up," a line Odets had previously used in his play, *Golden Boy*. And faced with a situation where things have gone wrong and he has to talk his way out of it, Falco says, "Watch me run a fifty yard dash with my legs cut off."

With Hunsecker, Odets created a different character, someone who is in a position of power and knows it. Unlike Falco, he doesn't need to be on the move all the time. People come to him, as the film makes clear with Hunsecker sitting at his usual table in a nightclub while agents and politicians and others try to ingratiate themselves. In one scene Falco joins him and Hunsecker savagely turns on the press agent as he explains to some other people just who and what Falco is:

> "Mr Falco, let it be said at once, is a man of forty faces, not one, none too pretty and all deceptive. See that grin? It's the charming street urchin's face. It's part of his 'helpless' act he throws himself on your mercy. I skip the pleading nervous bit that sometimes blends over into bluster. The moist grateful eye is a favourite face with him - it frequently ties in with the act of boyish candour: he's talking straight from the heart, get it? He's got about half a dozen faces for the ladies, but the real cute one to me is the quick dependable chap - nothing he won't do for you in a pinch. At least, so he says! Tonight Mr Falco, whom I did not invite to sit at this table, is about to show in his last and most pitiful role: pale face with tongue hanging out. In brief, gentlemen and Jersey Lily, the boy sitting with us is a hungry press agent and fully up on all the tricks of his very slimy trade."

It is, admittedly, virtually impossible to know exactly how much of Lehman's script remained in the end. He was given co-writer credit with Odets for the screenplay, so must have contributed a reasonable amount of the material to merit that status. Even so, I think it's possible to see Odets' hand at work just about everywhere and, if the stories about the script being written (or re-written) as filming was in progress are accurate, then he may well have done the major part of the work. Ernest Lehman himself said that "Clifford Odets had done some brilliant rewrites." There is too, a significant departure from Lehman's portrayal of Hunsecker in the novella and it is almost certainly something that Odets introduced into the script.

Lehman did not show Hunsecker to be overtly political, but in a key scene in the film which climaxes in a confrontation between Hunsecker and the musician, the columnist is seen preparing for his TV show and making comments about the American way of life: "From Washington through to Jefferson, from Lincoln and F.D.R., right up to today the Democratic way of life! That's what the man said. Nowadays it doesn't export too well....But you know....and I know....that our best secret weapon is D-E-M-O-C-R-A-C-Y".

Odets knew from personal experience how patriotic sentiments expressed in this way were often a cover for scoundrels to boost their own reputations, as with Joseph McCarthy and other members of the committees investigating supposed un-American activities, and introducing this scene must have been his idea. It also points to the growing power of television to influence opinions, with the more astute columnists realising that they needed to switch to that medium as newspapers lost some of their capacity to shape the public's perceptions.

Comparing the script of *Sweet Smell of Success* to the novella it's obvious that the film offers much harsher portraits of Falco and Hunsecker. In the novella Falco does seem to falter at times and almost question his lust for success. He has some contact with his family and appears to be upset because they view him as someone who has sold his soul to the Devil. And there is a woman he turns to for comfort. But the film shows him as compulsively pushing himself deeper and deeper into a frantic series of machinations. He has no redeeming characteristics, and as one of the other characters says to him: "You're an amusing boy, but there isn't a drop of respect in you for anything alive - you're too immersed in the theology of making a fast buck" This is almost certainly something written by Odets and nothing like it is in the published story.

On the whole, the film version of *Sweet Smell of Success* is a darker, more cynical story than the novella. There is, however, a hint of hope for at least some of the characters in the ending of the film. In the novella Falco is responsible for the arrest and brutal beating of the singer and is then lured to Hunsecker's apartment by the sister, who makes it appear that Falco has tried to molest her. Hunsecker arrives and the story ends as he savagely attacks Falco. Susan, in this version, is a tougher person than in the film, where she is portrayed as extremely vulnerable. The musician in the film is arrested and beaten, Falco does go to Hunsecker's apartment and is found there by the columnist, who assumes the worst and, as an act of revenge, informs the police that Falco has framed the musician by planting drugs in his coat pocket. Falco is then arrested and beaten, and the film ends as Susan leaves, presumably to go to the musician. As the script says, she "moves into a patch of early morning sunlight, then walks away towards a new day."

Alexander Mackendrick said that there never was a proper shooting script for the film, but a published script does exist and is essentially the same as what is seen on the screen. And it has been rightly acclaimed as one of the finest screenplays to come out of Hollywood. Films are a group activity and in *Sweet Smell of Success* it is obvious that James Wong Howe's brilliant black-and-white photography, Elmer Bernstein's edgy, jazz-tinged score and the work of Chico Hamilton's group, the direction and the editing, not to mention the acting, including contributions from a first-rate supporting cast, combined with the script to make the film work successfully. But I don't think it's exaggerating to say that without the script, and what seems to be Odets' major contribution to it, *Sweet Smell of Success* might have turned out to be just another competent Hollywood production. Odets took it far beyond that.

## NOTES

The screenplay of *Sweet Smell of Success* was published by Faber, London, 1998. Ernest Lehman's novella and his other Falco/ Hunsecker stories, are available in *Sweet Smell of Success*, The Overlook Press, New York, 2000.

There is a chapter about the making of the film in *The Bad and the Beautiful: A Chronicle of Hollywood in the Fifties* by Sam Kashner and Jennifer MacNair, published by Little Brown, London, 2002.

A video of the film was released in the MGM Vintage Classics series in 1998.

Most surveys of Odets' work concentrate on his stage plays. There are brief discussions of his film work in Gabriel Miller's *Clifford Odets*, Continuum, New York, 1989, and Gerald Weales'

*Odets:The Playwright*, Methuen, London, 1985.

For a recent and revealing look at the role of writers in Hollywood it's worth referring to Woody Haut's *Heartbreak and Vine: The Fate of Hardboiled Writers in Hollywood*, Serpent's Tail, London, 2002. Although this deals with writers from a specific genre (crime fiction) it offers many insights into the general problems faced by writers in Hollywood.

# ABSTRACT EXPRESSIONISM: THE BEBOP MYTH

In recent years it has become fashionable for young academic art critics and historians to draw parallels between developments in painting, jazz, poetry, and other activities in the 1940s and 1950s. A 'culture of spontaneity' is said to have arisen, one that derived much of its inspiration from jazz. And the abstract expressionists, in particular, are said to have been influenced by bebop, the modern jazz of the 1940s. According to William B. Scott and Peter M. Rutkoff, in their book, *New York Modern: the Arts and the City* 'the post-war jazz of Parker, Gillespie, Clarke, Monk, and Coltrane anticipated the artistic and political concerns that New York abstract expressionists explored visually in their equally revolutionary painting.' Thrown in at the end of a chapter about jazz and before one about painting, a statement like that seems more designed as a device for establishing a link, however tenuous, than providing useful ideas about parallels that could have existed. And the inclusion of Coltrane's name is enough to discredit it, his 'revolutionary' contribution to jazz not coming until the late 1950s, by which time the abstract expressionists were well established and, some might say, almost part of the establishment.

Even more controversial is another comment by Scott and Rutkoff: 'Jackson Pollock found bebop's speed and jarring harmony an apt analogue to his own work.' I'll say something about Pollock's jazz tastes a little later but first let me refer to other dubious suggestions about his supposed interest in bebop. In Daniel Belgrad's *The Culture of Spontaneity: Improvisation and the Arts in Postwar America,* we are told that 'Lee Krasner has asserted the profound influence of bebop on Jackson Pollock's painting during the crucial year, 1946, when he developed his gesture-field style of painting.' And in Ann Eden Gibson's *Abstract Expressionism: Other Politics,* it is claimed that 'Pollock... painted to the music of Charlie Parker and Dizzy Gillespie.' Both writers appear to be confident in their assertions that Pollock knew about, liked and was influenced by bebop, but the facts of the matter point to the contrary.

Belgrad's basis for 'the profound influence of bebop' appears to be Lee Krasner's reminiscences, as quoted in B.H. Friedman's biography of Pollock: 'He would get into grooves of listening to his jazz records - not just for days - day and night, day and night, for three days running... He thought it was the only other really creative thing happening in this country.' Had Belgrad delved a little further, however, even in Friedman's book, he would have read about Pollock playing 'his favourite Fats Waller and Jimmy Yancey records', and going to Jimmy Ryan's club in New York to listen to a Chicago-style group. And that's where his jazz interests lay, in the older forms of jazz, and certainly not with bebop. There is no evidence to support Ann Eden Gibson's description of Pollock painting while listening to Parker and Gillespie and she doesn't offer any. It simply seems to be an idea that has currency in academic circles and is repeated as books on the subject are written.

Insofar as Pollock's musical tastes were concerned there are accounts of him listening to classical music, usually at the behest of other people, but all those that touch on his liking for jazz make it clear that he preferred the world of Dixieland and Swing. It's interesting that the CD compiled from Pollock's own record collection and sold at the 1999 retrospective at the Tate didn't contain a single bebop item. As an American jazz magazine pointed out, 'Pollock's canvases may have pushed abstract art to its outer limits, but his taste in music turns out to be as rectilinear as the frames he stretched his canvases on.' According to the people who compiled the CD, 'Pollock owned a lot of schlock', and they had to 'eliminate the Andre Kostelanetz' when choosing the records to use.

The selection wasn't at all bad, and included Louis Armstrong, Count Basie, Duke Ellington, Jelly Roll Morton, and Coleman Hawkins, but it hardly points to Pollock being in touch with what Charlie Parker was doing in the 1940s. And we can add to this Ruth Kligman's account of trying to interest Pollock in Parker's and Gillespie's music. 'I don't get it,' he said, and 'I like Dixieland music, that's what I grew up on.'

Other painters associated with abstract expressionism have been linked to bebop, usually with little hard evidence to sustain an argument about the supposed influence of the music. An article by Mona Hadler, 'Jazz and the New York School', referred to the fact that Robert Motherwell had, in 1946, shown paintings in an exhibition, 'Homage to Jazz', which took place at the Kootz Gallery. I'm not sure what one or two paintings in a group exhibition are likely to prove, and Kootz happened to be Motherwell's dealer at the time so that was one good reason for being represented. No young painter is likely to turn down an opportunity to exhibit. But there's a telling comment in Motherwell's *Collected Writings* where he talks about his friendship with the sculptor David Smith. Motherwell and Smith shared enthusiasms for food, cars, and other things, but Motherwell adds, "There were of course minor blind spots on both sides; he liked to go to the Five Spot to hear Charlie Mingus or whoever might be there, while I've never been attracted to popular music, no matter how great." Motherwell's tastes ran to classical music, as he makes clear by his frequent references to Mozart, Bartok, Bach, Berg, and others. It may be worth mentioning at this point that Mark Rothko, though he had a great love of music, doesn't appear to have been interested in jazz. Like Robert Motherwell, he preferred classical music.

Daniel Belgrad says that Franz Kline and Willem de Kooning were 'modern jazz aficionados', but he doesn't specify just what they listened to. Kline, in fact, painted a tribute to King Oliver as late as 1958 and Oliver was associated with traditional jazz. This doesn't necessarily mean that Kline was unaware of modern jazz, but if he was knowledgeable about bebop it isn't well documented. He was a gregarious man, fond of hanging out in bars and clubs, and he probably did visit places where modern jazz was played, but I'd guess it was to socialise as much as listen to the music. There are anecdotes about Kline in Greenwich Village jazz clubs in the mid 1950s, but his own work was well developed by then and it's hardly likely that what he heard had a great effect on how he painted. As for de Kooning, who also sometimes frequented bars and clubs in New York, Carter Ratcliff, in *The Fate of a Gesture: Jackson Pollock and Postwar American Art,* pointed out that although de Kooning had 'an ear for songs from the jukebox... he believed that his art occupied a plane far higher than that of... popular music.' There is, incidentally, nothing in Elaine de Kooning's short memoirs of de Kooning and Kline to suggest that either thought jazz of key importance to their work.

Abstract expressionists on the West Coast did show some interest in jazz, though again the emphasis was on the older forms. Thomas Albright's *Art in the San Francisco Bay Area* notes that at the California School of Fine Arts, 'a small coterie of teachers and students - notably Hassel Smith, Deborah Remington, and Ernest Briggs - were avid followers of contemporary jazz.' What is meant by 'contemporary jazz' is unclear as the next sentence mentions a 'traditional jazz combo', in which Douglas MacAgy and David Park played. Hassel Smith and David Park were important members of the West Coast abstract expressionist group but neither was known as a fan of bebop. Smith indicated where his jazz sympathies were directed in his 'Homage to Bob Scobey', a painting dedicated to a white Dixieland trumpeter. Elmer Bischoff reminisced how he and his contemporaries often went to hear Muggsy Spanier, Kid Ory, Earl Hines, and Lu Watters, none of them connected to bebop. And he said that he thought the music fitted 'very well with the paintings Park, Diebenkorn, Smith and I were doing.' It is worth bearing in mind that, in the late 1940s, San Francisco was known as a place where traditional jazz held sway. The California beboppers congregated in Los Angeles.

That many artists from the 1930s through to the 1950s were interested in jazz is not in dispute. What may be questioned is whether or not this interest developed into influence. The evidence that it did seems slim in many cases and usually adds up to little more than Kline being seen in jazz clubs, Philip Guston reputedly having a large collection of swing records, and Pollock liking to play some sorts of jazz in his studio. There is hardly anything to show that most of the abstract expressionists were inclined towards bebop at a time when that music was new and their painting styles were being formed. If they were influenced by jazz it was usually the earlier types that Parker and Gillespie were moving away from. There may well be parallels to be drawn between what happened in jazz when bebop came along and what happened when abstract expressionism hit the art world, but it reduces art history and the wide experiences of the painters if we try to insist that they took their lead from jazz. The history of abstract expressionism is far too interesting to allow that to happen.

# ROBERT MCALMON'S POETRY

Few people today read Robert McAlmon's poetry. He's remembered mostly as a member of the expatriate circle in Paris in the Twenties, the publisher of Hemingway, Stein, and others, drinking companion of James Joyce, friend of Kay Boyle, and a memoirist whose *Being Geniuses Together* offers a lively view of life among the writers who congregated in the French capital. But there was more to McAlmon than the gregarious, hard-drinking, sardonic image suggests. He wrote several short novels and collections of short-stories, the best of which are still worth reading. And he produced a fair amount of poetry, though little of it has seen print since it was first published in the Twenties and Thirties. In its day his work was considered interesting enough to he printed in magazines like *Poetry, The Little Review, transition*, and the *Objectivists Anthology*. And it was praised by Louis Zukofsky, Ezra Pound, and William Carlos Williams. Zukofsky even went so far as to suggest that McAlmon's long poem, *North America: Continent of Conjecture*, was an essential text of modern poetry, along with *The Waste Land, The Cantos*, and Wallace Stevens' *Harmonium*. Time may well have shown that the flaws in McAlmon's poems lessened their chances of survival but I'm not sure that these flaws represent sufficient reasons for the poems to be totally forgotten.

I've written about McAlmon elsewhere so don't think it's necessary to repeat too many of the biographical details. He was born in 1896 and, after a brief spell in Chicago just after the First World War, arrived in Greenwich Village in 1920. His early poems appeared in Harriet Monroe's *Poetry*, the Chicago-based magazine, and show him to be competent with a routine kind of free verse. The following lines are from a series of short pieces referring to experiences McAlmon had in the Air Corps and they show how he was perhaps trying too hard to be sensitive and write in what he imagined to be a kind of poetic language:

In pale spaciousness
I blend with subtle infinity.
The wing wires of my plane
Whistle a monotone
That lulls my earthy unrest

To sleep.
The faint blur before me
Of whirring propellers
Soothes my eyes.

A longer poem, *The Via Dolorosa of Art,* also published in *Poetry* about this time, was more interesting and pointed to McAlmon's desire to deal with ideas in his poems. It reads as being somewhat overwrought on the whole, though there are passages which are nicely realistic and have a flat kind of rhythm:

But there was breakfast to have
The day was never his without his coffee.
So he thought of coffee:
In his mind the universe - thinking
Alone of coffee - sieved his self-perceptions.
Coffee - with not too much cream and sugar.

I don't want to spend too much time with these early McAlmon poems, though they are not without interest, and in 1921, when he was in London, a small collection of prose and poetry was published by the Egoist Press. McAlmon's own later comment on it was that, "as nobody paid it any attention I need not apologise and can dare to say that much worse has been done before and is being done yet by others."

By the mid-Twenties, when McAlmon was firmly established with the expatriates in Paris, he was involved with writing long poems. He had met and talked with Eliot in London and was familiar with *The Waste Land.* McAlmon's longer poems follow the pattern of Eliot's masterpiece, in so far as they often utilise different voices, but it would be unwise to claim that they match Eliot in terms of conciseness and overall completion. But then, McAlmon didn't have Ezra Pound handy to prompt him into making cuts and changes, nor was he patient enough to self-edit his work to any great degree. It isn't true to say that he didn't re-write but it would seem that he too often let things stand if they appeared to be sufficiently successful in saying what he had in mind. But he often lacked an overall sense of what he was aiming for so that the poems tend to work haphazardly, with successful passages alongside others which are pedestrian and only partially realised. McAlmon's *The Revolving Mirror* was an attempt to describe the age he lived in, with various figures from his own life appearing in the different sections. Among them were Sir John Ellerman, the British ship-ping-magnate and McAlmon's father-in-law, some of McAlmon's cafe friends from Paris, and James Joyce:

> That he had been and continued to be praised
> pleased his vanity at moments
> but when drunk,
> a drunk distinguished foreigner
> distinguishably drunken
> drinking
> he wept.

That passage is done as a character study, elsewhere dramatic monologues are used, and some fragments comment on Mussolini or pick up pieces from overheard conversations:

> Of course Mary had French in her
> and she was gay. She needed it in those days.
> Darnley, you know, was a homosexual.
> Yes.....O didn't you know ?
> Page boys and all that sort of thing.

McAlmon's intentions were clearly ambitious, whatever the out-come, and not without parallels in other American writing. Think of John Dos Passos' *U.S.A* , for example, and, though it may seem flippant to make the suggestion, the 'lost' pages of Joe Gould's *Oral History of the World*, a work which may never have existed other than in a few fragments and the imagination of its creator. But Gould's plan to portray his society through the overheard and the everyday, through bits and pieces culled from any source avail-able, and with anything that came to hand, was not without some similarities to what McAlmon wanted to do in a more systematic way.

*The Revolving Mirror* was flawed but interesting and has been de-scribed as "rhythmic prose............saved from flat failure by its humour and topicality." But it has also been said of it that it was a kind of response to Eliot, often almost a parody of his verse. "There is no nostalgic yearning for a glorious past here, no longing for a Golden Age now lost. McAlmon accepts what is, without sugar coating or regrets."

In the late-Twenties, McAlmon published another long poem, *North America: Continent of Conjecture*, which again attempted a wide-ranging overview of its subject, this time American history.

By using certain historical facts as a kind of loose linking narrative and interspersing them with anecdotes often told by different voices and accompanying these with lyrical passages described as "blues"("Bootleg town blues," "Cult Religion Blues" and so on), McAlmon hoped to capture the essence of America rather than record its history completely. There is a critical evaluation, by Yvor Winters, of Hart Crane's *The Bridge*, which can equally be applied to McAlmon's poem:

> "The book cannot be called an epic, in spite of its endeavour to create and embody a national myth, because it has no narrative framework and so lacks the formal unity of an epic. It is not didactic, because there is no logical exposition of ideas; neither Homer or Dante will supply a standard of comparison. The structure we shall find is lyrical; but the poem is not a single lyric, it is rather a collection of lyrics on themes more or less related and loosely following out each other."

This is true enough in relation to McAlmon and his casual attempt to provide some sort of narrative framework simply hadn't worked. But individual passages in the poem do read well and the whole thing, if uneven and often written in what has been described as "dressed up prose," never fails to be of interest. It's hard not to be attracted to an excerpt like the following from a section headed "Society and Advertising Blues:"

> One success leads, to another,
> in business and society.
> Use soothing toilet paper,
> you just know who's its maker.
> Inferior goods make scabs
> that turn the best people to crabs.
> In this age we' re living in
> it's nothing less than a sin
> not to demand Sap's labelled tin.

It has to be admitted that McAlmon's choice of subjects to write about in this poem often appears arbitrary and without a general purpose. And maybe Robert E. Knoll's summing up is accurate: "But as usual McAlmon's initial conception is worthier than his execution. His was not a failure of imagination or of intellect; his failure, here and generally, was a failure of the will. He did not imagine more generously than his talent could execute; too easily bored, he failed to develop the possibility of his ideas." And yet, within his failed promise, he still produced something worth considering because it at least had ambition and was interesting, a factor that so many poems, past and present fail to take into account.

One of McAlmon's most succesful longer poems was *New England Victorian Episodes: Pennythinker*, published in *Pagany* in 1930 and satirising the refined kind of artist and intellectual who prefers to sit on the sidelines observing the world rather than participating in its activities. Pennythinker, an artist, considers how the world is there to accompany his moods:

> Spring brightened the village campus
> while students strolled on grassy lawns midst trees.
> Elders and weeping willows cast string shadows
> on bright frocks that young girls wore.
> Boys played rampantly with boisterous glee on sidestreets.
> Pennythinker strolled, and thought the scene
> "So young, fresh and exquisite.
> Just too much the last word in young and carefree beauty."

But, several scenes later and with Pennythinker frustrated in his designs on a boy he fancies, the mood has changed:

> Pennythinker, slumping back into his chair,
> glares with vulturish eyes of life-hate
> into the abyss of time of maddening, detail-filled space,
> of people passing and of incidents unemphasised.
> Only after two days of austere intellectualisation
> to freeze his sensibilities to disdain of human pastimes
> could he comment, "Christ, how I detest personal relationships."

There is a consistency about this poem, both in its rhythms and its tone, which helps it work, and it may have been that the narrower aim (McAlmon wasn't trying to handle a wide-ranging idea) allowed it to succeed. It isn't a major poem but it does have a capacity to entertain.

The long monologue, *Fortune Carraccioli*, which appeared in *Poetry* in 1931, was cast in the voice of an Italian immigrant, walking the streets of Chicago, describing the sights he sees and the people he encounters, and looking back to his boyhood in Firenze. It sustains its mood and its rhythm, though would have probably worked just as well as prose:

> The wife doesn't see the joke of red underwear
> dancing on clothes-lines against smoke-stacks.

> She thinks I jeer at people,
> feeling myself a precious superior man.
> I tell her I love these people.
> They have what I haven't
> strong bodies to do hard work,
> and they don't bother thinking things
> that get none of us anywhere.

McAlmon doesn't seem to have written any more long poems after the early-Thirties, or if he did he certainly didn't publish them, but his short poems continued to appear in magazines and, in 1937, New Directions published a collection, *Not Alone Lost*. It has to be said that James Laughlin, publisher of New Directions books, was against taking on McAlmon's book and was only persuaded to do so by William Carlos Williams. Laughlin's reluctance was justified as *Not Alone Lost* failed to attract a wide readership and was said to have been the worst selling title in the history of the press. It's not a strong collection but does have a few good poems, among them several which referred back to McAlmon's boyhood in the Mid-West, and one, *The Crow Becomes Discursive* which has always struck me as the most successful of his shorter pieces, its language and dry tone neatly matching the scenes described:

> Autumn has ruffled my feathers.
> If my voice is not hoarser than it was
> something gone from the air makes it seem so.
> The beginning chill of autumn disturbs me.
> I must sit on the fence with my head turned sidewise and think.
> I watch other birds departing.
> I wonder. Why do we crows always linger?

The final two poems in the book refer to the Spanish Civil War and show that McAlmon, never an overtly political writer, was sympathetic to the Republican cause and deplored the "arrogance of priest, landowner, bankers, arms-men," and noted the "everlasting explanations of non-intervention/becoming an international convention," a clear reference to the way countries like Britain and the United States kept up a pretence of not getting involved in Spain while turning a blind eye to the support that Germany and Italy provided for Franco.

The political angle was continued in a handful of poems which came out in 1941, just after McAlmon had returned to America.

He had remained in Europe long beyond the dates that most of the expatriates had gone home, and was, in fact, still in France when the Germans occupied Paris. He did manage to eventually escape via Lisbon towards the end of 1940. His poems hit out at Fascism, though without suggesting that other political persuasions were to be trusted. McAlmon was, if anything, an anarchist, with a healthy mistrust of all governments and institutions. In *Birds for Extinction* published in *The Clipper*, a magazine produced by members of the Hollywood Left, he reflected on his experiences in France as the war started. He watches a flight of swans pass overhead and compares it to some young French pilots he'd seen:

> Their flight no doubt was more secure
> than that of pilot lads not yet quite sure
> that training or their planes were worthy,
> nor aware that governments and leaders can be scurvy.
> But then they could not know the way all
> schemes of Empire politics wrought their betrayal.

*The Clipper* isn't listed in bibliographies of McAlmon's work, and it's usually suggested that his final poems in print appeared in 1942. But some years ago I managed to obtain a copy of *The Old Line*, a magazine published by the University of Maryland. The April, 1943 issue was designed as "a literary challenge to Hitler's threat to wipe out culture in the modern world," and was effectively guest-edited by Norman Macleod, a left-wing novelist, poet, and academic, who got contributions from a wide range of authors, among them Pablo Neruda, Hugh McDiarmid, Langston Hughes, Kenneth Patchen, and Robert McAlmon. His *Autumn after the Fall* covered some of his time in France after the Germans had arrived, with an officer saying to him, "I hope America won't be foolish and get into the war," and the local people, who had initially fled when the enemy advanced, returning to find their houses and shops looted. It's not a particularly good poem, the rhythm and general structure coming across more like prose, but it is vivid in its portrayal of how the war affected life in the French countryside. Little details bring out the changes. A local drunk, once tolerated in his dissipation by the villagers, now has a face "no longer red with alcohol./Too few of the villagers had wine or the money to pamper him." And the horses have been taken from the fields, weeds are pushing up in places where flowers and vegetables once grew, and even the stray dogs have disappeared and cats are rare.

This probably was the last poem McAlmon published and, with the exception of a short prose piece about William Carlos Williams, the last example of his work to appear in print in his lifetime. He had gone to the South-West when he returned to America and had a job in a surgical goods store owned by his brothers, but the years of drifting and drinking in Europe had taken their toll and ill-health finally forced him into retirement. A forgotten man, he died in 1956.

It may be that the problems I've referred to - the flaws, the unfulfilled promise, the untidiness, the failure to develop ideas - will cause readers of this piece to think that McAlmon's work deserves to be forgotten. He was never a "good" writer, in the sense of his prose or poetry being polished, well-written, and capably achieved. He moved too quickly for that, his wandering life-style matching his movements in writing from one piece to the next. When he got bored he moved on. And yet I doubt that he ever wrote anything that lacked interest. McAlmon may be irritating with his writing but he's never boring. He didn't write poems complaining about the problems of being a writer-in-residence and the drawbacks of having to teach creative writing. There was a much bigger world out there that McAlmon wanted to get to know and to deal with in his poetry. That he failed as a poet (and he's not alone in that) doesn't lessen his efforts to write something of imagination and intelligence rather than just take the easy way out with fashionable complaints and bright comments. I'd sooner read a flawed McAlmon poem than any amount of supposedly "good" contemporary verse.

NOTES:

Some of McAlmon's prose has been reprinted in recent years and for information on this see my "Talking of Geniuses: Robert McAlmon" in *Beats, Bohemians and Intellectuals* (Trent Books, 2000). Most of the poetry remains buried in the small press books and little magazines of the Twenties and Thirties, the only exception that I know of being a reprint of *North America: Continent of Conjecture* (Dark Child Press, Pocatello, Idaho, 1983), and even this is not an easy item to track down.

*New England Victorian Episodes:Pennythinker* was reprinted in *A Return to Pagany*, 1929-1932 (Beacon Press, Boston, 1969), an anthology from the magazine, but it would seem that this book was withdrawn from circulation shortly after publication due to copyright problems, so copies are not easy to find. It is a wonderful collection and brilliantly captures the period and places McAlmon in context.

Robert E. Knoll's *Robert McAlmon: Expatriate Publisher and Writer* (University of Nebraska Press, Lincoln, 1959) is still worth looking at and does have some critical evaluations of the poetry. So does Sanford J. Smoller's *Adrift Among Geniuses: Robert McAlmon, Writer and Publisher of the Twenties* (Pennsylvania State University Press. University Park, 1975).

# BIRD BREAKS DOWN

In December, 1945, Charlie Parker arrived in Los Angeles as a member of a bebop group which included Dizzy Gillespie, Milt Jackson, Al Haig, Ray Brown, and Stan Levey. They were scheduled to fulfil an engagement at Billy Berg's Club in Hollywood and, by doing so, effectively introduce the new sounds in jazz to a West Coast audience. Bebop wasn't completely unknown in California, because records had filtered through from New York, and a few local musicians, such as Teddy Edwards and Sonny Criss, had quickly absorbed the bop message. And the outstanding trumpeter Howard McGhee had travelled to California with a Coleman Hawkins band and had become something of a catalyst among the young modernists in Los Angeles. But the arrival of Dizzy and Bird meant that musicians and fans would, for the first time, be able to hear the acknowledged leaders of the new music performing live.

There was a problem. Parker was known to be unreliable and Gillespie had added Milt Jackson to the group as a safety measure. Bird was deep in the throes of drug addiction and had suffered withdrawal symptoms on the long train journey across America. When he got to Los Angeles he found that the situation there was difficult. Marijuana was easily available, but hard drugs, such as heroin, were almost impossible to obtain and were highly priced. Bird's stay in Los Angeles would be complicated by the lack of a regular supply of heroin, and his behaviour became increasingly erratic. He often failed to turn up on time at Billy Berg's and sometimes didn't arrive at all. When Bird could get the narcotics he needed he produced music that overwhelmed the musicians and hipsters who came to the club. Pianist Hampton Hawes, who was just seventeen when he heard Parker at Billy Berg's, described the experience as a musical awakening.

Although the engagement at Billy Berg's initially attracted large audiences it would seem that for much of the time the club was mostly frequented by musicians and dedicated fans of bebop. They were in tune with what Bird and Dizzy were doing, but not everyone on the West Coast felt the same way. Parker later commented: "What made it worst of all was that nobody understood our music out on the coast....I can't begin to tell you how I yearned for New York." But he stayed in Los Angeles longer than he expected due to circumstances I'll discuss later. In the meantime some of his problems had been temporarily resolved when one of his devotees, Dean Benedetti, an alto saxophonist who gave up playing when he heard Bird and took to following him around and recording him whenever he could, found a reasonably steady source for drugs.

A man named Emry Byrd, nicknamed "Moose the Mooche," owned a shoe-shine stand on Central Avenue where he also sold jazz records. And he dealt in marijuana and heroin. Bird became one of his regular customers. With a steady supply of the necessary narcotics he settled into the routine of playing at Billy Berg's and making occasional radio and concert appearances. There are recordings from December 1945, including a studio session with Slim Gaillard and some airshots from Jubilee shows, and he plays well on them all.

Parker's presence in Los Angeles, and the influence he had on other musicians, came to the attention of Ross Russell. He had used the money he'd earned serving in the merchant marine during the war to open the Tempo Music Shop on Hollywood Boulevard, his intention being to sell traditional jazz and swing records. But the shop was soon almost taken over by hipsters and boppers and "became a headquarters for followers of the new music," though he admitted that it took him some time to come to terms with bebop. Once he did, however, he decided to establish a record company, Dial, to promote modern sounds. It had a shaky start in February 1946, when Parker turned up for a chaotic rehearsal (Russell described the musicians arriving "with a small army of hipsters and their women in tow") but failed to show for the actual recording session the following day. Tenorman Lucky Thompson took his place as he had when Bird wasn't on the stand at Billy Berg's. The stint at Billy Berg's had ended at the beginning of February and the group was scheduled to fly back to New York. But Bird couldn't be found, despite drummer Stan Levey checking all the likely places where he might be. His ticket was left at the airline office and Bird cashed it in and used the money to buy drugs. He was soon in need of more funds so formed a group to play at the Finale, a small club in the black section of Los Angeles. With him were Miles Davis, who had arrived in Los Angeles with the

Benny Carter orchestra, and a white pianist, Joe Albany, who became something of a legendary figure in the world of modern jazz though, like Parker, he had a major drugs problem. Bird also participated in a couple of Jazz at the Philharmonic concerts and recorded several sides for Dial at a session where Ross Russell noted his "impressive display of disciplined musicianship." One of the tracks was called *Moose the Mooche* as a tribute to Bird's drug connection, and in a way it anticipated an action of his that would affect his earnings. It turned out that he'd signed half of the royalties he got from Dial over to Emry Byrd, presumably as part of a drugs deal.

The Finale Club closed down due to pressure from the police and Emry Byrd was arrested when there was a drugs crackdown, so Bird was left without any sort of regular income or supply of heroin. He disappeared and it was only after Howard McGhee searched for him that he was found living in a garage. He hadn't eaten for several days and was trying to deal with his need for drugs by drinking large amounts of cheap wine. McGhee moved him to his own house and gave him a job in the band he'd formed for club work in Los Angeles. But Bird was, in Ross Russell's words, "a sick man that spring." And though he wanted to make more records for Dial both Russell and McGhee had "serious doubts about what would happen in the studio." Russell finally agreed to organise a recording date with Bird, McGhee, and three little-known musicians, pianist Jimmy Bunn, bassist Bob Kesterson, and drummer Roy Porter. It wasn't just Bird that Russell was bothered about. He had confidence in Howard McGhee but was worried in case the rhythm section wasn't strong enough. But the date was set for July 29th, 1946, and the results would become part of jazz history, even if not necessarily for the right reasons.

It was obvious that when Bird arrived in the studio he was in bad shape. He didn't appear to be interested in what was going on and sat slumped in a chair. Although he was supposed to be the leader of the group he hadn't planned anything and, when asked by McGhee what they would play, he merely grunted in reply. McGhee, familiar with Parker's erratic behaviour, quickly assumed control and prodded the altoist into warming up his horn. A few faltering notes followed. Then there was a suggestion that the group play *Max is Making Wax*, a fast bebop number that Bird should have been familiar with from his days on 52nd Street in New York. It was probably a mistake to pull Parker into a performance that would have tested even the most skilled and healthy musician, and Bird was clearly in no condition to handle the frantic tempo and tricky theme statement. Nor could he think quickly enough to produce anything worthwhile during his solo. By contrast, Howard McGhee's solo highlighted his brilliant technique and his fertile improvising. Despite Russell's misgivings the rhythm team proved to be competent enough and Jimmy Bunn was a good pianist with a bebop-influenced style.

Details of the session had been kept secret so that the studio wouldn't be swamped by Bird's followers, but Ross Russell had invited a few people to be present, including Elliott Grennard, a journalist who wrote for the music magazine, *Billboard.* He watched what was happening, took notes, and later wrote a short story, "Sparrow's Last Jump," in which a fictional saxophone player, Sparrow Jones, cracks up at a recording session. Years later, when asked about the actual events, he recalled Ross Russell's despair as he watched Parker struggling to play. "Oh Christ," Russell said, "I've just lost a thousand bucks tonight."

The next tune that the group recorded became the best known side from the session. Jimmy Bunn played a slow introduction and Bird, though slightly late in starting his solo, moved into *Lover Man.* There have been many arguments about this track over the years, and Bird himself dismissed it as one of his worst records, but it is not a totally a bad performance. Howard McGhee thought that "the sound came out fine," and added, "there were no wrong notes." The difficulty now, of course, is that it's almost impossible to detach *Lover Man* from the day's events and hear it simply as a musical performance. We know that Parker was battling the demons of drug addiction so the music has a poignancy that transcends any limitations evident in his playing. He stayed fairly close to the melody as written and seemed to be carefully choosing which notes to play. Bird made another version of *Lover Man* in 1951 with Red Rodney on trumpet, and it was certainly technically superior, but there is something compelling about the earlier one, though the non-musical associations might be an element in hearing it.

Parker's condition was worsening as the session progressed, and

McGhee remembered: "Bird was really disturbed. He was turning around and around and his horn was shooting up in the air." Elliott Grennard said, "he was staring into space. He had a tic." The group tried another slow number, *The Gypsy*, but Parker's playing was almost amateurish, with incomplete phrases and missed notes. In Elliott Grennard's story Sparrow Jones plays a number that parallels Bird's performance on *The Gypsy*, and Grennard wrote: "You know how the neighbour's kid sounds when he's practising his new lesson, squeaky and scratchy but earnest - so damned earnest?". He perhaps exaggerated a little, but not much, and *The Gypsy* was a poor display by any standards. Incredibly, at this point, when Parker was close to collapse, another fast number, *Bebop*, was started, but he was unable to play the tune in unison with McGhee and could only fumble through his solo. McGhee and Jimmy Bunn luckily saved the track from being a complete failure. Ross Russell had been standing behind Parker, steadying him so that his nervous twitches wouldn't pull him away from the microphone.

It was obvious that Bird would be unable to play any more and he was sent back to his hotel in a taxi. In the studio it was decided that Howard McGhee and the rhythm section would record a couple of numbers so as to get something worthwhile from the session. *Trumpet at Tempo* and *Thermodynamics* were dazzling performances by McGhee and showed him to be one of the leading bop trumpeters, though like so many of his contemporaries he had a career that was badly affected by drug addiction. But listening to his work throughout the *Lover Man Session*, as it is now known, makes one realise that, had Bird been in good shape, some classic bebop would have been recorded.

Bird's behaviour in the studio was a foretaste of what was to come. He was put to bed in his room at the hotel but then left his room and wandered into the lobby to use the pay-phone. But he was naked and was taken back to his room. He again left it and, again, was escorted back by the manager who then locked the door. A little later it was reported that smoke was coming from under the door. Bird had somehow set his bed on fire. Police and firemen were called and Parker, after being subdued by the police, was arrested. Ross Russell eventually tracked him down in the Psychopathic Ward of the county prison. He was in a straitjacket and was handcuffed to a bed, and was due to be charged with indecent exposure, resisting arrest, and arson. It was only after intervention by Russell and Marvin Freeman, a lawyer and jazz fan who was a partner in Dial Records, that Parker was committed to Camarillo State Hospital, a relatively liberal establishment where his drug addiction and mental condition could be treated.

Bird's stay in Camarillo (he later commemorated it in a recording called *Relaxing at Camarillo*) and his subsequent release and return to New York after a couple of successful Dial sessions, belong in a separate article, and I want to complete this one by referring to Elliott Grennard's story, "Sparrow's Last Jump," which was published in *Harper's* in 1947 and quickly reprinted in a couple of leading anthologies of short stories. Its wide circulation, and the fact that people recognised the events it described as being based on the Dial session, may have persuaded Ross Russell to issue the records, an act that Parker never forgave him for. According to Grennard, Bird never spoke to Russell again, except about money, and in Russell's *Bird Lives!* , his biography of Parker, he tells of an incident in a club in late 1954. Parker demanded money from Russell and argued with him for releasing *Lover Man* years before. Later, Russell was advised to leave the club because Bird was said to have a gun and was threatening to shoot Russell.

Was Russell right to release the tracks that Parker recorded at the *Lover Man* session, or should he have written off the money he'd invested in hiring the studio and other expenses? It's easy to understand that he would want to recoup his losses. Dial was a small label, still struggling to stay alive in 1947, and Russell, after all, had taken a chance by recording bebop. It was a music that was never likely to become widely popular, at least not in its purest form, so Dial needed to make the most of any material it produced if it was to stay in business. Russell may also have felt that the Parker records deserved to be issued out of historical interest, though Bird himself wouldn't have agreed with that view.

In an interview he said: "If you want to know my worst on wax, though, that's easy. I'd take *Lover Man*, a horrible thing that should never have been released - it was made the day before I had a nervous breakdown. No, I think I'd choose *Bebop*, made at the same session, or *The Gypsy*. They were all awful."

On balance, I'd tend to agree with Bird's opinion that the records should never have been issued, though I also think that they may well have been worth preserving for Howard McGhee's work alone. But the fact of the matter is that they were released and so became a part of the Charlie Parker story and jazz history generally.

## NOTES

The best source for the four sides from the *Lover Man* session is *Charlie Parker on Dial:The Complete Sessions* (Spotlite SPJ-CD 101-4), a superb 4-CD set which sets them in context. They have been included in other collections of Parker material but the Spotlite issue is the best documented. The two tracks recorded by Howard McGhee after Parker's collapse can be found on *Howard McGhee on Dial: The Complete Sessions* (Spotlite SPJ-CD 131).

Ross Russell's *Bird Lives!* (Quartet Books, London, 1973) is worth reading for its eye-witness account of the *Lover Man* session, and his novel, *The Sound* (Cassell, London, 1962), has a central character based on Bird and paints a vivid picture of the bebop era. Elliott Grennard's "Sparrow's Last Jump" was included in *Jam Session* (Peter Davies, London, 1958), edited by Ralph J. Gleason.

# HARRY BISS

Who was Harry Biss? Most jazz musicians can be allocated some sort of identity from the usual sources - reference books, old magazines, etc - and it's true that Biss's name crops up in various discographies, but little or no information seems to exist to say when and where he was born or when and where he died.

He appeared on the music scene in the mid-1940s, which suggests he was probably born in the early 1920s. In 1944 he was with Georgie Auld's big band and can be heard on transcription recordings of tunes such as *Short Circuit* and *Mandrake Root* playing in the style of Count Basie. Of course, the nature of the arrangements may have required Biss to have played that way, so it's impossible to tell how developed he was as a soloist. But the Auld band was considered to be forward-looking in its approach, and Biss came into contact with enthusiastic young modernists Sonny Berman, Al Cohn, Serge Chaloff, and Art Mardigan. He continued to work with Auld through 1945 and into 1946 and can be heard, if only briefly, on *Airmail Special* and *Let's Jump.*

Biss had also recorded with trumpeter Billie Rogers in 1945 and discographies show him as a member of an interesting group (with Aaron Sachs, Frank Socolow, and Chuck Wayne) which recorded in Cincinatti, though the results do not appear to have ever been released. After leaving Auld he was with Herbie Fields (there is a brief piano solo on *Among My Souvenirs*), Buddy Rich, and Boyd Raeburn. All these involvements would have placed him alongside musicians and arrangers who were alert to the new sounds of Be-bop. He was certainly one of a group of young boppers who got together in Brooklyn to listen to records and socialise. Terry Gibbs, George Handy, and Tiny Kahn were also present. And in 1947 Biss was in guitarist Bill De Arango's group at the Three Deuces in New York. Gibbs was also there, along with bassist Charlie Leeds and drummer Art Mardigan. A review in *Down Beat* dated June 18 1947 praised all the musicians for playing 'softly with good dynamic control' and producing 'some startling solos.'

There are other indications of Biss's participation in the modern scene of the late 1940s and early 1950s. Bassist Phil Leshin, talking about the period, remembered going to 'Verland Studios, over a firehouse on 47th or 48th Street. A lot of the guys involved in modern jazz showed up at the sessions - Allen Eager, Al Cohn and Zoot Sims, pianists Harry Biss and Harvey Leonard, guitarist Charlie Byrd.' Terry Gibbs, who seems to have known Biss fairly well, described him as 'a complete nervous idiot. He looked like a Virgil Partch cartoon.' Partch was a famous American cartoonist who often drew oddball characters ('nerds' would be the term used now) and it's easy to see what Gibbs meant by comparing photos of Biss with some Partch drawings. Gibbs also recalled an incident when Biss, annoyed with his girlfriend because she was back-seat driving, stopped his car at a red light and then got out and walked away.

Discographies sometimes list a Brew Moore session for Savoy in December, 1947, with Biss playing piano, though the tracks were not issued. But it occurs to me that there may be a mix-up with a Moore date in 1948 when Gene Di Novi filled the piano chair. And Biss is occasionally credited with a role in the Gene Roland orchestra that was assembled for rehearsal purposes in 1950. Recordings of it do exist, but when they were issued on Spotlite some years ago the pianist was shown as 'unknown'. If he was present it would be another pointer to his links to the modern fraternity in New York. Charlie Parker, Red Rodney, Zoot Sims, Eddie Bert, Jimmy Knepper, and many more, took part in the Roland rehearsals.

The early 1950s gave Biss greater opportunities to display his solo skills on records. In August, 1951, he was in a Zoot Sims quartet that recorded for Prestige and the advent of LP recording meant that the musicians could spread out on a couple of long numbers as well as producing the conventional three minute performances. *East Of The Sun* and *Zoot Swings The Blues* threw the spotlight on Sims but Biss also got ample solo space and showed himself to be a thoroughly modern stylist with an approach that often gave the impression of notes bubbling up from the piano. His work wasn't hackneyed, in that it never lapsed into fashionable quotes, and he was skilful at backing Sims.

A couple of weeks after the Sims date Biss recorded with Terry Gibbs for Savoy, though he was essentially limited to a background role and the vibraphonist and Hal McKusick took the solo honours. In early 1952 trombonist Eddie Bert hired Biss for a Discovery session. What is interesting about the piano solos on tracks such as *The Ming Tree* and *All The Things You Are* is that there seems to be something of a Lennie Tristano-type touch to them. Had Biss studied with Tristano at some stage, or had he just heard him in clubs and on records? Later in 1952 he was in a Terry Gibbs group that appeared at Birdland and was recorded while broadcasting. Biss can only be heard in brief introductions to *What's New?* and *Perdido* and the others in the group - Gibbs, Allen Eager, Phil Urso, Don Elliott, and trumpeter Fats Ford - were given the solo opportunities.

I've noted that Biss played with big bands in the 1940s, and the available information suggests that, in addition to those I've named, he also worked with Tommy Dorsey, Louis Prima, Sonny Dunham, Art Mooney, and Billy Butterfield. In the early 1950s he was with Tex Beneke, who had a good band and was using some modern arrangements as well as Glenn Miller related material. Sorting out personnels for bands isn't easy, but it's probable that Harry Biss (often listed as Henry Biss) was the pianist on various transcriptions from 1951, including *Blue Moon* and *Dancer's Delight.*

It's in 1953 that the Harry Biss story comes to an end. He was with Charlie Parker when the altoist played what should have been a season at the Latin Quarter, a club in Montreal. Things went wrong from the start, with the musicians (Art Mardigan, trumpeter Benny Harris, and bassist Conrad Henry made up the rest of the group) said to have been dirty and dishevelled when they arrived. The club owner claimed that it was obvious there had been no rehearsals and added: 'Their performance was pitiful. Mr Parker personally did his best but the others, especially the pianist, didn't match him at all; the piano player was always in a fog; half of the time he didn't play. Didn't know where he was.' A local musician took over the piano at one point, and the engagement was terminated after three days. It's impossible to know what Biss's problem was, though one can guess that drugs lay behind it.

Harry Biss disappeared from the jazz scene after 1953. Did he quit music altogether? Did he die young? There are many questions and research hasn't turned up any answers to them. He remains a mystery man of jazz.

NOTE: Thanks to Dave Brown, Dave Moore, and Geoff Wills, for help with trying to track down information about Harry Biss.

# BUDDY WISE

1955 was a bad year for modern jazz. Charlie Parker passed away in March, Wardell Gray died in mysterious circumstances in Las Vegas in May, and the promising young baritone saxophonist, Bob Gordon, was killed in an automobile accident in August. There was another death, though it was less well-reported than those, and the musician concerned has not been remembered in the way that Parker, Gray and Gordon are. Tenorman Buddy Wise tends to be mentioned only when Gene Krupa's band of the late-1940s is discussed, but he was for a short time highly regarded in modern jazz circles.

Robert Raymond Wise was born in Topeka, Kansas, in February, 1928. Like so many musicians of his generation he made his professional debut as a teenager, working with bands led by Hal Wasson and Mal Hallett in 1943 and 1944. Pianist John Williams, who himself went on the road when he was 16, remembered being with Wise in Hallett's outfit, along with trumpeters Don Fagerquist and Sonny Rich and trombonist Dick Taylor. They were all interested in the new sounds then being created by Charlie Parker and Dizzy Gillespie. Fagerquist and Taylor moved on to the Gene Krupa orchestra, and it was Fagerquist who, in 1945, recommended Wise as the replacement for Charlie Kennedy, who was about to be conscripted into the army. The 17-year-old Wise was soon in a saxophone section which included Charlie Ventura.

Ventura was a featured soloist with Krupa, and Wise initially had to be content with section work. But in 1946 Ventura left to form his own band and Wise took over the jazz chair. Krupa's band was a popular one and its book in the late-1940s included a number of modern arrangements by Gerry Mulligan and Ed Finckel. In January 1947, Krupa recorded Mulligan's *Disc Jockey Jump*, a bright number which neatly combined straightforward swing with some boppish licks and also gave Wise solo space. He steps out of the ensemble with a striking phrase and demonstrates that he's firmly in the modern camp, his sound being clearly derived from Lester Young. It may give an indication of his leanings if it's mentioned that he once named Al Cohn and Zoot Sims as his favourite tenormen.

216

Airshots and other similar recordings indicate that Wise was well featured with Krupa. And in December 1947, he was given solos on two of the band's more bop-inclined studio sides, *Calling Dr Gillespie* and *Up an Atom*. Both were arranged by Ed Finckel and they show the Krupa band at its best, the scores skilfully incorporating the latest ideas but also preserving a basic swing approach. Wise's solos again demonstrate that he favoured a style that might best be described as virile cool, his tone and phrasing being firm and rounded.

Wise continued to work with Krupa throughout 1948 and 1949, and in January of the latter year he was featured on the band's energetic version of George Wallington's *Lemon Drop*, a tune also recorded by Chubby Jackson and Woody Herman. There is, incidentally, a short film from this period in which Krupa's orchestra plays this particular number. It's interesting that Wise had stayed with Krupa for so long at a time when the line-ups of big-bands often changed with bewildering frequency. But working with a well-known leader certainly gave him the right exposure and he was one of the band's major soloists. An idea of how central he was to its performances can be gained from recordings made at the Hollywood Palladium in April, 1949. Wise can be heard on several tracks, including *Mulligan Stew, Lemon Drop, After You've Gone*, and *G Bop*, playing with a great deal of skill and confidence. The fast tempo, and the fact of having to follow Roy Eldridge, don't seem to bother him on *After You've Gone*, and enthusiastic shouts greet his lively solo on *Lemon Drop.*

In February, 1950, the Krupa band recorded an album of Fats Waller songs which spotlighted Wise and trumpeter Don Fagerquist. These sides, which appear to have been almost forgotten in recent years, caught the Krupa musicians in first-class form, and Wise's solos on tunes like *Ain't Misbehavin, A Handful Of Keys,* and *Honeysuckle Rose*, were well-shaped and cleanly played. The word pretty was sometimes used to describe Wise's playing, and it's true enough in the sense that he never forced the pace nor tried to get too intricate in his solos. He was relaxed, even on up-tempo tracks.

It's worth noting that his name often cropped up in the pages of *Metronome* around this time. The January 1950 issue, which listed the winners of the annual poll, included him in the top 30 tenor players. The March issue had a review of an appearance by the Krupa band at Bop City and said that among the best soloists was 'Buddy Wise on tenor, especially in slower tunes where his pretty tone showed off.' In May there was a review of Krupa's *These Foolish Things*, a feature for Wise, though it was less than positive, describing his style as 'Lester Young, right down to the one-note honk, behind-the-beat lingering, double-time blowing, sometimes cogent, sometimes mechanical.' A review of the Krupa/Waller records in the June issue was better, with Wise singled out for playing good tenor.

The June issue of *Metronome* also had a review of the Woody Herman band at Bop City which referred to Buddy Wise blowing some pretty tenor. He had left Krupa and joined the Herman Herd in time for its opening at the club, though he doesn't seem to have been hired for his jazz skills. Bob Graf was named as the featured tenor soloist on most numbers, and when Herman went into the Capitol studios and recorded *Music to Dance to* and *Sonny Speaks* it was Graf who took the tenor solos. Wise was with Herman for just a few months, leaving around September, 1950.

He had thought about forming his own band but was soon offered a job with Ray Anthony, whose orchestra was becoming popular in the early-1950s. Wise was with Anthony for about 18 months, presumably leaving sometime in 1952, and he was given solo spots on several numbers. Ray Anthony was, of course, a much more commercially-inclined leader than either Krupa or Herman, with a book that mixed standards, popular songs of the day, novelty numbers, imitations of Glenn Miller, and a few swing items. His arrangers, and they included the excellent George Williams, generally held things within a framework that would keep dancers and non-jazz listeners happy. I'm not knocking Anthony when I say this. He never claimed to be fronting a jazz organisation, but his music was always efficiently played and entertaining, and he helped keep the big-band spirit alive when audiences were rapidly turning to other kinds of music. And he occasionally let his musicians loosen up a little, as they do on a 1952 transcription of *Perdido*, with Wise and his tenor partner, Billy Usselton, producing spirited solos. It isn't always easy to pinpoint exactly which Anthony tracks have contributions from Wise. Usselton was also from the cool school, though perhaps less direct in his phrasing, and different versions of some of Anthony's best-known numbers are scattered around various LPs and CDs. Wise is usually credited with the tenor solos on the studio recordings of *Trumpet Boogie* and *Mr Anthony's Boogie*, and he's named by the announcer on a non-studio version of the latter. He's also featured on *De-lovely*, recorded for Capitol in 1952, and a studio version of *Perdido* from 1951 as well as a 1950 transcription of *Sleepy Time Gal*.

When Wise left Anthony he stayed in California, and in September, 1954, he was in a small group led by baritone-saxophonist Virgil Gonsalves which recorded for Nocturne. Hearing him in this context, where he has the opportunity to stretch out, emphasises his good tone and attractive phrasing. He's in fine form throughout, but particularly effective on *Too Marvellous for Words* and *Bounce*. This was, surprisingly, the only small group session in which Wise participated, but he possibly thought that the increased activity on the West Coast might lead to more work in the jazz field. It didn't happen that way. It would seem that, at some point, he re-joined the Ray Anthony orchestra, and when it was working in Las Vegas he was arrested on a drugs charge and died in prison in July, 1955.

Buddy Wise clearly never got to show how well he could function in an outright jazz setting. His work was mostly confined to big-band recordings of the late-1940s and early-1950s, but it deserves to be remembered for its consistency.

Sources

Sleevenotes to HEP LP 26. John Williams interviewed by Steve Voce *Jazz Journal,* June, 1994. Letters from Frank Touhey and John Robinson.

Recommended records

Gene Krupa: Columbia CD CK 65678; Hep CD 51; CBS LP BPG 62290; First Heard LP FH26; RCA Camden LP INTS 1072. Ray Anthony: Montpellier CD 006; Aerospace RACD 995; Capitol CDP 744079-2; Jasmine JASCD 345 and JASCD 351; Circle CCD-96. Virgil Gonsalves: Fresh Sounds NR3CD-101

# BIRD LIVES!

I've met old men and women who can clearly remember where they were when the final result of the 1945 General Election was announced, and I've met younger men and women who know exactly what they were doing when Kennedy was killed. Myself, I can tell you where I was, and what I was doing, when I heard that Charlie Parker had died.

It was March, 1955, and I was in the army in Germany. We were billeted four to a room on the third floor of a one-time German Army barracks, and the soldiers I lived with, three older, regular corporals, tolerated the mild eccentricities of "the kid," and let me listen to occasional jazz programmes on the radio that was on the table in front of the window. It sometimes almost went through the window, especially when Michael, an Irishman of indeterminate age and established drinking habits, staggered in and stood on the table, while talking about the sadness of his existence and threatening to throw himself onto the parade ground below. He usually calmed down after we'd dragged him back and assured him that he was fine, life was fine, and the bars would be open again next day.

Anyway, that particular night, a Friday if memory serves me right and the nearest one after March 12th, I was lying in bed listening to a programme on the American Forces Network called Hot House which was presented by a character named "The Baron of Bounce." The normal pattern was for the linkman to say, "And now Hot House," and the theme music, the sinuous strains of Benny Goodman's bop-influenced *Undercurrent Blues*, would introduce the programme. But something different happened. The voice did say, "And now, Hot House," but then there was a slight pause and a sombre-sounding "Baron of Bounce" announced, "Bird is dead," and instead of *Undercurrent Blues* the music that followed was Charlie Parker with Strings playing *Dancing in the Dark*.

I can still feel the tension of that experience, and I continue to think it was probably the most important event of the past fifty years. But then, I share the attitude of clarinet-player Tony Scott who, during a panel discussion at a jazz festival some years ago, became emotionally overwrought because he couldn't get the other participants to agree that Bird was not only the greatest musician, but also the greatest human being, of the Twentieth Century. He was exaggerating, perhaps, but only slightly, and only in relation to the question of Parker's status as a man. As a musician, he was the greatest.

Where did I first hear Bird? Most likely on the radio in the late-1940s. I had an older brother who was not a jazz fan but did tune in to programmes which had records of the big-bands of the day, and the divide between them and out-right jazz was often fairly slim. Jazz slipped in and out of popular radio shows and you could hear Woody Herman's *Lemon Drop* on Family Favourites, along with George Shearing's *September in the Rain* and other records which appealed to jazz fans and at least some of the general public. There were few actual jazz programmes on British radio in those days, so the devotees like myself grabbed at what we could and then looked to the Continent, tuning the dial to stations like Cologne, Hilversum, and Paris, not to mention the ever-reliable American Forces Network. The rest of the family retired to bed, leaving me crouched by the radio in the hunt for some authentic be-bop. The next day I would walk around with the sounds of the previous night's records spinning in my head. Brew Moore and Kai Winding playing *Sleepy Bop*, Stan Getz cool and poised on *As I Live and Bop*, and Fats Navarro, a brilliant trumpeter and early casualty of the drugs scourge, presenting a series of dazzling ideas on the strangely titled *Ice Freezes Red*. Surrealism came to me via be-bop and black-and-white Hollywood films and was a natural part of my life. Each Sunday morning I would hurry across town to the home of the only other person I knew who liked bop as much as I did, and we would trade notes about what we'd heard during the past week as a small portable record-player gave out with Wardell Gray and Dexter Gordon on *The Chase* or Charlie Ventura's *High on an Open Mike*. And we delighted in the bop jokes that highlighted the alienation of the central characters. Two boppers emerge from a mammoth jam session in a basement club and, from behind their dark glasses, peer at the outside world. "Man, dig that crazy, moon," says one, and the other replies, "Man, that isn't the moon, that's the sun." They walk on, arguing, and decide to ask a passer-by to adjudicate. "Tell us, man," they say, "Is that the sun or the moon?" and the passer-by says, "I don't know, I'm a stranger around here."

Pinning down the exact year when thinking back over forty-five of them isn't always easy, but it does stick in my mind that the first Charlie Parker record I bought, around 1950, was a thing called *Stupendous*. Now, I have to admit that I bought the record (a 78rpm, of course) primarily because the other side was Howard McGhee's *High Wind in Hollywood*, and I'd seen a photograph of McGhee, drape-suited and sporting dark-glasses, and he was, I thought, the epitome of hip. His music was that way, too. The nervous energy of his muted trumpet playing, with some excitable tenor saxophone from Teddy Edwards and Dodo Marmarosa's probing piano, appealed to my youthful mood of wanting something different. I don't think I'd then heard of Ezra Pound, but "make it new" was an idea I understood. The excitement of those days was infectious, and even now I only need to hear the names of the musicians - Red Rodney, Allen Eager, Serge Chaloff, Bud Powell - for the adrenalin to start flowing.

There weren't all that many jazz records available, and in any case there wasn't much money to buy them. I scraped together what I could from a paper-round and helping out in a local shop, and I managed to build up a tiny collection of bop records on labels like Esquire, Vogue, and Melodisc. I soon began to notice that Charlie Parker had a distinctive voice and a fund of ideas that made him stand head and shoulders above most of the others, good as some of them were. I was reading about him, and the other boppers, in early issues of *Jazz Journal*, and I obtained a copy of Leonard Feather's pioneering book, *Inside Be-bop*, from Dobell's shop in Charing Cross Road, and studied it as closely as any book I've read since. It went into detail about Bird and Dizzy Gillespie, but also had a fund of information about the minor figures of the bop movement. I still have my original copy, and the records it mentions have been ticked off as I tracked them down over the years, determined to find even the most obscure of them. I recall being sent to stay with relatives in Whitehaven after an illness and, exploring the small seaport and mining town, I discovered a run-down music shop. I asked if they had any jazz records, and the owner dragged out a couple of cardboard boxes and told me to sift through them and I could have what I wanted at half-price. Chubby Jackson's *The Happy Monster* and Illinois Jacquet's *Jivin' with Jack the Bellboy* came into my possession that way. On another occasion, I was made to go to Morecambe for a short holiday, and bored with watching the gulls circling over the damp sands, I wandered into an arcade which had a stall selling second-hand records and, to my delight, came across a worn, but playable copy of Lucky Thompson's *Boppin' The Blues*. Neal Hefti's trumpet solo on that, with its paraphrases of Stravinsky, still comes over as one of the most striking of the era.

When I went to work, taking a job in a cotton mill because I had to and not because it offered any prospects, I had a little money and saved enough to buy myself rail tickets to London, where I went to Dobell's and other shops and bought what I could. I lived on packets of crisps and bags of greasy chips, but came home with wild recordings that I could play only when the house was empty. Fats Navarro and Howard McGhee duetting fiercely on *The Skunk*, Don Lanphere strangely laconic and introverted on *Spider's Web*, and Charlie Parker setting the standards for everyone on *Bird's Nest* and *Relaxing at Camarillo*, while Dizzy Gillespie roared through *Manteca* and *Stay On It*. The money I earned also enabled me to make the 1953 trip to Dublin to hear Stan Kenton's orchestra at its finest. A Musician's Union ban then prevented American bands from playing in Britain, so the *Melody Maker* organised two concerts and hundreds of us travelled by train, and ferry to see musicians like Conte Candoli, Lee Konitz, and Zoot Sims, taking Kenton's music firmly into the modern camp. In later years the experience (two rough overnight crossings of the Irish Sea) marked us out as veterans who had earned our status doing things the hard way. I went into the army the following year and remember the billet door opening one night and a voice asking, "Did anyone here see Kenton in Dublin?". "Yes," I replied, and made a good friend.

I carried *Inside Be-bop* with me wherever I went in the army, using it like a bible to reinforce my faith and keep the corruptions of the world at bay. Those corruptions were musical, and as the 1950s progressed they became ever more threatening as rock 'n' roll took over the airwaves. I recall that the first time I heard Elvis Presley's *Heartbreak Hotel* echoing down the corridor of a barracks block I thought it was a joke. I still do. It was significant that the noise level seemed to increase, along with the determination of its supporters to force it on everyone, when "pop" achieved dominancy. Meanwhile, I held onto my belief in bop and the modern jazz styles that followed it. Miles Davis and Lennie Tristano gave birth to the cool, Gerry Mulligan, Chet Baker, and Shorty Rogers floated smooth West Coast sounds, and by the mid-1950s a hard, New York mood was driving the music of Art Blakey, Kenny Dorham, and Horace Silver. I was transferred to another camp and had a less-tolerant group of room-mates, so I curled up under the blankets and held a radio close to my ear late into the night. Today, when I hear a Warne Marsh record I can almost smell army life. And Les Brown's *Montoona Clipper* (not be-bop, but with a good tenor solo by Dave Pell) makes me think of nights in a dark and empty camp assembly-hall, using the record-playing equipment so I could listen to the right kind of music without interruption. There were always little surprises as well to lighten the load. On a train journey from Bielefeld to the Hook of Holland I met a musician from an army band and we talked enthusiastically for several hours about bop and Bird and Thelonious Monk. A night in a German bar produced a bored saxophone player going through the routines of the dance-music he had to play, but he came alive when I mentioned Lester Young. And a fleeting visit to our unit by a truckload of American troops got me talking to a New Yorker who had been to Birdland. It was like having a conversation with someone who had been to Lourdes.

When I came home from the army I had my copy of *Inside Be-bop*, along with various records I'd bought in Germany. I also had an army exercise book, marked "For Official Use Only," in which I'd pasted cuttings from the *Melody Maker*, the weekly paper I'd bought for years and had mailed to me from England. I still have this makeshift scrapbook, and the mixture of record reviews and news items about Bird and Dizzy and J.J. Johnson and Duke Jordan and Al Haig evokes an era in a way that few jazz history books can do. Looking for it recently, I came across another exercise book, this one from the Grammar School I attended between 1947 and 1952, and which I'd also used to collect cuttings from the *Melody Maker*. Glancing through it took me back before my army days, and reminded me that there was a music teacher who, if only to appear liberal-minded, allowed me to play a jazz record at the end of each period of musical study. The rest of the class were permitted to leave if they wanted to, and usually only myself, the teacher, and a couple of the curious, stayed to listen to Charlie Barnet's *O'Henry*, Dizzy Gillespie's *A Night in Tunisia*, and Kenny

Clarke's *Conglomerations*. The baffled teacher was a pleasant-enough man, and no doubt meant well, but his notion that I would "grow out" of such interests amused me. I doubt that he's still around, but I'll doff my beret to his memory because he at least tried to talk to me about the music, and he was unusual in that respect.

But to return to the post-army days. I settled back into civilian life, had a couple of girlfriends who couldn't understand why I wanted to listen to jazz, met someone who did, and eventually married and got into the routine of work and family life and everyday activities. But I still looked to jazz, and especially the music of Charlie Parker, to provide a theme around which to improvise the necessary. Interestingly, by this time, the late 1950s, Bird's music had become almost fashionable amongst middle-class, university-educated intellectuals, who were influenced by the Beat and related-literature then breaking into print. References to Parker could be found in the posh Sundays and weekly magazines. It hadn't been that way in the early-1950s, though, and the audience for Bird and bop in Britain had been small. There was a little clique of modern jazzmen (who remembers Denis Rose, Tommy Pollard, and Hank Shaw?), some big-band musicians who didn't play bop but had the musical knowledge to admire it, and scattered fans who, even in London huddled together in tiny clubs. Did anyone else visit the Acton Bop Club, and if I take you to Great Newport Street, off Charing Cross Road, can you show me where the Studio '51 club used to be? I recall a night there when Les Condon and Johnny Rogers bopped their way through *Dance of the Infidels*, and another when Dizzy Reece blew high notes from a corner by the piano as Phil Seaman pushed him along with shimmering cymbals and crisp rim shots. I'd guess that both musicians and audience were mostly from working and lower-middle class backgrounds, though they formed a new, classless kind of bohemia. More-conventional middle-class types often preferred traditional jazz or rural blues, largely, I suspect, because those styles seemed authentically ethnic. They tied in with folk-music, and went along with orthodox socialism (the boppers were anarchists, if they were anything), coffee-bars, duffle-coats, and, a few years later, CND marches. The sharp-suited boppers I knew wouldn't have been seen dead wearing a duffle-coat or sitting in a coffee-bar, nor would they have put in an appearance at Aldermaston. It wasn't that they supported the State, but rather that they preferred to ignore it and listen to Bird. As the pianist Walter Bishop said, when asked about his dedication to music in the 1950s: "For me it was be-bop or bust." But I would always feel a twinge of amusement at their ignorance, mixed with a surge of anger at their arrogance, when intellectuals who had "discovered" Bird after 1955 would question my experience of having heard his music for years before that. It was as if they assumed that he only had credibility once they had acknowledged him.

So, I get out the old records, aware that they can make for an exercise in nostalgia, particularly if they relate to periods in one's life that were significant for some reason or other - an affair, a time of intellectual transition, a moment of promise - but also conscious that the best of them, and Bird's music most of all, transcend that limitation. Charlie Parker died in 1955, as I recall quite clearly, but all I have to do is play one of his records and Bird lives!

# Index

*44 Gravel Street,* 46
*A Casebook on The Beat,* 171
*A Discourse on Hip,* 162, 181
*A Handful Of Keys,* 217
*A Letter From San Francisco,* 171
*A Night in Tunisia,* 224
*A Portrait of the Hipster,* 151, 156, 161
*A World to Win,* 15, 119
Abstract Expressionism, 8, 192
Acton Bop Club, 225
*Acts of God,* 44
*After You've Gone,* 217
Agee, James 148, 158
*Ain't Misbehavin,* 217
*Airmail Special,* 212
Albany, Joe 207
Algren, Nelson 15, 126, 170
*All The Things You Are,* 214
*American Caravan,* 29, 62
American Forces Network, 220, 221
*American Mercury,* 12, 29
*American Sexual Imperialism,* 149
*American Voices,* 80
Amis, Kingsley 161, 172
*Among My Souvenirs,* 212
*An Autobiographical Novel,* 91
Anderson, Sherwood 27, 91, 174
Anonymous Movement, 76
*Answering a Trade Union Man,* 178
Anthony, Ray 218, 219
*Anvil,* 13, 14, 15, 20, 119
Apotheker, Lillian 76
Appel, Benjamin 119
Aragon, Louis 79, 80
Arnold, Buddy 107
*Aroused By Books,* 153, 156, 160
*Art in the San Francisco Bay Area,* 195
Artaud, Antonin 101, 102, 144
*As I Live and Bop,* 221
Asch, Nathan 61
Ashleigh, Charles 52, 54, 59
*Atlantic Avenue,* 31, 32
*Atlantic Monthly,* 56, 57
Auld, Georgie 212
*Autumn after the Fall,* 202

Babb, Sanora 68
Bailey, Blake 38, 41, 160
Baker, Chet 224
Balchowky, Ed 116
*Ballad of Reading Gaol,* 57
Barker, George 166, 168, 170
Barnet, Charlie 224
Barrett, Will 148, 158
*Bars and Shadows,* 53, 59
Bazelon, Dave 148, 158
*Beat Coast East,* 135, 142, 143, 145
*Beat Down To Your Soul,* 158
*Beatitude Anthology,* 135, 137, 138
*Beatitude,* 7, 116, 135-141
Bebop, 8, 205, 209, 210, 212
Beckett, Samuel 77
Beecher, John 71, 72, 81
Beeching, Jack 71
Beiderbecke, Bix 27
*Being Geniuses Together,* 196
Belgrad, Daniel 192, 194
Bellamy, Edward 12
Bellow, Saul 148, 154, 158
Beloit, Roger 108
Benedetti, Dean 206
Beneke, Tex 214
Berg, Billy 205, 206
Berman, Sonny 212
Berman, Wally 93
Bernstein, Walter 46, 48, 49, 50
Bert, Eddie 213
Bessie, Alvah 81
*Between Worlds,* 142, 143
*Big Table,* 144
*Billboard,* 208
*Bird Lives!,* 8, 9, 210, 211
*Birds for Extinction,* 202
*Bird's Nest,* 223
*Birth of the Beat Generation,* 164
Bischoff, Elmer 195
Bishop, Walter 226
Biss, Harry 8, 212-215
Black Mountain, 67, 72, 80, 172
Black Sparrow Press, 168
*Black Spring,* 78
Blake, Olive 103,
Blake, William 121
Blakey, Art 224
Block, Joan 146

227

*Blockade*, 86
Bloor, Ella Reeve 64
Blossom, Roberts 145
*Blue Moon,* 214
*Blues*, 19, 199
Bly, Robert 81
Bodenheim, Maxwell 43, 46, 53, 113, 114, 173-182
*Boppin' The Blues*, 223
*Bounce,* 219
Bowles, Paul 168, 170
Boyle, Kay 196
Bremser, Ray 142, 143
Brent, John 146
Breton, André 101, 154
Briggs, Ernest 195
Brossard, Chandler 9, 91, 122, 125, 148, 149, 156-158, 160-165
*Brother, The Laugh is Bitter,* 92
Browder, Earl 89
Brown, John 57
Brown, Ray 205
Broyard, Anatole 9, 91, 101, 122, 126, 131, 148-163, 165, 168
*Bruno in Venice West,* 94
Bukowski, Charles 67, 73, 81, 161
Bunn, Jimmy 207, 208, 209
Bunting, Basil 82
Burroughs, William 91, 102, 103, 105, 121, 130-134
Butterfield, Billy 214
Byrd, Charlie 213
Byrd, Emry 206, 207

Cafe Metro, 81
Cage, John 76
Caldwell, Erskine 167
*Calling Dr Gillespie*, 217
Camarillo State Hospital, 210
Candoli, Conte 223
Cantine, Holley 167
Carpenter, Maurice 71
Carraccioli, Fortune 200
Carrefour Press, 77
Carson, Rachel 181
Carter, Benny 207
Cassady, Neal 88, 99, 102, 124
Cassandra's Coffee House, 136
Cassill, R.V. 9, 126, 160
*Cavalier*, 97, 156
Chaloff, Serge 212, 222
Chambers, Whittaker 61, 64
Chance, John 139

Chaplin, Ralph 52, 58, 59
Charters, Ann 158
Chicago, 27-30, 52, 56, 59, 91, 92-94, 97, 113, 144, 173, 174, 180, 193, 196, 200
*China Strikes Back*, 46
*Circle*, 170, 219
Clarke, Kenny 224
*Cloaks and Suits,* 18
*Close Encounters,* 145
Clurman, Harold 186
*Coastlines,* 67, 69-74
Cohn, Al 212, 213, 216
Coltrane, John 9, 192
Combs, Tram 143
Comfort, Alex 166, 170
*Commentary*, 149, 158, 161
Commuca, Ricci 108
Communist Party, 11, 13, 14, 17, 21, 29, 35-38, 40, 43, 47, 53, 55, 56, 64, 75, 78, 79, 85-89, 91, 100, 101, 112, 114, 132, 179, 187
*Compass*, 167
Condon, Les 225
*Conglomerations,* 225
Connolly, Cyril 170
Conroy, Jack 11-16, 119
Corso, Gregory 72, 81, 114, 130, 133, 135, 137, 143, 144, 161
*Cosmopolitan*, 184
Cott, Jonathan 76, 84
Count Basie, 162, 193, 212
Cowley, Malcolm 11, 63, 143
Crane, Hart 77, 78, 168, 199
Creeley, Robert 130
Criss, Sonny 205
Croft, Andy 71
Crosby, Harry 76
Cruden, Robert 12
Cummings, e e 53, 166
Curtis, Tony 186, 187

Dadaists, 91, 154
Dahlberg, Edward 146
Dameron, Tadd 108
*Dance of the Infidels,* 225
*Dancer's Delight,* 214
*Dancing in the Dark*, 220
*Dante Called You Beatrice*, 168
Darwin, Charles 121
Davis, Miles 9, 109, 206, 224
Day, Dorothy 180
De Arango, Bill 212

*Deadline at Dawn,* 183
Debs, Eugene V. 89
Delattre, Pierre Henri 137, 140
Dell, Floyd 53, 56
Des Pres, Terrence 70
*Desolation Angels,* 109
Di Novi, Gene 213
di Prima, Diane 134
*Dial,* 28, 206, 207, 210, 211
Dickens, Charles 27
Diebenkorn, Richard 195
Dienstag, Alan 139, 141
*Disc Jockey Jump,* 216
*Discovery,* 126, 149, 152, 156, 159, 214
Donovan, Kitty 146
Dorham, Kenny 224
Dorsey, Tommy 214
Dos Passos, John 11, 27, 167
Dostoevsky, Fyodor 35, 121
*Down Beat,* 212
*Downriver,* 170
Dreiser, Theodore 27
Dublin, 223
Duchamp, Marcel 143
*Dude,* 157
Duncan, Robert 95, 168, 170
Dunham, Sonny 214
Durem, Ray 81
*Dynamo,* 22, 45, 71

Eager, Allen 107-111, 213, 214, 222
*East Of The Sun,* 213
Eastman, Max 56
Eberhart, Richard 166
Edwards, Teddy 205, 222
*Egoist Press,* 197
Eldridge, Roy 217
*Elegy for a Broken Bird,* 143
Eliot, T.S. 18, 23
Ellington, Duke 193
Elliot, Jack 110
Elliott, Don 214
Ellison, Ralph 154
*Engagement,* 62
*Episodes,* 137, 140, 203
*Epoch,* 125
*Esquire,* 65, 127, 222
Ettor, Joe 56
*Everett, November Fifth,* 55
*Evergreen Review,* 145
Everson, William 167, 168
*Excusology of the Ocean,* 145

*Exile From a Future Time,* 24
Fagan, Ruth 179
Fagerquist, Don 216, 217
Faier, Billy 110
*Falcon Press,* 168, 169, 171
Farber, Manny 148, 158
Farmer-Labour Party, 22
Farrell, James T. 15, 113, 114, 167
Faulkner, William 27, 46, 167, 170, 171
FBI, 28, 31, 61, 65, 67, 73, 75, 94, 184
Fearing, Kenneth 22, 28, 46
Feather, Leonard 108, 222
Federal Writers' Project, 15, 178
Ferlinghetti, Lawrence 80-82, 95, 97, 132-134, 137, 138, 143
Ferrer, Francisco 57
Field, Ben 71
Fields, Herbie 212
Finckel, Ed 216, 217
Fisher, Stanley 135
*Flee the Angry Strangers,* 125, 163, 165
Fles, John 144, 145
*For He's a Jolly Good Fellow,* 152
*For Kerouac in Heaven,* 145
Ford, Charles Henri 19, 168
Ford, Fats 214
*Forward,* 91, 92
Foster, William Z. 89
Fraenkel, Michael 76
*Freedom,* 166
Freeman, Marvin 210
Freidman, Bob 146
French, Warren 136, 137, 139, 140
Freud, Sigmund 76, 150, 151
*From an Exposition of Power and Industrial Machinery,* 75
Frontier Films, 46
Frost, Anne 139
Frost, Robert 168
Frumkin, Gene 67, 71
Fruscella, Tony 109
Funaroff, Sol 17, 22, 23, 24, 25

*G Bop,* 217
Gaddis, William 157, 159
Gaillard, Slim 206
Galler, David 146
Gardiner, Wrey 166, 168-172
Gardner, Lew 139
Gascoyne, David 168, 170, 171

*Gaslight Poetry Review*, 142-144, 146
Gates, Henry Louis 158
*Gemini,* 139
Genet, Jean 48, 101, 102
*Georgie May,* 176
*Get Home Free*, 127, 129
Getz, Stan 109, 110, 221
Gibbs, Terry 212, 213
Gibson, Ann Eden 192, 193
Gillespie, Dizzy 76, 109, 110, 122, 126, 192, 193, 195, 205, 216, 222, 223, 224
Ginsberg, Allen 32, 43, 44, 58, 72, 80, 85, 87, 90, 91, 96, 97, 99, 101-103, 105, 106, 112, 114, 121, 122, 124, 127, 128, 130-139, 142-144, 153, 159, 160, 164, 170
Giovannitti, Arturo 43, 44, 52, 56, 57, 58, 59
Gitler, Ira 108
*Give Us This Day*, 83
Gladnik, Robert 40
*Glory Days in Greenwich Village*, 146
*Go*, 70, 123-125, 127, 129, 165
*God's Little Acre*, 47
Gold, Michael 17, 25, 29, 44, 56, 57, 117
*Golden Boy*, 188
Gonsalves, Virgil 219
*Goodbye, Union Square*, 28, 31
Goodman, Benny 220
Goodman, Paul 146, 166, 168, 170
Gordon, Bob 216
Gordon, Dexter 107, 123, 221
Gordon, Don 70, 81
Gorki, Maxim 12
Gould, Joe 198
Grad, David 40
Graf, Bob 218
Graham, W.S. 166, 170
Gray, Wardell 107, 123, 216, 221
Greenberg, Clement 148, 158
Greenwich Village, 19, 30, 55, 56, 103, 108, 113, 114, 116, 120, 125, 144, 145, 148, 151-153, 155-165, 173, 176, 177, 179, 194, 196
Grennard, Elliott 208, 209, 210, 211
Grey Walls Press, 168, 169, 171
Gumbiner, Richard 139
Guston, Philip 195
Guthrie, Woody 35, 110

*Ha! Ha!*, 150, 156
Hagglund, Ben 13, 15
Haig, Al 205, 224
*Hallelujah, Thine the Glory*, 52
Hallett, Mal 216
Halper, Albert 27-32
Hamalian, Linda 167, 169
Hamsun, Knut 27
Handy, George 212
*Harmonium,* 196
*Harper's,* 29, 127, 210
Harrington, Alan 122, 124
Harris, Benny 214
Haut, Woody 183, 191
Hawes, Hampton 205
Hawkins, Coleman 107, 193, 205
Haynes, Roy 110
Haywood, Big Bill 52, 91
*Heartbreak Hotel,* 223
Hecht, Ben 174, 179
Hecht, Harold 185
Hefti, Neal 223
Hemingway, Ernest 27, 62, 63, 76, 167, 170, 171, 196
Henry, Conrad 214
Herbst, Josephine 11, 61-65
Herd, Herman 218
Herman, Woody 217, 218, 221
*Hermanos!*, 38, 39, 41
Herrick, William 34-42
Herrmann, John 61-65
*High Noon*, 47
*High on an Open Mike*, 221
*High Wind in Hollywood*, 222
Hikmet, Nazim 82
Hines, Earl 195
Hiss, Alger 61, 64, 65
*Holiday,* 126
Holiday, Billie 126
Hollingworth, Ambrose 146
Hollywood, 43, 44, 46-50, 52, 68, 69, 71, 86, 89, 100, 145, 165, 171, 175, 183-186, 190, 191, 202, 205, 206, 217, 221
Holmes, John Clellan 7, 105, 112, 121-129, 132, 165
*Home Alone*, 145
*Home Relief Bureau,* 178
*Honeysuckle Rose,* 217
*Horizon*, 84, 101, 170
House UnAmerican Activities Committee, 47, 67, 69, 70, 171, 183, 185
*How Brave We Live*, 7, 163, 165

INDEX

*Howl*, 43, 44, 58, 91, 94, 101, 102, 104, 106, 126
Hughes, Langston 202
Hurwitz, Leo 48
Huston, John 46, 48, 49

*Ice Freezes Red,* 221
*Images of Poverty*, 44
*Imagine the South*, 167
*In Secret Battle*, 92
*In The Bronx and Other Stories,* 119
Industrial Workers of the World, 34, 51, 52, 54, 55, 56, 59, 60, 112
*Inside Be-bop,* 222-224
*Inside Out*, 48, 50
International Brigades, 36, 83, 87
*Intoxicated By My Illness,* 148, 152
*Intruder In the Dust*, 46
*It's What's Happening, Man*, 97

*Jabberwhorl Cronstadt*, 78
Jackson, Chubby 217, 222
Jackson, Milt 205
Jacquet, Illinois 222
James, Harry 109
*Jazz Journal*, 8, 219, 222
*Jazz Monthly,* 169
*Jivin' with Jack the Bellboy*, 222
Joans, Ted 142
*Johnny Guitar*, 47
Johnson, J.J. 224
Jones, Leroi 81, 144
Jordan, Duke 224
Joyce, James 27, 59, 62, 76, 196, 198
*Junky*, 131, 133

*Kafka Was The Rage*, 155, 156
Kahn, Tiny 212
Kalar, Joseph 12, 17, 20-22, 24, 25, 117
Kaminsky, Max 122
Kamuca, Richie 108
Kart, Larry 107, 110, 111
Kaufman, Bob 81, 112, 132, 136, 137
Kazan, Elia 48
Kazin, Alfred 125, 148, 155, 158
Kees, Weldon 148, 158
Kelly, John 136, 137
Kenny, Beverly 162
Kenton, Stan 108, 223
Kerouac, Jack 27, 30, 31, 85-91, 96, 99, 100, 102-105, 107-111, 112, 114-

116, 121-134, 137, 153, 159, 160, 161, 164, 165
Kesterson, Bob 207
KGB, 61
Kibbee, Roland 185
*Kill Memory*, 39, 40, 41
Kirby, Anabel 137
*Kiss the Blood off My Hands*, 46
Kligman, Ruth 193
Kline, Franz 114, 117, 121, 194, 195
Klonsky, Milton 126, 148, 158, 160-162, 173, 181
Knepper, Jimmy 213
Knoll, Robert E. 199, 204
Konitz, Lee 223
Kooning, Willem de 194
Kootz Gallery, 194
Kostelanetz, Andre 193
Kramer, Aaron 180
Krasner, Lee 192
Krebs, Richard 87
Kreymborg, Alfred 174
Krim, Seymour 112, 135, 143-145, 148-150, 156, 158-163, 168
Krupa, Gene 216, 219
*Kulchur,* 144
Kupferberg, Tuli 143

Lamantia, Philip 166, 170
Lancaster, Burt 184, 185, 186
Landesman, Jay 122, 128
Lanphere, Don 223
Larkin, Philip 161, 172
Lary, Ben 108
Laughlin, James 167, 201
Law, Oliver 36
Lawrence, Lars. *See Philip Stevenson*
Lawson, John Howard 86, 100
Le Sueur, Meridel 14
Leeds, Charlie 212
Legman, Gershon 128
Lehman, Ernest 184, 188, 190
*Lemon Drop,* 217, 221
Leonard, Harvey 213
Leshin, Phil 212
*Let's Jump*, 212
*Letter to an Imaginary Friend*, 69, 70
*Letter To The Past,* 166
Levertov, Denise 81, 167
Levey, Stan 205, 206
Lewis, H. H. 12, 13
Lewis, Sinclair 27
Lieber, Maxim 28, 31

Liebnecht, Karl 57
*Life and Loves in Greenwich Village,*
180
*Lights in the Valley,* 178, 179
Lindsay, Vachel 57, 113
Lipton, Lawrence 73, 91, 97
Little, Frank 57, 59
*London Magazine,* 94
London, 7, 8, 25, 26, 30, 41, 54, 55,
59, 84, 94, 109, 116, 144, 167, 168,
169, 182, 190, 191, 197, 211, 223,
225
London, Jack 12, 116
*Lonesome Traveller,* 109
Lorca, Frederico Garcia 39
Los Angeles, 48, 67, 69, 70, 71, 73,
74, 91, 95, 96, 195, 205-207
*Love and Terror,* 39, 40, 41
*Lover Man,* 208, 210, 211
Lowenfels, Walter 75-84
Lubin, Bob 146
*Lucky Jim,* 172
Lunacharsky, Anatoli 133
Lyons, Eugene 88

MacAgy, Douglas 195
MacColl, Ewan 22, 24, 25
Machito, *(Francisco Raúl Gutiérrez
Grillo)* 109
Mackendrick, Alexander 185, 186,
187, 190
Macleod, Norman 19, 25, 117, 202
Maddow, Ben 25, 43-50, 58
Malamud, Bernard 154
Maltz, Albert 11, 71, 171
Manchester, 22, 25, 109
Mandel, George 125, 163, 165
*Mandrake Root,* 212
Mangione, Jerry 178
*Manteca,* 223
Marat, Jean-Paul 57
Mardigan, Art 212, 214
Margolis, William 137, 138
Margulies, De Hirsch 76
Markham, Edwin 81
Marmarosa, Dodo 222
Marsh, Warne 110, 224
*Max is Making Wax,* 207
*May Days,* 43, 53, 54, 59
Mayakofsky, Vladimir 24
Maynard, John Arthur 93, 98
McAlmon, Robert 61, 62, 76, 196-204
McCarthy, Albert 169

McCarthy, Mary 150
McCarthy, Senator Joe 73, 74, 85,
181, 186, 189
McClintock, Harry 51
McClure, Michael 135, 137
McDarrah, Fred 142, 143, 164
McDiarmid, Hugh 202
McDonald, Dwight 167
McGhee, Howard 109, 205, 207-209,
211, 222, 223
McGrath, Thomas 68, 69, 71, 73, 81,
132, 146
McKay, Claude 53
McKusick, Hal 213
McNally, Dennis 86
*Melodisc,* 222
*Melody Maker,* 223, 224
Meltzer, David 137
Melville, Herman 35, 125
*Men in War,* 47
*Men, Women and Other Anticlimaxes,*
155, 156, 160
Mencken, H.L. 12
*Merlin,* 92
*Metronome,* 217, 218
Meyerbach, Raymond Samuel 137
Michel, Louise 57
Micheline, Jack 7, 112-120, 132, 134,
142, 143, 145
Miller, Glenn 214, 218
Miller, Henry 35, 77, 78, 95, 101,
143, 166, 168, 170
Milne, Ewart 71
Mingus, Charlie 194
*Minna and Myself,* 174
*Moby Dick,* 125
*Modern American Poetry,* 17, 25, 43,
57, 59
*Modern Reading,* 170, 171
*Modern Writing,* 149, 152, 156, 159
Monash,Paul 163, 164, 165
Monk, Thelonius 192, 224
Monroe, Harriet 196
*Montoona Clipper,* 224
Mooney, Art 214
Moore, Brew 107-111, 170, 171, 181,
213, 221
Moore, Reginald 170
*Moose the Mooche,* 206, 207
Morgan, Ted 131
Morris, William 143
Morton, Jelly Roll 193
*Mothers of Invention,* 109

Motherwell, Robert 193
*Mozart in Hell,* 143
*Mulligan Stew,* 217
Mulligan, Gerry 109, 216, 224
Murger, Henry 138
Murtaugh, John 107
*Music to Dance to,* 218
*My Wandering Boy,* 51

*Naked Lunch,* 131, 133, 134
*Naked on Roller Skates,* 177
Navarro, Fats 108, 221, 223
Neiman, Gilbert 143
Nelson, Cary 17, 25
Neruda, Pablo 202
Neugass, James 83
*Neurotica,* 103, 122, 126, 149, 156, 159
*New American Poetry,* 135
*New American Review,* 162
*New British Poets,* 172
*New Directions,* 41, 149, 150, 156, 159, 167-169, 201
*New Lines,* 172
*New Masses,* 13, 15, 21, 22, 31, 43, 45, 62, 63, 86, 87, 121, 173, 178
*New Republic,* 22
*New Theatre,* 22
*New World Writing,* 94, 149, 156, 159
New York, 12, 14, 15, 17, 18, 21, 22, 25, 28, 29, 30, 32, 35, 37, 38, 41, 42, 44, 49, 50, 56, 59, 61-64, 67, 69, 71, 72, 80, 83, 84, 91, 93, 96, 99-103, 105, 106, 108-110, 116, 121-123, 126, 127, 142-146, 148, 150, 153, 155, 159, 165, 167, 168, 170, 172, 174, 175, 179, 180, 181, 183-186, 190, 193, 194, 205, 206, 208, 210, 212, 213, 224
Newman, Charles Henry. *See Funaroff*
Nick's-in-the-Village, 122
Nin, Anaïs 77, 97, 154, 168
*Ninth Avenue,* 177
*None But the Lonely Heart,* 183
Norris, Frank 12
*Not Alone Lost,* 201
*Nothing More to Declare,* 128
*Now,* 48, 54, 166
*Nugget,* 126, 127, 145
*Nykino,* 45

O' Connor, Philip 166

*Objectivists Anthology,* 196
Odets, Clifford 8, 183-190
*Of Thee I Sing,* 77
*Of This Time, Of That Place,* 170
O'Hara, John 27
Oliver, King 27, 194
Olson, Charles 96, 168
*On The Road,* 91, 94, 103, 104, 107, 126
O'Neill, Eugene 55
*Only an Inch From Glory,* 30
*Oral History of the World,* 198
Orlovsky, Peter 144
Orwell, George 166, 167
Ory, Kid 195
*Outlaw Of The Lowest Planet,* 169
Ozieblo, Barbara 181

*Pagany,* 28, 200, 203
*Palantir,* 104, 128
Paris, 38, 40, 61-63, 75-78, 80, 82-84, 92, 101, 109, 110, 134, 144, 154, 196, 197, 202, 221
Park, David 195
Parker, Charlie 9, 19, 101, 109, 110, 122, 142, 143, 192, 193, 195, 205-211, 214, 216, 221, 225, 226
Parkinson, Thomas 171
Parrish, Jon 126
Partch, Virgil 213
*Partisan Review,* 14, 18, 45, 101, 122, 148, 149, 151, 156, 158, 159
Patchen, Kenneth 25, 95, 139, 146, 166, 168, 169, 202
*Pearson's Magazine,* 91
Pell, Dave 224
Pell, Mike 87
*Perdido,* 214, 218
*Perfect Fools,* 129
Perkoff, Stuart 93, 95, 96, 112, 132
Pillin, William 71, 73
*Playboy,* 97, 127
*Poetry Los Angeles,* 69
*Poetry Quarterly,* 168
*Poetry,* 122, 174, 200
*Politics,* 167
Pollard, Tommy 225
Pollock, Jackson 121, 192, 193, 195
Popular Front, 11, 14, 36, 46, 79
Porter, Bern 170
Porter, Roy 207
Poster, Herb 148, 158
Poster, Willie 148, 158

Potts, Paul 168, 171
POUM, 37
Pound, Ezra 18, 76, 196, 197, 222
Powell, Bud 222
Presley, Elvis 183, 223
Prima, Louis 214
*Proletarian Literature in the United States*, 22, 45, 114, 178
Propper, Dan 145
*Protest*, 91, 104, 127, 152, 156, 159
*Provincetown Review*, 145
Putnam, Samuel 91

Raeburn, Boyd 212
*Rainbow at Midnight*, 94
Raine, Kathleen 171
Rajk, Laszlo 37, 41
*Rambling Kid*, 54, 55, 58, 59
Ransom, John Crowe 168
Ratcliff, Carter 194
*Rebel Poet*, 13, 20
Reece, Dizzy 225
Reed, John 35, 56, 63, 88
Reel, Pat 87, 88
*Relaxing at Camarillo*, 210, 223
Remington, Deborah 195
Replansky, Naomi 70, 71
*Replenishing Jessica*, 175
*Revolutionary Girl*, 178
Rexroth, Kenneth 20, 80, 91, 92, 94, 124, 139, 166-170, 172
Reynolds, Mack 143
Reznikoff, Charles 28
*Rhymes to be Traded for Bread*, 113
Rich, Buddy 108, 212
Rich, Sonny 216
Ridge, Lola 43
Riley, Peter 170
*River of Red Wine*, 115
Rivers, Larry 126
Rodney, Red 208, 213, 222
Rogers, Billie 212
Rogers, Johnny 225
Rogers, Shorty 95, 224
Roland, Gene 213
Rolfe, Edwin 17, 25, 70, 71
Romney, Hugh 146
Rose, Denis 225
Rosenberg, Harold 84
Rosenfeld, Isaac 148, 158
Rosenthal, Irving 144
Roskolenko, Harry 18, 143, 166
Roth, Samuel 180

Rothko, Mark 194
Rothschild, Connie 146
*Royal Roost*, 108
Rukeyser, Muriel 46
*Run, Sheep, Run*, 177
Russell, Ross 127, 206-211

*S.S. Utah.*, 87
Sachs, Aaron 212
*Sailor Off The Bremen*, 38, 41
*Salaam!*, 54
Sampas, Sebastian 27, 86, 88, 89
*San Francisco Review*, 145
San Francisco, 25, 41, 52, 67, 71, 72, 80, 92, 94, 95, 96, 106, 109, 110, 114, 134, 136-138, 140, 143, 144, 167-169, 172
San Remo, 164, 179
Sandburg, Carl 44, 53, 57, 81, 91
Saroyan, William 27, 100, 168, 170
Savage, Derek 170
Schechner, Mark 162
Schwartz, Delmore 148, 157, 158
Schwerner, Armand 81
Scott Fitzgerald, F. 27, 77, 169
Scott, Tony 220
Scottsboro Boys, 78
*Scribner's*, 63, 65, 165
Seaman, Phil 225
*September in the Rain*, 221
*Shadows and Wolves*, 39, 41
Shaw, Hank 225
Shaw, Irwin 38, 41
Shearing, George 221
Sherman, Jory 137, 139
*Short Circuit*, 212
Silver, Harvey Martin. *See Micheline, Jack*
Silver, Horace 224
Sims, Zoot 213, 216, 223
Sinclair, Iain 170
Sinclair, Upton 12
*Six American Poets*, 143, 145
Skerl, Jennie 133
*Skinny Dynamite*, 119
*Sleepy Bop*, 221
Slesinger, Tess 28
*Slow Vision*, 177, 181
Smart, Christopher 57
Smith, David 194
Smith, Hassel 195
Smith, Johnny 162
Snyder, Gary 97, 112, 132

Socolow, Frank 212
*Solidarity*, 52
Solomon, Carl 89, 99-106, 112, 122, 132, 144
*Some Deaths*, 80, 84
*Songs of the Workers*, 51, 59
*Sonny Speaks*, 218
*Sons of the Fathers*, 30
*Southern Labour Organiser*, 178
Spain, 36, 37, 38, 39, 40, 46, 86, 87, 116, 201
Spanier, Muggsy 195
Spanish Civil War, 7, 38, 39, 42, 71, 80, 81, 83, 86, 87, 114, 201
*Spartacus*, 57
*Spearhead*, 167, 171
Spector, Herman 17-22, 117
Spengler, Oswald 121
*Spider's Web*, 223
Spier, Leonard 13, 14
Stalin, Josef 34, 80, 133
Stamm, Claus 146
*Stay On It*, 223
*Steel*, 79
Stein, Gertrude 62, 76, 196
Steinbeck, John 167
Stern, Marvin 36
Stevens, Wallace 25, 169, 196
Stevenson, Philip 68
Straight, Charlie 27
Stravinsky, Igor 223
*Studs Lonigan*, 113
*Stupendous*, 222
*Summer is Ended*, 63
*Sunday Worker Magazine*, 15
Surrealism, 154, 221
*Swank*, 144, 145
*Sweet Bye and Bye*, 51
*Sweet Smell of Success*, 8, 184-186, 189, 190
Swenson, May 146
Swingler, Randall 71

Tate, Allen 161, 168
Taylor, Dick 216
Tempo Music Shop, 206
*Ten Days That Shook the World*, 88
Thaelmann, Ernst 78
The American Feature Writers Syndicate, 31
*The Asphalt Jungle*, 46, 49
*The Balcony*, 48
*The Beat Scene*, 116, 135, 142-146

*The Beats*, 116, 127, 132, 133, 135, 145, 152, 156, 159
*The Big Knife*, 183
*The Bridge*, 199
*The California Quarterly*, 67-71, 73, 74
*The Canticle of the Wanderer*, 139
*The Cantos*, 196
*The Chase*, 221
*The Chicago Review*, 125, 144
*The Chute*, 30, 32, 33
*The City*, 43, 44
*The Clipper*, 69, 202
*The Contact Collection of Contemporary Writers*, 62
*The Country Girl*, 183
*The Crow Becomes Discursive*, 201
*The Daily Worker*, 56, 79, 85, 87 112, 177
*The Dark Thorn*, 166, 168
*The Disinherited*, 12, 13, 15, 119
*The Escalator Movement*, 91
*The Exile*, 18
*The Expatriates*, 143
*The Fate of a Gesture*, 194
*The Finale Club*, 207
*The Fire Sermon*, 22
*The Flowering Moment*, 168
*The Foundry*, 29, 32, 33
*The Fourth Horseman of Miami Beach*, 31, 33
*The Gentle Furniture Shop*, 181
*The Go Hole*, 124
*The Great Gatsby*, 145
*The Great Rememberer*, 32, 123, 128
*The Gypsy*, 209, 210
*The Happy Monster*, 222
*The Hegira Cycle*, 139
*The Holy Barbarians*, 91, 95, 98
*The Horn*, 126
*The Industrial Worker*, 53
*The Itinerant*, 37, 38, 41
*The Jazz Word*, 144
*The Kid From Hoboken*, 38, 41
*The Liberator*, 53, 55, 56
*The Little People*, 30, 32
*The Little Red Songbook*, 51, 59
*The Little Review*, 55, 62, 174, 196
*The Man from Colorado*, 46
*The Man With the Golden Arm*, 126
*The Masses*, 43, 53, 55, 56, 118
*The Menorah Journal*, 28
*The Mephisto Waltz*, 48

*The Midland,* 28
*The Ming Tree,* 214
*The Miscellaneous Man,* 138
*The New York Times Magazine,* 125
*The New York Times,* 125, 153, 155
*The New Yorker,* 41, 173
*The Old Line,* 202
*The Outsider,* 116, 138
*The Phoenix and The Tortoise,* 169
*The PI Yearbook of Jazz,* 169
*The Poetry of The Forties,* 169
*The Preacher and the Slave,* 51
*The Prisoners,* 80
*The Provincetown Players,* 181
*The Quincy Girls,* 129
*The Real Bohemia,* 136, 137, 138, 140
*The Recognitions,* 157
*The Red Decade,* 88
*The Red Drum,* 109
*The Revolving Mirror,* 197, 198
*The Salesman,* 65
*The San Francisco Poetry Renaissance, 1955-1960,* 136
*The Savage Eye,* 48
*The Sea Around Us,* 181
*The Secret Swinger,* 122
*The Senate of the Dead,* 57
*The Skunk,* 223
*The Sound,* 127, 211
*The Spider and the Clock,* 23
*The Subterraneans,* 108, 109
*The Tale of the Amazing Tramp,* 145
*The Tenants,* 154
*The Town and the City,* 30, 122, 125
*The Trembling Lamb,* 144
*The Unforgiven,* 48
*The Via Dolorosa of Art,* 197
*The Walker,* 57
*The Waste Land,* 196, 197
*The Way West,* 48
*The West is Dead,* 54
*The Wide Skirt,* 25
*The Wild Ones,* 47
*The Young and Evil,* 19
*There Is Power in the Blood,* 51
*Thermodynamics,* 209
*These Foolish Things,* 218
*This Coffin Has No Handles,* 69
*This Quarter,* 20, 62
Thompson, E.P. 69
Thompson, Lucky 206, 223
*Three Deuces,* 212
*To An Imaginary Daughter,* 83, 84

Tolley, A.J. 169
Tolstoy, Leo 35, 121
*Too Marvellous for Words,* 219
*transition,* 18, 20, 62, 196
Travis, Nick 162
Trilling, Lionel 170
Tristano, Lennie 214, 224
Trocchi, Alexander 92
*Tropic of Cancer,* 35
Tropp, Stephen 143
Trotskyism, 14
*Troubador,* 174
Trumbo, Dalton 71
*Trumpet at Tempo,* 209
Twain, Mark 27
Tyler, Parker 19

*U.S.A,* 198
*Undercurrent Blues,* 220
*Underhound,* 139
*Union Square,* 29, 31, 32, 33
*United Action,* 46
*Unrest,* 13, 43
Untermeyer, Louis 43, 57, 59
*Up an Atom,* 217
Uronovitz, B. 137
Urso, Phil 214
*USA with Music,* 77
Usselton, Billy 107, 218

Valtin. *See Richard Krebs*
*Vanity of Duluoz,* 32, 86, 87
Venice West, 73, 91-94, 96, 98, 138
Ventura, Charlie 216, 221
Verland Studios, 212
*Vespers,* 55
*Views of a Nearsighted Cannonee*r, 161
*Visions of Cody,* 153, 159
*Vogue,* 222

*Waiting for Lefty,* 186
Wakefield, Dan 179
Waller, Fats 193, 217
Wallington, George 217
*Walls and Distances,* 146
Ware, Harold 64, 65
Washington Square, 110, 143, 180
Wasson, Hal 216
Watson, Steven 164
Watters, Lu 195
Wayne, Chuck 212
*We Gather Strength,* 17, 25

Webster, Ben 107
Weinberg, Harold 180
Weisburd, Mel 71
West, Nathanael 100, 169
Whalen, Philip 135, 137, 143
*What Happens,* 61, 62, 63
*What the Cytoscope Said,* 152, 156
*What's New?,* 214
*What's This Cat's Story,* 158, 159
*When The Sirens Blow,* 13
Whitehaven, 222
Whitman, Walt 44, 54-56, 58, 72, 81, 99
*Who Walk in Darkness,* 9, 125, 149, 157-165
*Wild River,* 48
Wilde, Oscar 57
Wilentz, Elias 135
Williams, George 218
Williams, John 216, 219
Williams, William Carlos 18, 82, 166, 168, 170, 196, 201, 203
Winchell, Walter 184
Winding, Kai 221
Wise, Buddy 8, 107, 216, 218, 219
Wixson, Douglas 11-15, 21, 25
Wobblies, 34, 51-59, 91, 112
Wolfe, Thomas 27, 63
Wolff, David 45
Wolof tribe, 130
Woodcock, George 166, 167, 169-171
Workers Film and Photo League, 45

Yancey, Jimmy 193
Yates, Richard 160
*Yet Other Waters,* 15
Young, Lester 107-110, 126, 216, 218, 224
*Yugen,* 116, 143

Z, Clara 40
Zappa, Frank 109
Zhdanov, Andrei 133
*Zoot Swings The Blues,* 213
Zukofsky, Louis 80, 196